Global Infrastructure Networks

Global Infrastructure Networks

The Trans-national Strategy and Policy Interface

Colin Turner

Heriot-Watt University, UK

Debra Johnson

Hull University Business School, UK

Edward Elgar
PUBLISHING

Cheltenham, UK • Northampton, MA, USA

Published by
Edward Elgar Publishing Limited
The Lypiatts
15 Lansdown Road
Cheltenham
Glos GL50 2JA
UK

Edward Elgar Publishing, Inc.
William Pratt House
9 Dewey Court
Northampton
Massachusetts 01060
USA

A catalogue record for this book
is available from the British Library

Library of Congress Control Number: 2017941902

This book is available electronically in the **Elgar**online
Social and Political Science subject collection
DOI 10.4337/9780857934413

ISBN 978 0 85793 440 6 (cased)
ISBN 978 0 85793 441 3 (eBook)

Typeset by Servis Filmsetting Ltd, Stockport, Cheshire
Printed and bound in Great Britain by TJ International Ltd, Padstow

Contents

Preface

Despite its widely recognised importance to economic, political and social systems, infrastructure remains a curiously under-explored area within the social sciences. Most approaches tend to be sector specific within an examination of impacts of the establishment or evolution of economic or social infrastructure within narrow domains. Other approaches have tended to be discipline specific, seeking to isolate specific events under specific conditions (as highlighted by the transaction costs approaches within transport economics) whilst others have tended to explore infrastructure in a more abstract fashion as witnessed by the burgeoning literature on the emerging area of 'infrastructure studies' (which in practice has tended to be an off-shoot of information studies and has a strong focus on ICT systems). Part of the issue is that the study of infrastructure is by its very nature multi-disciplinary, which can often mean that the subject matter can be difficult to isolate.

However, having made these points, to my mind there are very strong currents from within debates regarding critical infrastructures that are having a generally integrative effect across the multi-disciplines studying these core structures that underpin contemporary systems. The study of criticality within infrastructure systems attracts academic and practitioner interest from a diverse array of fields from engineering to security studies. In part this has been driven by an increased focus on systemic approaches to the study and design of infrastructures. Such approaches draw increasingly on narratives from complexity science and highlight the logic that any single piece of infrastructure is seen as part of larger system. This reflects growing academic interest in the practice of infrastructuring (defined here as the process whereby a body – usually a state – undertakes to develop the necessary infrastructure to support territoriality) involving the recognition of spatial and functional interdependencies within the design and operation of infrastructure systems. In functional terms, this operational complexity has been highlighted by the mutually supporting nature of contemporary infrastructure systems where one sector's infrastructure cannot operate without the existence and effective operation of infrastructure within at least one or more other sectors. Similarly, with spatial complexity (which is the primary focus of this work), the interdependencies within and between state-based national infrastructure systems can either promote or inhibit the global free movement of flows that is at the core of the Global Infrastructure System (GIS).

The approach followed within this work is one that adheres closest to the domain of International Political Economy (IPE), although in examining the establishment of infrastructure through this lens it is also necessary to draw on themes and literature from within related fields such as political geography. The IPE-based approach followed reflects on the interactions between states and markets within a globalised system of economic flows. More specifically (and following the logic of state primacy embedded within neo-realist perspectives), the work will focus on how states shape the emergent GIS. Whilst international infrastructure is not a new phenomena (one can trace such structures back to the 'Silk Road' and also the maritime infrastructures that supported colonialism), it is contemporary forces that are at the forefront of the analysis within this book; the contemporary forms of globalisation as identified by Held et al. (1999) with their 'extensity of global networks, the intensity of global interconnectedness, the velocity of global flows and the impact propensity of global interconnectedness' (p. 17).

The defining of GIS as being based upon the totality of and interaction between territorial national systems underscores the position that the efficacy of globality upon state is directly empowered by the physical structures that channel and direct these flows across and within borders. However, such a definition should not preclude the importance of soft infrastructure in also enabling or retarding global flows. This places attention on the role of National Infrastructure Systems (NIS) and of state infrastructuring in the process of state adaptability to global flows. This work (as outlined in chapters 1 and 2) treats state infrastructuring as innate state strategy to secure and/or enhance its territoriality. This is conceptualised through what is termed the state's infrastructural mandate, which ties the state's main functions (i.e. control, security, integration and prosperity) to the capabilities and design of its infrastructure system. Thus at the core of the work within this book is how states are adapting NIS to global flows and how this process of adaptation is shaping global flows and by implication the GIS. With these overarching research objectives, the research within the book will progress as follows.

Chapter 1 identifies the main themes within the book. Initially the chapter will examine the nature of infrastructure. This is drawn from a multi-disciplinary literature source and highlights the increasingly amorphous nature of what can be considered infrastructure. The chapter then moves on to examine the form and nature of NIS as the bedrock of the GIS. This involves exploring the components of the infrastructural mandate. The chapter examines how infrastructure aids the realisation of a number of key components of state functioning. Chapter 2 dovetails into the themes engendered within the formative chapter through seeking to address how the forces of globality are altering many, if not all, of the components of the state's infrastructural mandate. Within the context of these adaptive tensions, the second chapter outlines the nature and structure of the GIS to be utilised within the work, noting not just the key components of territorial components but also the importance of non-territorial and transit systems to the operation of the GIS.

Chapters 3, 4 and 5 offer a sectoral analysis of the broadly defined economic infrastructure sectors (namely transport, energy and information). To aid the consistency of analysis, a common structure is employed across these chapters. Initially each chapter focuses on the form and nature of the global/international component of the respective system. In so doing, each chapter examines the nature and volume of cross-border flows and the main enabling infrastructures (notably the main links and nodes) within the global system of flows for the respective infrastructural component. Thereafter, the respective chapters move on to examine the main forces for integration and fragmentation within each of the global infrastructure sectors. In each of the sectors, there seems to be a common pattern of integration but with state-based forces seeking to limit the intensity and velocity of flows across borders. These reflect both the unevenness of infrastructure across space, differing geo-economic/geo-political concerns and the varying salience states place upon enabling global flows. In short, a paradoxical situation of restrictive integration appears as the norm. Such themes as well as issues for further research are addressed within the final chapter.

REFERENCES

Held, D., McGrew, A., Goldblatt, D. and Perraton, J. (1999) Global Transformations: Politics, Economics and Culture. London: Polity Press.

Abbreviations

ATS	Air traffic services
bcm	Billion cubic metres
btoe	Billion tons of oil equivalent
BRIC	Brazil, Russia, India, China
CITES	Convention on International Trade in Endangered Species
CSI	Container Security Initiative
ECT	Energy Charter Treaty
EIA	Energy Information Administration
FDI	Foreign direct investment
FLNG	Floating liquefied natural gas
FSU	Former Soviet Union
GATS	General Agreement on Trade in Services
GATT	General Agreement on Tariffs and Trade
GDP	Gross domestic product
GES	Global energy system
GII	Global information infrastructure
GIIC	Global Information Infrastructure Commission
GIN	Global infrastructure networks
GIS	Global Infrastructure System
GPN	Global production network
GSC	Global Standards Collaboration
GTI	Global transportion infrastructure
IATA	International Air Transport Association
ICANN	Internet Corporation for Assigned Names and Numbers
ICAO	International Civil Aviation Organization
ICT	Information and communication technology
IEA	International Energy Agency
IETF	Internet Engineering Task Force
IGU	International Gas Union
IMO	International Maritime Organization
IP	Intellectual property
IPE	International political economy
IPR	Intellectual property rights
ISP	Internet service provider

ISPS	International Ship and Port Facility Security
IT	Information technology
ITF	International Transport Forum
ITU	International Telecommunications Union
LDC	Less developed countries
LNG	Liquefied natural gas
mb/d	Million barrels per day
mboe/d	Million barrels of oil equivalent per day
MNC	Multinational company or corporation
MNIC	Multinational infrastructure company
mtce	Millions of tonnes of coal equivalent
NAFTA	North American Free Trade Area
NES	National energy system
NGO	Non-governmental organisation
NII	National Information Infrastructure
NIS	National infrastructure system
NTI	National transportation infrastructure
OBOR	'One Belt, One Road'
OECD	Organisation for Economic Co-operation and Development
OPEC	Organization of the Petroleum Exporting Countries
PPP	Purchasing power parity
SIDS	Small island developing states
TEN	Trans-European networks
TEU	Twenty foot equivalent
TNIC	Trans-national infrastructure companies
TPES	Total primary energy supply
TRIPS	Trade-Related Intellectual Property Agreement
UNCLOS	United Nations Convention on the Law of the Sea
UNCTAD	United Nations Conference on Trade and Development
WEF	World Economic Forum
WIPO	World Intellectual Property Organization
WTO	World Trade Organization

1. Infrastructure and Territoriality

Analysis of the Global Infrastructure System (GIS) and the forces shaping its form and evolution lie at the core of this book. Central to this analysis is the contention that the GIS is based on the interaction between and within state-based territorial infrastructure systems (termed here the National Infrastructure System, NIS). The approach is based on the proposition that states infrastructure as a means of establishing and sustaining territoriality, defined here as the 'behaviour that uses a bounded space, a territory, as the instrument for securing a particular outcome' (Taylor, 1995, p. 151). Throughout this book, the state is positioned as the main source of territoriality within the global system and, as a means of securing its objectives, the state will utilise and upgrade existing and establish new physical structures (i.e. infrastructure) across its territory. Infrastructuring is thus viewed as a state strategy designed to enable the control, integration, security and development of a demarcated space. Although such state centric positions have been increasingly questioned (for example, Elden, 2010; Keating, 2013), nevertheless the departure point in this volume is assessing how NIS are shaping and adjusting to the challenge of the globalisation of economic, political and social systems.

This chapter introduce the nature of infrastructure and explores its nexus within the forces of state territoriality. In so doing, the chapter begins to address the main issues shaping the capabilities of infrastructure to operate as an effective tool of state territoriality. This is addressed through the lens of what is termed here as the state's 'infrastructural mandate' (that is, how infrastructure via the NIS enables state territoriality). It is argued that it is this infrastructural mandate that drives state strategy, especially within the context of the GIS, and shapes its evolution.

THE TERRITORIALITY–INFRASTRUCTURE NEXUS

The etymological roots of the word 'infrastructure' stem from Latin and refer to 'the structure beneath' – that is, the basic physical and organisational structure needed for the operation of a society or enterprise or the supporting structure/base/foundation for a system or organisation. In its broadest context, and in the context of this volume, infrastructure refers to the support structure for economy and society. These core facilities support the basic activities needed for a society to function. In modern society this includes all forms of transport, communication, energy, etc. Transport, communications and energy are not of intrinsic value in themselves but rather it is their enabling function that is the source of their utility. For example, the act of being able to transport people or goods from one location to another has no value in itself, but it is what the movement of these people or goods represents in terms of production, security, consumption, etc. that is so important. In short, economic and social development would not have progressed so far without the underpinning support of roads, railways, communication and energy flows.

Over time, the understanding of what constitutes infrastructure has become more complex and ambiguous. Increasingly infrastructure is used as a rather amorphous term which has co-evolved with the development of socio-economic and political systems (for a review, see Howe et al., 2016). When viewed through the lens of territoriality, infrastructure – at its most basic – refers to those physical assets located within a space that enable the territorial authority to assert power over that space (for a fuller examination, see Brenner, 1999a). Contemporary treatments of infrastructure extend beyond a purely physical definition to include the 'soft' component of infrastructure systems. Different interpretations of what is meant by the terms 'hard' and 'soft' infrastructure can cause confusion. Fourie (2006), for example, distinguishes between economic (or hard) infrastructure which promotes economic activity such as transport, telecommunications and energy systems and social (or soft) infrastructure which promotes health, education and cultural dimensions and has an impact on the quality of life such as schools, libraries, universities, hospitals, courts, museums, theatres and recreational facilities. The two categories can and do overlap: education and health provision, for example, are not only important to the quality of life but are also essential for economic activity.

However, although Fourie is not alone in this approach and whilst infrastructure systems can be subdivided in a multitude of ways depending on the context (Neuman, 2006), the definition used within this volume is based on the following (see also Figure 1.1).

Hard infrastructure: this refers to the conventional conceptualisation of infrastructures as physical structures that enable and facilitate territoriality. These categories can be subdivided into three categories: communications infrastructures (that is, those that involve the transmission, processing and distribution of human-sourced flows such as transport and information); socio-technical (that is, those structures that enable the utilisation of – crude or processed – natural endowments to support human activity such as energy and water) and social infrastructures (that is, those physical assets that support social services such as hospitals, schools, etc. and which, according to Fourie constitute soft infrastructure). This volume focuses on those infrastructures that are national systems but which also have to channel extensively transnational flows, namely information, transport and energy infrastructures.

Soft infrastructure: the growing complexity of infrastructure in terms of functional and spatial operations, as well as its increased polycentrism, have increasingly drawn attention to soft infrastructure (Niskanen, 1991). Soft infrastructure constitutes the enabling institutions for the territorial infrastructure system that facilitate both the interworking of the individual and the mutually supporting components through defining the body of rules and regulations that govern their operation and interaction (Portugal-Perez and Wilson, 2012). The regulatory framework is essential to all levels of infrastructure (see later) but it is particularly important to transnational infrastructure, governing as it does issues of eligibility and interoperability in terms of access to particular infrastructure.

Definitions of soft infrastructure are also sometimes extended to include the financing of these systems as well as training programmes, etc. (Brooks and Hummels, 2005). Three main themes (see Figure 1.1) characterise soft infrastructure: institutional design (that is, how these systems are managed and configured to enable the NIS); institutional capability (that is, the human capital within these systems to support territorial needs) and institutional objectives (that is, the objectives of the institutions (in this case the state) and how these affect the configuration of the NIS).

Recognising the increasingly fluid concept of infrastructure (notably with regard to its soft and hard components as well as the interaction between them), Star and Bowker (1995) identify the following core characteristics of infrastructure:

- Infrastructure is embedded within social-economic and technological structures;
- Infrastructure is hidden in many of the tasks it performs and supports;
- Infrastructure has effects beyond a single point in time and space;
- Infrastructure usage has to be learnt as part of a 'community of practice';
- Infrastructure co-evolves with the form and nature of its usage (that is, how capacity is shaped by peak flows);
- Infrastructure becomes transparent through standardised interfaces;

- Infrastructure development reflects path dependencies within the system; and
- Infrastructure becomes visible when it breaks down.

Importantly, these characteristics underline that infrastructures are 'sunk' into socio-economic activities and are suggestive of a 'taken-for-grantedness' within infrastructure systems based on user expectations that infrastructure will work and that its existence only becomes obvious at the point at which it fails (Howe et al., 2016). This creates a paradox within infrastructure systems whereby infrastructure only tends to be noticed at the point in time or space when its stops operating as infrastructure and needs to be repaired or replaced. For Star and Bowker (1995), infrastructure only becomes infrastructure at the point of usage and that usefulness of infrastructure can vary across different socio-economic groups. This means that in establishing a universal and ubiquitous NIS, the state builds infrastructure that is not used by all, may be under-used or offers limited advantages to limited segments of the population. Star and Bowker (2006) see user groups as central because they generate learning processes which stimulate proper usage and engagement between users. This enabling function involves a more distributed set of activities, comprising an infrastructure system that involves technical, social and institutional factors, which reflects that infrastructure does not emerge from a simple act of being but from the relationships formed between users.

Positioning infrastructure systems as relational systems implies that they operate as enablers of territoriality. This reflects the conclusions of technology historians (for example, Hughes, 1987; Badenoch and Fickers, 2010) who stress how infrastructural relations have been shaped and stretched by the process of modernity. Modernity has generated user reliance on infrastructure systems as political, economic and social relations have become spatially spread (Edwards, 2003). In an era of welfarism, the activist state drove relationship formation as a key component of public policy as identified within the 'modern infrastructural ideal' (Graham and Marvin, 2001). Without infrastructure, users could not operate effectively as economic, political or social agents (Edwards, 2003). Within a state-based system of territorial authority, these characteristics define the logic of state infrastructuring as a means of turning space into territory through creating, forming and sustaining the relationships between itself and all non-state agents located and operating within that space (Mann, 1984; Lefebvre, 1991; Brenner, 1999a). It is the provision of these structures (and the relations created and sustained over them) that enables that space to be controlled, secured, integrated and/or economically developed/grown.

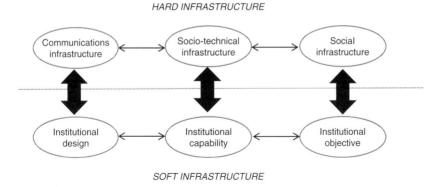

Figure 1.1   The national infrastructure system

State infrastructuring (as a strategy to enable territoriality) seeks not only to facilitate usage to build relations that enable the infrastructural mandate (see later) but also to set terms of usage and limits, controls, and to outlaw or deter those that are contrary to this objective. This increasingly stresses individual responsibility in usage (Rose and Miller, 1992; O'Malley, 1996; Rose, 1996; Cruikshank, 1999; Henman, 2004) with the state exercising power to make agents behave in certain ways within the context of its mandate. This has its most evident expression within the control aspect of the infrastructural mandate (addressed later) which also links with issues of security, integration and development/growth (Jackson et al., 2007). However, using relational systems as a means of attaining territoriality has been made more complex through what Graham and Marvin (2001) term the 'splintering' of user demands. This means that not only do infrastructural relations vary between users over space and time (Star and Bowker, 1995) but also within and between communities/user groups as users focus on those infrastructures they need as part of their membership of communities and their immediate or semi-immediate functioning (Frischmann, 2005). This pattern suggests infrastructural relations are dynamic and reflect the learning processes within communities surrounding and utilising these systems as both technologies and user groups change (Star and Bowker, 1995; Star and Ruhleder, 1996).

These narratives underscore the core role of what is termed 'secondary infrastructure' in the establishment, development and utilisation of the relational infrastructure systems. These secondary infrastructures are the technologies that directly facilitate access to networked infrastructure. It is through these access technologies that infrastructural relations are created and sustained, subject to issues of congestion, externalities, capacity and politics (Edwards, 2003). Typically, such technologies include, most obviously, vehicular capacity (maritime, land and air-based) within the transport system, portable and semi-portable information and communication technology (ICT) devices in telecommunications and portable liquefied natural gas (LNG) facilities in energy. These secondary infrastructures exhibit many of the characteristics of infrastructure identified by Star and Ruhleder (1996), not least of which is the 'taken for grantedness' based on their embeddedness in everyday activities and conventions and their being easy to use, access and understand. Thus, as the spread of access technologies depends on affordability, skills and their absorption in the system and, as such, these technologies are integral to the infrastructure system (Star and Bowker, 2006). These qualities render them a core focal point for state power because they enable the state to control access, and thus the form and type of usage within a territory.

Theoretically, there is no compulsion for users to build relations with infrastructure but there is a clear sense of value derived from the creation, sustenance and progression of such relations. As harnessed by the features of the aforementioned modernity (for a review, see Howe et al., 2015), user welfare became increasingly reliant upon these systems which legitimised state activism in NIS to drive relation formation and how – in the era of welfarism – the state was pro-active in driving infrastructural relations as a key component of public policy as identified within the 'modern infrastructural ideal' (Graham and Marvin, 2001). As modernism has evolved into post-modern systems, the needs of the system have changed from nation state construction and consolidation through to system sustainability and dealing with uncertainty that is ultimately difficult to predict (Edwards, 2003) based on the certainty, adaptability and reliability of connectivity, access, interoperability and quality differentiated systems with variable infrastructural flexibility, adaptability, capacity and connectivity (Johnson and Turner, 2007).

Debates within international political economy on territoriality have focused on whether territoriality is synonymous with the state (as defined by internationally recognised borders). Many argue that such a treatment is too narrow (Agnew, 1994) because it results in a narrow methodological nationalism, assumes the historical fixity of territory and implies that infrastructure will only form around the territorial confines of the state (see, for example, Sack, 1983). Moreover, the state-based treatment of territoriality suggests that infrastructural relations can be confined to the borders of the state where infrastructures are channels through which users (of which the state and its agents are just one set) can possess the capability to interact with – and where necessary influence – other users. However, this purely methodological national approach is challenged, given that NIS are often built on preceding territorial configurations and that these systems cannot always be operationally confined to within the borders of the state (Sassen, 2013). As Brenner (1999a) argues, territorialisation is historically specific and, as a result, infrastructures – as territorial configurations – are under a constant process of change and are updated and reconfigured as the demands placed upon them alter (Harvey, 1982).

This leads on to the second perspective, namely where territory is defined more by the form and extent of relations than by state borders. This draws explicitly on the globalisation literature in which local processes are integrated into global chains in which actors selectively participate. This reflects the work of Castells (2009) who defines territory as the 'material support of simultaneity in social practice' (p. 19) which is increasingly divorced from the demarcated borders of the state, a process driven by advances in technology that render states mere nodes in the 'global space of flows'. To Castells (2009), it is these flows that are the focus of analysis and the territorial infrastructures merely form the enabling conduits. Painter (2010) argues that territory can be understood as the result of both 'networked social-technical practices' and the network of relations, with the result that – according to Sassen (2013) – key elements of the state's mandate can no longer be conceptualised as purely national because they function in a larger operational space which reflects processes beyond the borders of the state. These processes have been further supported by emergent geopolitical forces that have shaped transnational power relations. Keating (2013) suggests that although such approaches do not render states obsolete (as argued within more extreme de-territorialisation theses), they are not cornerstones of the system (for a review of the issues, see Murphy, 2012).

Keating (2013) comments that the differences between these two perspectives is largely empirical, with each having more in common with the other than first appearances might suggest. The choice of approach is often ontological. By focussing on a global system of national infrastructures, attention is drawn to such hybrid views of territory. This reflects that whilst the border infrastructure system is core to the establishment and evolution of the NIS it nonetheless is shaped by and adapts to global flows and the changing infrastructural relations embedded within such interactions. Thus, although states constructed NIS around existing infrastructures during state formation and these state-based systems continue to evolve with the state, it is argued that the state remains the core territorial building block of the global system and, as such, is the only meaningful actor forming the global infrastructure system. However, it is undeniable that not all infrastructural relations can be captured within the borders of the state (this is explored more fully in Chapter 2) and therefore states have to adapt the NIS accordingly. Some authors (for example, Bouzarovski et al., 2015) argue that the development of transnational transit systems demonstrates an erosion of state territoriality. However, these systems remain very much a derivative of the state system as it is often the state that finances, drives and legitimises pan-regional systems. Moreover, transnational infrastructural relationships cannot form without state sanction or legitimacy (a theme more fully explored in Chapter 2). This is not to assume spatial fixity of such systems. In examining how and why states infrastructure as a means of understanding the global system, it must be acknowledged that history suggests that new forms of territoriality will subsume existing infrastructure to meet their objectives (Hulten, 1996).

These debates find resonance in multi-scalar treatments of infrastructure systems. The multi-scalar approach distinguishes between six layers within a global infrastructure system, four of which are based on the state (community, urban, regional and national) and two are above the level of the state (transnational and global). In relational systems, users develop interactions with different types of networks to complete different tasks. At the individual level, proximity of and access to local and, to a lesser extent, national networks shape relations. This is different for multinational corporations and, maybe, for some smaller corporates. The important point is that local infrastructure is a key relation for all, whereas higher level relations tend to be more exclusive. Thus, in policy terms there is a greater focus on local networks and less on those above the nation state. In other words, infrastructure relations build from the bottom up with the degree of exclusion growing as infrastructures expand in spatial scope (Smith, 1984). These different levels are set out in Table 1.1 and reflect the conclusions of Brenner (1999a) regarding the redefinition of territoriality by processes at sub-national and international levels.

In focussing on the interface between national and international systems, sub-national systems are treated as a subset of the NIS as they are integral to the attainment of the state's infrastructural mandate. In the context of the relational NIS, the 'infrastructured state' seeks not only to create physical infrastructure channels but also to monitor, stimulate, manage and legitimise the infrastructural flows within and across its borders as part of its mandate to assert territoriality (Agnew, 2005). Implicit in the notion of the 'infrastructured state' is that the state has an incentive to control access to and the capabilities of gateway infrastructures (that is, those points of access to the NIS) as a means of asserting territoriality. Such a state-centred view has to contend with shifting relations where the integrity of the system is no longer solely shaped by the conditions within it. Agnew (1994) highlights that as territorial systems, states should not be divorced

Table 1.1   Multi-scalar infrastructure

Type	Scale	Definition
Community infrastructures	Sub-national	Infrastructures of either a limited spatial or user reach: these can be dedicated to a limited community of practice, be it a particular social group or corporate entity, and could include a private network in a building or road networks in a single site. This infrastructure tends to be highly localised.
Urban infrastructures	Sub-national	Spatially fixed infrastructures that cover an expansive area with a high density of users in an urban agglomeration.
Regional infrastructures	Sub-national	These infrastructures may or may not include single or multiple urban, sub-urban or rural areas within an expanded territory, usually within the borders of a single state.
National infrastructures:	National	These are the totality of all network infrastructures located within a territorial state. These are independent systems and reinforce state territoriality.
Transnational infrastructures	International	In areas of evolving inter-state integration (both formal and informal), these infrastructures support the creation of a virtual transnational system through the interaction between national systems. Systems remain territorial but are open, interoperable and interconnected to ensure the seamlessness of the system at the point of intersection (that is, borders).
Global infrastructures	International	These are territorial and non-territorial infrastructures whose interaction and interdependencies enable seamless global flows. These include the global commons but also the desire of states to limit institutional barriers to global flows.

from their context and that territoriality through the infrastructure system also has to reflect that the state cannot command sovereignty over all forces operating within or impacting upon it. In other words, what is domestic and international cannot be easily delineated. As Brenner (1999a) suggests, the territorial state is but one layer in a multi-scalar system: it is part of an institutional mosaic comprising multiple overlapping levels that are neither congruent, contiguous nor co-extensive with each other to the extent that infrastructural relations can never be fully internalised.

THE NATIONAL INFRASTRUCTURE SYSTEM AND THE INFRASTRUCTURE MANDATE

The NIS (a term increasingly deployed by policymakers) represents the totality of networked infrastructure (that is, stand-alone and interacting communication, socio-technical, soft and social infrastructure systems) located within the borders of a state. Within the literature on territoriality, the salience of the NIS is based on the state's 'infrastructural mandate' – that is, a necessity by a state to infrastructure if it is to demonstrate territoriality. It is through the NIS that the state is able to establish and sustain the relationships between it and civil society and business that enable it to assert sovereignty over a demarcated space (Mann, 1984; Lefebvre, 1991; Brenner, 1999b). This implies a need for the state not only to build, maintain and sustain physical, interconnected links but also to enable flows across and between these physical components. The infrastructural mandate reflects the intimacy between the capability of the state to fulfil its major social, political and economic functions and the existence of a supporting infrastructure through which these capabilities are to be realised (Samli, 2010). These four state functions (territorial integration, control, security and economic growth/development – see later) reflect an amalgam of perceived roles from diverse, multi-disciplinary literature (for example, Hartshorne, 1950; Mann, 1984, 2008; Taylor, 1995). These are inherent to what is termed here the 'infrastructured state' – that is, the capability of the state to exert territoriality through a mature, spatially complex NIS.

As a state strategy, the complexity of the infrastructure creates a number of challenges for the sustained operation of the NIS as a support to state territoriality:

1) Obsolescence: this emerges when the NIS is no longer relevant to the needs of the state as the infrastructure becomes divorced from its shifting context (that is, economic growth and development, productivity, climate change and environment, population and demography and technology).
2) Senescence: this emerges as the NIS structure and capabilities erode through degradation generated by the ageing process and the slowness of the system to change, with the result that the infrastructure begins to fail more often and with greater disruptive effects.

3) Complexity catastrophe (Kauffman, 1996): this occurs when infrastructure and its interlinkages grow so complex that it can fail in a multitude of ways, many of which are not readily evident. This can often stem from the fact that systems can change too fast, creating new interconnections without full comprehension of the risks created by such complexity. This is more fully explored with reference to the spatial complexity generated by globalisation in Chapter 2.

4) Failing soft infrastructure: this reflects the inability of the supporting institutional systems to stimulate NIS adaptation. Examples of such failure include limits to modular-driven innovation and systemic liberalization; the absence of appropriate enforcement and failure to build user groups, etc.

5) Failing nodes (McKelvey, 2002): this is based on connectivity failure where human failure generates a loss of capability and inadequate coverage to sustain the system. This can be created by the absence, failure and/or obsolescence of social infrastructure which is central to creating institutional capability.

In addition to these legacies from the complex operation of infrastructure, state infrastructuring also faces other practical issues. First, the infrastructure mandate is increasingly realised through polycentric infrastructure systems (Scholte, 2005) in which the state is but one source of power. Moreover, the state is increasingly becoming more of a client/user of infrastructure over which it seeks to exert influence or attempts to develop in a manner that suits its objectives and not those of the asset owner (Willke, 1986). In a market-led NIS, the state retains a role largely through addressing issues of market failure. Second, as identified by Graham and Marvin (2001), there is increased splintering away from the 'infrastructural ideal' because value from and quality of the system offered can vary widely across space, time and socio-economic clusters. Thus the infrastructural mandate (which relies upon ubiquity and uniformity) can be compromised. Third, the infrastructure mandate depends upon learning processes as a means of generating inclusiveness (Star and Bowker, 1995) which can also vary widely over space, time and socio-economic groups. Fourth, as mentioned earlier, user focus on those segments of the NIS that are needed as part of their membership of communities limits systemic perspectives at the point of usage (Star and Ruhleder, 1996). In combination, these characteristics of the NIS create pressures upon the state in the attainment of its infrastructural mandate because the complex structures, through which the process is attained, are not always responsive to state pressure.

THE FOUR DIMENSIONS OF THE INFRASTRUCTURE MANDATE

Based on a multi-disciplinary approach, the relationship between the state and the NIS can be synthesised into the four inter-related processes of the infrastructural mandate: control, security, integration and growth/development. The identification of the infrastructural mandate offers a neo-Weberian perspective on the state, namely that the state is a social body/social organisation that pursues specific goals (Palan et al., 1996). This is also reflected in Auster and Silver (2012) who argue that the state functions to sustain itself through the provision of structures that enable security, protection, control and economic welfare gains. This work reflects themes embedded within the logic of the competition state and of a zero sum mentality in state strategy as each state seeks to maximise the welfare of their respective populations (Jackson and James, 1993). These structures are examined in more depth next.

Control

Infrastructure operates as an intermediate platform for power relations between the state and all agents located and operating within a territorially (both horizontal and vertical) (Elden, 2013) demarcated space (Mann, 1984; Brenner, 1999a). Under this treatment, infrastructures are channels through which users (of which the state and its agents are just one set) possess the capability to influence the actions of other users. Mann (1984) refers to the occurrence of infrastructural power, stressing how these structures are key to enabling the state to penetrate civil society and to exert power over territories. Such power is not necessarily malign and may also reflect security or integration concerns. Political control depends upon the ability of the state to move the resources of control around a territory. In his categorisation of social power, Mann (2008) states that ideological, economic, military and political power are all reliant upon infrastructures to be effective. Infrastructure represents the channels through which information and commands are transmitted. These themes have been rather perversely reflected within the state failure literature (Brenner and Elden, 2009; Eriksen, 2011; Sundsoleriksen, 2011; Wolff, 2011) which notes that the state – where it is at risk of loss of control over a territory – has an incentive to under-develop, destroy or control access to infrastructure.

Power comes from relations becoming reliant and – in a Foucauldian sense – control is embedded throughout the system, not merely through formal methods but through social, cultural and personal norms all shaping the form and intensity of the infrastructural relationship (Rose and Miller, 1992; O'Malley, 1996; Rose, 1996; Cruikshank, 1999; Henman, 2004). These are frequently not the high politics shaping the infrastructural mandate, but lower level everyday interactions within the system that shape its functioning but can impact upon attaining the objectives within the infrastructural mandate. The state seeks to facilitate usage to build infrastructural relations that enable the infrastructural mandate, but also to set the terms of usage and limits, controls and outlaws those actions that are contrary to this objective. This increasingly stresses individual responsibility in usage (O'Malley, 1996; Rose 1996) with the state exercising power to seek to make agents behave in certain ways within the context of its mandate. Integral to this are rules over access to, control of and usage of infrastructure that become a key element of control within the economic system. This involves the social goods from learning about what is beneficial usage and what runs contrary to this.

Control also extends to the nature of the Anthropocene where infrastructure is used to control natural environmental processes and events to enable human activity to be sustained both within and across territories. Consequently, long-term environmental processes have implications for infrastructure because they place pressure upon the state to adapt the NIS to actual and anticipated environmental change. For the state, such adaptations are driven by the challenge to the sustenance of territorial control implied by these processes where territorial integration is threatened/ undermined and growth/development impacted. The underlying logic is that failure to control (or at least militate against) these territorial changes arising from long-term environmental change can – via its infrastructural impacts – have a widespread impact on state territoriality.

The final element of control relating to the NIS concerns the sustaining influence over an NIS where it is but one player among several. The polycentric NIS (where established) has to be compliant with the state's infrastructural mandate. Consequently, as users establish relations with or are transferred to non-state components of the NIS, the government will seek to steer users towards specific aims that support its territorial objectives (Braithwaite and Drahos, 2000; Moran, 2003). This is achieved through a mix of methods including business model legitimisation (Kostova and Zaheer, 1999), universal service obligations and firm/ industry specific regulation.

Integration

For the state, the integrative aspect of the NIS is reflected in how the spatial and temporal compression promotes economic, social and political cohesion within a territory (Munnell, 1992; Rietveld, 1995; Edwards, 2003).

Hartshorne (1950) argued that the role of the state is to bind together assorted social and territorial segments into an effective whole (see also Martin and Rogers, 1995). This is a vertical process for social groups and a horizontal process for territorial groups. The integrative aspect of the infrastructural mandate reflects the operation of the NIS at the confluence of a range of policies, notably social and regional policies. It also reflects a need on the part of the state to establish the NIS as a scalable system that enables flows at sub-national levels to integrate with the broader national system and to ensure that flows within the borders of the state have the capability to penetrate both territorially and across all socio-economic groups. This is seen as beneficial for both the state and the targeted regions/groups (Mann, 1984). As argued in Chapter 2, the trend towards globalism is extending this integration to enable all parts of a state's territory to access the main global infrastructure channels as a stimulant to welfare enhancement (for a review, see Puga, 2002) through a focus on those segments of the NIS that facilitate the proactive competition state (notably key gateways and hinterland systems).

Integration is reflected in Lefebvre's notion of abstract space: that is, space that has the explicit goal of homogeneity through the enabling of social, political and economic relations (Brenner, 1999a) where only the state – so Lefebvre (1991) argues – has the capability to organise space on such a grand scale. Conventionally, these themes were embedded within a welfarist approach (Gramlich, 1994) to NIS development encapsulated within the aforementioned 'modern infrastructural ideal' (Graham and Marvin, 2001). The shift to neo-liberalism within NIS has shifted priorities towards an NIS that enhances welfare through enabling growth (Rose and Miller, 1992; Estache and Fay, 2010; Majone, 1996). This refocus has seen some splintering of the system as infrastructure varies according to user requirements rather than a simple universal system (Graham and Marvin, 2001), resulting in access to and quality of infrastructure varying markedly across socio-economic strata (Offner, 1999) and potential power asymmetries across a territory (Massey, 2005), with a resultant inhibition of territoriality (Poulantzas, 1978; Mann, 1984).

Security

Security is defined here as the external threats to the military, political, societal, environmental and economic security of the state (Agnew, 1994; Williams, 2003) that can be mobilised through the interaction between and within NIS. Economic, technological and environmental changes have – both singularly and in combination – exposed infrastructure systems to both man-made and naturally occurring events and processes that can disrupt the relational system to the extent that users are unable to function and their mandate is compromised (Rinaldi et al., 2001). In contrast to notions of control, security within the infrastructural mandate is borne of the interaction of the NIS with other systems (Held et al., 1999; Scholte, 2005). Consequently, debates within critical infrastructure strategies (see later) reflect anticipation that the threats to security across NIS increase as the intensity of flows increases. This occurs when complexity and global change have created uncertainty over the stability and sustenance of relational infrastructure systems (Moteff, 2012). The efficacy of systems is not only impaired by harmful external flows but also by events beyond the borders of the state that hinder the capabilities of the NIS. These challenges can be sourced from the global commons (Murphy, 2010), such as choke points (see chapters 3 and 5), from cyberspace (see Chapter 4) or from other NIS, either through transit or direct links.

In view of these security concerns, the core challenge is that interdependent networks are largely, as mentioned, under private control but are central to the state's strategic interests. This suggests that there is the need for a strong legitimisation process to ensure that those who control such strategic assets do not operate counter to the long-term interests of the state. There is a clear mandate within the process that state involvement and interaction can be legitimised within the domain of critical infrastructure (see later) where the state potentially seizes either control or ownership of such assets to ensure its objectives are met. In prioritising infrastructure, this process recognises that not all infrastructures within a particular system have the same salience. Evidently, the core assets within the infrastructure system are those that offer the greatest knock-on effect and spill over into other infrastructures.

Growth/Development

Conventional approaches to the nexus of prosperity and the NIS are formed around the consensus – as part of the process of territorial economic integration – on enabling intra-state exchange as economic relations become stretched (Gritsch, 2005). Infrastructure plays a core role in organising and rationalising resources within a state by fostering communication and exchange and by shaping the economic geography of the state (Aschauer, 1989; Easterly and Rebelo, 1993; Canning et al., 1994; Sanchez-Robles, 1998; Canning and Pedroni, 2004). The infrastructure narrative within international economics reflects a desire to militate against the impact of the absence of and/or deterioration of infrastructure upon transactions costs. The logic is that investing in infrastructure decreases the cost of undertaking trade, thereby increasing the potential for trade. In reflecting a Foucauldian discourse on the role of the state, the economic growth/development narrative implies that the NIS has a function – especially within the context provided by the logic of the competition state – as a key component of the state's export system. The NIS is the means by which commodities and fully and part-finished products are moved through the state's gateways. These gateways are shaped by the economic need to interact with the global system, and the NIS is seen as a catalyst and sustainer of these value creating relationships.

The logic of the competition state is embedded within policy discourses in which the NIS is positioned as a platform for the global positioning of the state (Romp and de Hann, 2007; Röller and Waverman, 2001). This reflects a broad consensus on the impact of the state of the NIS on growth (as reflected within Porter, 1990). As markets integrate, NIS are focused on making markets work more efficiently by facilitating and stimulating flows (both within and external to the state) that enhance strategic positioning (Palan et al., 1996). This is based on the state pushing users towards those infrastructures and types of uses that have positive feedback on performance, reflecting that growth is a function of usage rather than absolute levels of provision. The erosion of the welfarism of the positive state has given way to the growth focus of the competition state (Fougner, 2006). This reflects a Foucauldian perspective that the core welfare focus of the state is to generate economic growth. Glykou and Pitelis (2011) suggest that the most effective industrial strategy in the context of global markets is to reduce the production and transaction costs faced by firms as a means of generating productive efficiency. Infrastructure represents one of the main channels through which such efficiencies can be attained by improving internal and external facing logistical systems.

THE INFRASTRUCTURE MANDATE THROUGH THE AGES

The four main dimensions of the infrastructure mandate – control, security, integration and growth/development – are not new and have played a significant role in infrastructure development for centuries. As is the case today, the predominance of each dimension has varied, depending on the prevailing political, economic and social context. However, it has been commonplace for more than one dimension simultaneously to play a significant role in infrastructure strategy and policy. A long-term perspective on infrastructure development reveals that major changes have occurred on the back of technological change and that new dominant powers have emerged through military or economic means or a mixture of both, and have frequently exploited infrastructure in a pioneering way which has yielded advantages over competing powers.

Until the nineteenth century, transport infrastructure was the only significant form of infrastructure; energy, telecommunications and related infrastructure only came to prominence as a result of industrialisation. In pre-industrial days, both road and water-borne transportation played an important role in the economic and political evolution of the most successful civilisations and seemingly drew on the four dimensions of the infrastructure mandate. The Roman Empire provides an early example of this phenomenon. Roman roads, which reportedly incorporated over 86,000 kilometres of paved roads in addition to many more minor roads, were originally built to facilitate rapid movements of troops and supplies, and provided key communication links between Rome and its imperial offshoots (Chevallier, 1976). They were thus important in the consolidation, or integration, of the Empire and helped its rulers control and secure its territory as well as facilitating trade with far-flung parts of the Empire.

Not only did the roadmap of the Roman Empire delineate the extent of Roman influence politically and economically, but it also influenced the reach of arts and religion, thereby further integrating the imperial territory. The spread of Christianity was linked to the pattern of Roman roads, some of which served as major pilgrimage routes in medieval times. As well as acting as a conduit for the military and trade, Roman roads thus helped bind the different races and regions of the Empire together, a phenomenon which continued to exercise an influence on the evolution of modern Europe long after the demise of the Roman Empire.

Although its roots can be traced back several centuries prior to the emergence of the Roman Empire, the Silk Road, a network of overland trade routes linking Europe with China, began to develop in earnest during the first century of the Han dynasty (206BC–220AD) and reached its heyday during the Mongol Empire in the thirteenth century. During its long existence, the Silk Road saw and helped foster the rise of several civilisations, acting as a conduit for conquering, trade and the transmission of cultural and religious values. Frankopan (2015) attributes the spread of Zoroastrianism, Judaism, Christianity, Buddhism and Islam, in part, to links made possible by the Silk Road. Frankopan (2015) also repeats the theory that it was the Silk Road trade routes that played a key role in spreading the Black Death during the fourteenth century.

The first Silk Roads were essentially overland routes and were more suitable for low volume, high value goods such as silk (which prompted great interest in Rome) and spices. However, maritime transport provided opportunities to trade a greater array of goods over longer distances and potentially supported the control and security dimensions of infrastructure.

In addition to roads, the Romans also used coastal sea routes to support their empire and opened shipping routes between Europe and India. From the ninth century onwards, Arab traders started to develop their own sea trading routes down the coast of Africa and to the east, gradually diminishing the importance of the Silk Roads.

Waterborne transport was at the heart of logistical developments in the medieval period. Rivers and coastal waters facilitated trade in both northern Europe and the Mediterranean. The Hanseatic League, a federation of merchant guilds and towns, had its origins in the German city of Lübeck. By the peak of its influence in the late fourteenth century, it involved towns spanning northern Europe from England to Russia and dominated trade throughout the Baltic and northern Europe. Its influence also extended beyond the commercial sphere into a military and diplomatic dimension to defend its trade routes. Its rules and regulations are also an early example of the role and power of soft infrastructure.

The Hanseatic League was essentially concerned with short sea transport, but from the fifteenth century onwards European powers increasingly sought alternative long distance maritime trade routes to the traditional overland east–west routes, prompted in part by the fall of Constantinople in 1453. Portugal and Spain were among the first to find success. The former quickly established domination of trade and of a greater part of the world than any other power for a short period. By the mid-sixteenth century, Portuguese influence stretched along the east and west coasts of Africa and through the Persian Gulf and Indian Oceans, resulting in Portuguese control of the Ceylonese and Indonesian spice trade, which also enabled Portugal to establish a presence in China and Japan. Spain turned its ambitions towards transatlantic trade, hoping to find an alternative route to Asia. Consequently, it established trade and colonial territories throughout South America, in the Caribbean, notably Cuba and Hispaniola (the modern day Haiti and Dominican Republic), Mexico and into southern and western parts of what became the US.

Other European powers were not far behind. The Netherlands, largely through the offices of the Dutch East India Company, established powerful trading bases in Asia, notably in modern day Sri Lanka and Indonesia, whereas France gained influence in the Caribbean and West Africa. England, latterly Britain, developed the most extensive overseas trading networks accompanied by political and diplomatic supremacy in several parts of the world. This maritime and political supremacy reached its peak in the second half of the nineteenth century when it was increasingly challenged by the US and Germany in particular.

Major economic breakthroughs have been accompanied throughout history by improvements in technology, production, communications and logistics. That is not to say that communications improvements cause economic transformation but they have often been necessary to it. Given their superior organisation, the Romans travelled faster than medieval man. Indeed, during medieval times, the transport system deteriorated (Leighton, 1972) and, significantly, there were no major changes in the organisation of economic life. The domestic inland transport systems of the post-medieval European empires were initially less advanced than their long-distance maritime transport, but during the eighteenth century the supply and quality of inland transport in England improved; for example, in the 40 years from 1780, according to Girard (1965), the duration of the road journey from London to Manchester fell from five days to 36 hours. Along with the development of canals, and later railways, these changes provided conditions for the industrial age to commence earlier in England than elsewhere. Transport innovations extended the market for goods, thereby facilitating the introduction of mass production and the creation of factories. Manufacturers were also guaranteed more reliable and continuous supply and delivery of raw materials and goods.

It was no accident, therefore, that the first canals, and later the first railways, were built to service the coal mines which were essential to the steam age which began in the early nineteenth century. As the century progressed, steam transformed maritime transport and enabled the spread of railways which, according to Wolmar (2009, p. 26), 'between the first and last quarter of the nineteenth century, . . . transformed the world from one where most people barely travelled beyond their village or nearest market town, to one where it became possible to cross continents in days rather than months.' Consequently, production and consumption no longer needed to be located in close proximity to each other, opening up the possibility of large-scale production, specialisation and the development of new industries, along with attendant social changes in terms of urban development and working practices. The railway revolution began in Britain but quickly spread to the rest of Europe and to the US where it helped open up vast swathes of territory for settlement. Railways were also used by the British to consolidate their imperial power in terms of commerce (the prosperity dimension) and security and control in Africa and India (see later).

Rick Szostak (1991) has argued that it was the absence of an effective transport system which inhibited industrial modernisation in France during the eighteenth century. However, by the mid-nineteenth century, Britain's continental rivals were beginning to catch up economically. The Second Empire's (1852–1870) rail policy under Napoleon III demonstrates how politicians and financiers were becoming increasingly aware of the potential political and economic power derivable from railways (Blanchard, 1969). In 1852 only 3,000 kilometres of track were in use – lines were discontinuous and split between companies. By the time of the Empire's demise in 1870, almost 20,000 kilometres of rail track were in operation and were organised in a few coherent units. Blanchard (1969) maintains that this transformation was only possible as a result of deliberate policy by a strong government and far-sighted financiers who conceived the rail system as a distinct network rather than as an accumulation of individual lines and which settled the pattern of French industrialisation.

Napoleon III also encouraged the restoration of French influence and prestige in neighbouring countries and was prepared to use economic means, including control over railways, to achieve this. A prime example, albeit not the only one, of this policy (Blanchard, 1969) occurred in 1868–9 when the French Compagnie de l'Est bought several short and unprofitable lines serving Belgium and Luxembourg with a view to integrate them seamlessly into its own network and to develop a direct link with Dutch lines, especially those providing access to Rotterdam. This development posed threats to the prosperity of the port of Antwerp and gave rise to Belgian fears that French iron interests, which exercised control over Compagnie de l'Est, would interfere with the export of iron ore from Lorraine to Belgium's iron and steel industry. Detecting a French plot to dominate Belgium economically, and perhaps even to occupy it, the Belgian government alerted Britain and Prussia to what was happening and the project failed to materialise.

The French example demonstrates the potential use of railways to increase political and economic influence in neighbouring countries, whereas the development of the German rail system highlights rail's potential to foster political unification and integration (Henderson, 1975). Early German rail development occurred on an ad hoc basis with a mixture of state and private provision and frequent bitter rivalry between states and between towns and cities in the same state. However, even during the early days of the German rail system in the 1830s, figures like Friedrich List warned that short-sighted rivalries between states should not be allowed to inhibit the development of a German rail network and that co-operation in communications, especially in relation to rail building, would substantially enhance the advantages accruing from the Zollverein (the customs union), which was established on 1 January 1834.

List's warnings were ignored. However, the railways mushroomed and stimulated economic growth: new firms of contractors and engineers were established; jobs were created; iron foundries flourished on the backs of the railways and markets for agricultural and industrial products were extended. Once the railways reached the ports, particularly Hamburg and Antwerp, goods previously only consumed within small local regions were exported. In the longer run, claims Henderson (1975), railways helped unite Germany and broke down long-standing local rivalries and isolationism. The railways, together with the Zollverein, sowed the seeds for German unification in 1871 and, it can be argued, were a prime example of the integration dimension of the infrastructure mandate.

In Russia towards the end of the nineteenth century railroads, which had been a force for modernisation and economic dynamism elsewhere, were used to maintain Russia's autocratic system of government. Following the assassination of the liberal Tsar Alexander II in 1881, Alexander III reverted to a more conservative style of government which involved asserting his absolute dominance over all aspects of life. The construction of the Trans-Siberian Railroad (Marks, 1991) was a case in point. Poor communications were a weak link in Russia's control of its eastern territories and rendered the country vulnerable to foreign aggression in the Pacific region. Central to Russia's internal policy during this period were attempts to overcome internal political division and to promote a unified Russian state through government intervention, centralisation and Russification. The railroad was intended to bring Siberia into contact with the rest of Russia, thereby destroying its uniqueness and individuality which provided ammunition for Siberian regionalists and separatists Marks (1991, p. 45) concluded that 'Russification and the extension of political control to the region were to be gained through the construction of a railroad and economic development.'

In this sense, infrastructure was being used as a political tool to facilitate further political integration and to exercise control over the territory. In relation to external policy, various writers (Marks, 1991; Wolmar, 2013) argue that the result of building a railroad which could transport troops to the Pacific and bring about the de facto annexation of northern Manchuria was an important contributor to the outbreak of the 1904/5 Russo–Japanese War, failure of which helped provoke the 1905 uprising in Russia.

Although it had been the tsar's decision to build the railway based purely on 'his personal motivations and his assessment of its military and political value' (Wolmar, 2013, p. 76), Russia's Finance Minister (later Prime Minister) Sergei Witte had prior experience in the development of Russia's railways and recognised the economic potential of rail for Russia and, according to Wolmar (2013), regarded railways, and the Trans-Siberian Railway in particular, as a key driver in Russia's modernisation and industrialisation. It was this economic push which he anticipated, wrongly, would help maintain the tsarist regime.

As the example of the Trans-Siberian Railroad demonstrates, railways were one way of extending a nation's influence and territory. During the nineteenth century, European powers used railroads to consolidate their power and influence in their colonial territories and to prevent incursion in these territories by competing powers. Rail investment also served to tie many of these territories into the international economy as producers of primary commodities. Many of the railroads were built with private capital but were harnessed by European governments to serve bigger imperial strategies.

By the late nineteenth century, the so-called 'Scramble for Africa' was in full swing with railroads playing a key part. The moving force behind this for the British was Cecil Rhodes whose main aim, in popular mythology at least, was to link all the British colonies of Africa through construction of the 'Cape to Cairo' railway. Reality was more complex than this: the activities of Rhodes in the late-nineteenth century reflected a complex mixture of factors in which the drive to extend British influence throughout Africa was co-mingled with entrepreneurial objectives. The major impact of the railroads in Africa was at a sub-imperial level. The Rhodesian railway through Northern Rhodesia (in which Rhodes's British South Africa Company was a driving force) and Lord Salisbury's Uganda line, built in part to frustrate a possible French threat to British control over the Suez route to the East, were examples of this. These routes acted as bricks for nation building, opened up new land for settlement and enabled the colonial territories to be integrated into the economic systems of the imperial power as providers of primary commodities. In India, British rail policy also served both as a tool of commercial policy and as a way of exerting political control over the princely states of India (Sethia, 1991).

During the twentieth century, transport infrastructure continued to play a role in the life of nations beyond simple involvement in ensuring movements of goods and people. In Nazi Germany, for example, the construction of the autobahns, commonly known as 'Hitler's highways', became an important symbol of the new regime. Shand (1984, p. 48) argues 'the propagandistic exaltation of the Reichsautobahnen melded together three fundamental strands of Nazi ideology; national unity, national greatness, and party leadership in a strong state'. Hitler himself certainly attributed great importance to the development of the autobahns: within two weeks of becoming Reich Chancellor in 1933, the need to improve the condition of German roads and to construct new highways was discussed in Cabinet and Fritz Todt was given the task of pushing this forward (Seidler, 1988). Hitler was also interested in rail and, according to Albert Speer (2009) aspired to build a transcontinental rail network to link together economically all parts of his anticipated future empire.

Although many of these examples of the promotion of infrastructure for broad political and economic motives may be adjudged to have failed to fulfil their ambitious objectives, the concept of infrastructure as a powerful political and economic tool has nevertheless exercised a powerful influence over policy makers and over the interpretation of historical trends. This influence remains strong to this day. In Europe, for example, the Trans-European Network (TEN) Initiative has attempted, with patchy success, to promote cross-border infrastructure across the EU with a view to stimulate economic growth and greater integration (Johnson and Turner, 1997) in line with two of the four dimensions of the infrastructure mandate.

However, the 'One Belt, One Road' (OBOR) project announced by the Chinese government in 2013 represents the most ambitious and far-reaching cross-border initiative of modern times and has the potential to serve all four dimensions of the infrastructure mandate. The OBOR is a two-pronged plan to improve connectivity within and between Eurasia, East Africa and Oceania through construction of new and the improvement of existing infrastructure, namely ports, airports, roads, railways, pipelines, fibre-optic networks and logistics hubs. The first component is the Silk Road Economic Belt, which comprises several land corridors to link China, Central Asia, West Asia, the Middle East and Europe, involving countries along the original Silk Road and also links between China and South and South-East Asia. The second component is the Maritime Silk Road intended to foster collaboration and investment through the South China Sea, the southern Pacific and the Indian Ocean, thereby spreading the reach of OBOR to East Africa.

Given the relative newness of the OBOR concept, opinions vary regarding its implications and the relative salience of each of the four dimensions of the infrastructure mandate. The economic aspirations, albeit diverse, are the clearest. For China, the OBOR is intended to increase prosperity by increasing investment and trade. Reflecting the multi-scalar, multi-actor scope of the project, the increased economic activity will benefit the less developed provinces of western and central China in particular and China's large state-owned enterprises and construction companies as a result of the massive engineering projects involved (estimated at US\$4 trillion plus over the coming decades). Once the projects are in place, trade should become faster and easier. The OBOR will also help China source much needed raw materials and supplies for its own growth and, through the stimulation of trade, bolster markets for its own goods. Moreover, the OBOR is anticipated to enhance China's security by reducing reliance on the bottleneck formed by the Malacca Strait. It is the political implications of the OBOR which are less clear cut in terms of the perceived ambiguity of China's objectives and of the uncertainty over whether China will be able to overcome the many economic and political challenges involved in implementing the OBOR. Such uncertainties include the role of major international players such as the US and India (Blanchard, 2016; Luft, 2016) who have their own concerns about what the OBOR might mean for the global and regional balance of power. Other challenges include the sheer scale of the funding required and the ability/willingness of countries along the various transport corridors to participate and contribute.

CRITICAL INFRASTRUCTURE AND THE INFRASTRUCTURE MANDATE

The value of the infrastructural mandate as a conduit for territoriality is increasingly expressed through themes of critical infrastructure. Although there are assorted definitions on what constitutes 'critical' infrastructure (Organisation for Economic Co-operation and Development, OECD, 2008) it can be broadly defined as those segments of the NIS whose failure would directly compromise state territoriality as expressed in the infrastructure mandate. Across states, assets and activities such as banking, food supply, medical facilities and the military can be and are often included in the definition of critical infrastructures. However, as stated earlier, this volume concentrates on economic infrastructures.

Debates upon critical infrastructure have been shaped by a number of themes. The first is the aforementioned shift towards polycentric NIS, especially within the many developed economies in which the state has replaced the direct ownership and control of infrastructure with a more 'regulatory approach' (Majone, 1996; Moran, 2003). This regulatory approach does not downplay the importance of infrastructure but implies that attaining the objectives as expressed within the infrastructural mandate does not always necessitate direct state ownership. As such, as Braithwaite and Drahos (2000) argue, the state begins to steer the system towards its objectives via regulatory controls and other incentives and/or controls (for review of the UK system as an exemplar of this process, see Stern, 2014). Second, the impact of globality (see Chapter 2) combined with increased security concerns has highlighted a need by the state to ensure that these points within the system are secure and can effectively filter out and monitor threats to the state. Third, technological change has introduced new vulnerabilities that have further exposed these systems to disruption. This is highlighted by the increased pervasiveness of ICTs across all infrastructures.

These adaptive tensions within NIS as a result of these and other changes highlight their increased functional and spatial complexity. The spatial complexity of NIS (where the impact of externally sourced or destined flows can impact on the efficacy of the NIS) is discussed in the following chapter. However, there is a need to consider (largely due to its links to globalising forces) functional complexity within NIS insofar as it impacts on state territoriality. The burgeoning literature on 'criticality' has stemmed from a number of disciplines but common to all of them is the idea of NIS as complex adaptive systems in which no single piece of infrastructure is divorced from any other because they mutually interact and depend upon each other for their functionality. Rinaldi et al. (2001) identify the following interdependencies: cyber interdependency where the success of infrastructure depends on information transmitted through information infrastructure; geographic interdependency where a local event can generate change in all connected (both direct and indirect) systems and logical interdependency where the state of each piece of infrastructure depends upon the state of others.

For states, such complexities matter because they create uncertainty over the attainment and retention of territoriality. It is possible with functional complexity that the erosion and failure and/or disruption to a single piece of infrastructure can have cascade effects (see Chapter 2) throughout the NIS which challenge a number of components of the infrastructural mandate. The danger for states from such complexity is the lack of knowledge as to how exactly infrastructures can fail, which, in turn, generates limited understanding of how such events/processes will impact upon territoriality. Moreover, this also places an emphasis on soft infrastructure systems to fully create an awareness of the risk and to militate against perceived and/or actual ignorance of system complexity and its legacy. This underscores the importance of the aforementioned challenges to the system and that the state not only needs to infrastructure but also to continually re-infrastructure as a means of securing territoriality.

CONCLUSION

This chapter has focused on identifying the form and nature of infrastructure systems and their intimate link with the territorial state. Infrastructure systems are relational systems; they are the physical channels through which interactions occur between users. This renders them central to the operation of the territorial state through the establishment and evolution of the NIS. The NIS is shaped by what is termed here the 'infrastructure mandate'. This mandate underlines the notion that the core functions of the state (i.e. improving the welfare of citizens and ultimately preserving state territoriality and retaining its sovereign position over this space) are dependent upon the provision of a spatially extensive infrastructure within the borders of the state. However, key to the successful support of the state's functions by the NIS is its ability to adapt to its shifting context. At the core of adaptive tensions within territorial systems is the global stretching of relations that are altering the nature of territoriality.

REFERENCES

Agnew, J. (1994) 'The territorial trap: the geographical assumptions of international relations theory', *Review of International Political Economy*, *1*(1), 53–80.

Agnew, J. (2005) 'Sovereignty regimes: territoriality and state authority in contemporary world politics', *Annals of the Association of American Geographers*, *95*(2), 437–61.

Aschauer, D.A. (1989) 'Is public expenditure productive?', *Journal of Monetary Economics*, *23*(2), 177–200.

Auster, R.D. and Silver, M. (2012) *The State as a Firm: Economic Forces in Political Development* (Vol. 3). Dordrecht, NL: Springer.

Badenoch, A. and Fickers, A. (eds.) (2010) *Materializing Europe: Transnational Infrastructures and the Project of Europe.* Basingstoke, UK: Palgrave Macmillan.

Blanchard, J. (2016) 'Probing China's twenty first century Maritime Silk Road Initiative (MSRI): an examination of MSRI narratives', *Geopolitics, 22*(2), 246–68.

Blanchard, M. (1969) 'The railway policy of the Second Empire', in Crouzet, F., Chaloner, W.H. and Stern, W.M. (eds.), *Essays in European Economic History 1789–1914*. London: Arnold, pp. 98–111.

Bouzarovski, S., Bradshaw, M. and Wochnik, A. (2015) 'Making territory through infrastructure: the governance of natural gas transit in Europe', *Geoforum*, *64*, 217–28.

Braithwaite, J. and Drahos, P. (2000) *Global Business Regulation.* Cambridge: Cambridge University Press.

Brenner, N. (1999a) 'Globalisation as reterritorialisation: the re-scaling of urban governance in the European Union', *Urban Studies*, *36*(3), 431–51.

Brenner, N. (1999b) 'Beyond state-centrism? Space, territoriality, and geographical scale in globalization studies', *Theory and Society*, *28*(1), 39–78.

Brenner, N. and Elden, S. (2009) 'Henri Lefebvre on state, space and territory', *International Political Sociology*, *3*, 353–73.

Brooks, D.H. and Hummels, D. (2005) *Infrastructure's Role in Lowering Asia's Trade Costs: Building for Trade.* Cheltenham, UK: Edward Elgar.

Canning, D. and Pedroni, P. (2004) *The Effect of Infrastructure on Long Run Economic Growth*, mimeo, Harvard University.

Canning, D., Fay, M. and Perotti, R. (1994) 'Infrastructure and growth' in Bsaldassarri, M., Paganetto, M. and Phelps, E.S. (eds.), *International Differences in Growth Rates.* New York, NY: St Martin's Press, pp. 285–310.

Castells, M. (2009) *The Rise of the Network Society. The Information Age: Economy, Society, and Culture* (Vol. 1), 2nd edn. Chichester, UK: Wiley Blackwell.

Chevallier, R. (1976) *Roman Roads.* London: Batsford.

Cruikshank, B. (1999) *The Will to Empower: Democratic Citizens and Other Subjects.* Ithaca, NY: Cornell University Press.

Easterly, W. and Rebelo, S. (1993) 'Fiscal policy and economic growth: an empirical investigation', *Journal of Monetary Economics*, *32*, 417–58.

Edwards, P.N. (2003) 'Infrastructure and modernity: force, time, and social organization in the history of sociotechnical systems', *Modernity and Technology*, 185–225.

Elden, S. (2010) 'Land, terrain, territory', *Progress in Human Geography*, *34*(6), 799–817.

Elden, S. (2013) 'Secure the volume: vertical geopolitics and the depth of power', *Political Geography*, *34*, 35–51.

Eriksen, S.S. (2011) '"State failure" in theory and practice: the idea of the state and the contradictions of state formation', *Review of International Studies*, *37*(01), 229–47.

Estache, A. and Fay, M. (2010) *Current debates on infrastructure policy*. Commission on Growth and Development Working Paper No 49, Washington, DC: World Bank.

Fougner, T. (2006) 'The state, international competitiveness and neoliberal globalisation: is there a future beyond "the competition state"?', *Review of International Studies*, *32*(01), 165–85.

Fourie, J. (2006) 'Economic infrastructure: a review of definitions, theory and empirics', *South African Journal of Economics*, *74*(3), 530–56.

Frankopan, P. (2015) *The Silk Roads: A New History of the World*. London: Bloomsbury.

Frischmann, B.M. (2005) 'An economic theory of infrastructure and commons management', *Minnesota Law Review*, *89*, 917–1030.

Girard, L. (1965) 'Transport', in Habbakuk, A.J. and Postan, M. (eds.), *The Cambridge Economic History of Europe*, Vol. 6. Cambridge: Cambridge University Press, pp. 227–38.

Glykou, I. and Pitelis, C.N. (2011) 'On the political economy of the state, the public–private nexus and industrial policy', *Policy Studies*, *32*(4), 461–78.

Graham, S. and Marvin, S. (2001) *Splintering Urbanism: Networked Infrastructures, Technological Mobilities and the Urban Condition*. London: Routledge.

Gramlich, E.M. (1994) 'Infrastructure investment: a review essay', *Journal of Economic Literature*, *32*(3), 1176–96.

Gritsch, M. (2005) 'The nation-state and economic globalization: soft geo-politics and increased state autonomy?', *Review of International Political Economy*, *12*(1), 1–25.

Hartshorne, R. (1950) 'The functional approach in political geography', *Annals of the Association of American Geographers*, *40*(2), 95–130.

Harvey, D. (1982) *The Limits to Capital*. Oxford: Blackwell.

Held, D., McGrew, A., Goldblatt, D. and Perraton, J. (1999) *Global Transformations: Politics, Economics and Culture*. Cambridge: Polity Press.

Henderson, W.O. (1975) *The Rise of German Industrial Power, 1834–1914*. London: Temple Smith.

Henman, P. (2004) 'Targeted! Population segmentation, electronic surveillance and governing the unemployed in Australia', *International Sociology*, *19*(2), 173–91.

Howe, C., Lockrem, J., Appel, H., Hackett, E., Boyer, D., Hall, R., Schneider-Mayersom, M., Pope, A., Gupta, A., Rodwell, E., Ballestero, A., Durbin, T., el-Dahdah, F, Long, E. and Mody, C. (2016) 'Paradoxical infrastructures: ruins, retrofit and risk', *Science, Technology & Human Values*, *41*(3), 547–65.

Hughes, T.P. (1987) 'The evolution of large technological systems', in Rijker, W.E.,

Hughes, T.P. and Pinch, T. (eds.), *The Social Construction of Technological Systems: New Directions in the Sociology and History of Technology.* Cambridge, MA: MIT Press, pp. 51–82.

Hulten, C.R. (1996) *Infrastructure Capital and Economic Growth: How Well You Use It May Be More Important Than How Much You Have*, (No. w5847). National Bureau of Economic Research.

Jackson, R.H. and James, A. (eds.) (1993) *States in a Changing World: A Contemporary Analysis.* Oxford: Clarendon Press.

Jackson, S.J., Edwards, P.N., Bowker, G.C. and Knobel, C.P. (2007) 'Understanding infrastructure: history, heuristics and cyberinfrastructure policy', *First Monday*, *12*(6).

Johnson, D. and Turner, C. (1997) *Trans-European Networks: The Political Economy of Integrating Europe's Infrastructure.* Basingstoke, UK: Palgrave Macmillan.

Johnson, D. and Turner, C. (2007) *Strategy and Policy for Trans-European Networks.* Basingstoke, UK: Palgrave Macmillan.

Kauffman, S. (1996) *At Home in the Universe: The Search for the Laws of Self-Organization and Complexity.* Oxford: Oxford University Press.

Keating, M. (2013) *Rescaling the European State: The Making of Territory and the Rise of the Meso.* Oxford: Oxford University Press.

Kostova, T. and Zaheer, S. (1999) 'Organizational legitimacy under conditions of complexity: the case of the multinational enterprise', *Academy of Management Review*, *24*(1), 64–81.

Lefebvre, H. (1991) *The Production of Space.* Blackwell: Oxford.

Leighton, A.C. (1972) *Transport and Communications in Early Medieval Europe AD 500–1100.* Newton Abbot, UK: David & Charles.

Luft, G. (2016) 'China's Infrastructure Policy: why Washington should accept the new Silk Road', *Foreign Affairs,* September–October.

Majone, G. (1996) *Regulating Europe.* London: Routledge.

Mann, M. (1984) 'The autonomous power of the state: its origins, mechanisms and results', *European Journal of Sociology*, *25*(02), 185–213.

Mann, M. (2008) 'The State: its origins', in Brenner, N., Jessop, B., Jones, M. and MacLeod, G. (eds.), *State/Space: A Reader.* Oxford: Blackwell, pp. 27–52.

Marks, S.G. (1991) *Roads to Power: The Trans-Siberian Railroad and the Colonization of Asian Russia 1850–1917.* Ithaca, NY: Cornell University Press.

Martin, P. and Rogers, C.A. (1995) 'Industrial location and public infrastructure', *Journal of International Economics*, *39*, 335–51.

Massey, D.B. (2005) *For Space.* London: Sage.

McKelvey, B. (2002) 'Managing coevolutionary dynamics'. *18th EGOS Conference, Barcelona, Spain.*

Moran, M. (2003) *The British Regulatory State: High Modernism and Hyper Innovation.* Oxford: Oxford University Press.

Moteff, J.D. (2012) *Critical Infrastructure Resilience: The Evolution of Policy and Programs and Issues for Congress.* Washington, DC: Congressional Research Service.

Munnell, A.H. (1992) 'Policy watch: infrastructure investment and economic growth', *The Journal of Economic Perspectives*, *6*(4), 189–98.

Murphy, A.B. (2012) 'Entente territorial: Sack and Raffestin on territoriality', *Environment and Planning, Part D*, *30*(1), 159.

Murphy, T. (2010) 'Security challenges in the 21st century global commons', *Yale Journal of International Affairs*, *5*(2), 28–43.

Neuman, M. (2006) 'Infiltrating infrastructures: on the nature of networked infrastructure', *Journal of Urban Technology*, *13*(1), 3–31.

Niskanen, W.A. (1991) 'Soft infrastructure of a market economy', *Cato Journal*, *11*, 233–44.

O'Malley, P. (1996) 'Risk and responsibility' in Barry, A., Osborne, T. and Rose, N. (eds.), *Foucault and Political Reason: Liberalism, Neo-Liberalism and Rationalities of Government*. Chicago, IL: University of Chicago Press, pp. 189–207.

Offner, J.-M. (1999) 'Are there such things as *"small networks"*?', in Coutard, O. (ed.), *The Governance of Large Technical Systems*. London: Routledge, pp. 217–38.

Organisation for Economic Co-operation and Development (OECD) (2008) Protection of 'Critical Infrastructure' and the Role of Investment Policies Relating to National Security, May 2008, accessed 12 June 2016 at www.OECD.org

Painter, J. (2010) 'Rethinking territory', *Antipode*, *42*(5), 1090–118.

Palan, R., Abbott, J. and Deans, P. (1996) *State Strategies in the Global Political Economy.* London, New York: Pinter.

Porter, M.E. (1990) *The Competitive Advantage of Nations.* New York, NY: Free Press.

Portugal-Perez, A. and Wilson, J.S. (2012) 'Export performance and trade facilitation reform: hard and soft infrastructure', *World Development*, *40*(7), 1295–307.

Poulantzas, N. (1978) *State, Power, Socialism.* London: Verso.

Puga, D. (2002) 'European regional policies in light of recent location theories', *Journal of Economic Geography*, *2*(4), 373–406.

Rietveld, P. (1995) 'Infrastructure and spatial economic development', *Annals of Regional Science*, *29*, 117–19.

Rinaldi, S.M., Peerenboom, J.P. and Kelly, T.K. (2001) 'Identifying, understanding, and analyzing critical infrastructure interdependencies', *IEEE Control Systems*, *21*(6), 11–25.

Röller, L.H. and Waverman, L. (2001) 'Telecommunications infrastructure and economic development: a simultaneous approach', *American Economic Review*, 909–23.

Romp, W. and de Haan, J. (2007) 'Public capital and economic growth: a critical survey', *Perspektiven der Wirtschaftspolitik*, *8*(S1), 6–52.

Rose, N. (1996) 'Governing "advanced liberal" democracies', in Barry, A., Osborne, T. and Rose, N. (eds.), *Foucault and Political Reason: Liberalism, Neo-Liberalism and Rationalities of Government.* London: UCL Press.

Rose, N. and Miller, P. (1992) 'Political power beyond the state', *British Journal of Sociology*, *43*(2), 173–205.

Sack, R.D. (1983) 'Human territoriality: a theory', *Annals of the Association of American Geographers*, *73*(1), 55–74.

Samli, A.C. (2010) *Infrastructuring: The Key to Achieving Economic Growth, Productivity, and Quality of Life.* Dordrecht, NL: Springer.

Sanchez-Robles, B. (1998) 'Infrastructure investment and growth: some empirical evidence', *Contemporary Economic Policy*, *16*, 98–108.

Sassen, S. (2013) 'When territory deborders territoriality', *Territory, Politics, Governance*, *1*(1), 21–45.

Scholte, J.A. (2005) *Globalization: A Critical Introduction*, 2nd edn. Basingstoke, UK: Palgrave Macmillan.

Seidler, F. (1988) *Fritz Todt: Baumeister des Dritten Reiches*, Munich and Berlin: Herbig.

Sethia, T. (1991) 'Railways, Raj and the Indian States: policy of collaboration and coercion in Hyderabad', in Davis, C.B. and Wilburn, K.E. (eds.), *Railway Imperialism*. New York and London: Greenwood Press, pp. 103–20.

Shand, J.D. (1984) 'The Reichsautobahn: symbol for the Third Reich', *Journal of Contemporary History*, *19*, 189–200.

Smith, N. (1984) *Uneven Development: Nature, Capital and the Production of Space*. New York, NY: Basil Blackwell.

Speer, A. (2009) *Inside the Third Reich*. London: Phoenix (first published in 1970 by Weidenfeld and Nicholson).

Star, S.L. and Bowker, G.C. (1995) 'Work and infrastructure', *Communications of the ACM*, *38*(9), 41.

Star, S.L. and Bowker, G.C. (2006) 'How to infrastructure' in Lievrouw, L. and Livingstone, S. (eds.), *Handbook of New Media: Social Shaping and Social Consequences of ICTs*. London: Sage, pp. 230–45.

Star, S.L. and Ruhleder, K. (1996) 'Steps toward ecology of infrastructure: design and access for large information spaces', *Information Systems Research*, *7*(1), 111–34.

Stern, J. (2014) 'The British utility regulation model: its recent history and future prospects', *Utilities Policy*, *31*, 162–72.

Sundsoleriksen, S. (2011) '"State failure" in theory and practice: the idea of the state and the contradictions of state formation', *Review of International Studies*, *37*, 229–47.

Szostak, R. (1991) *The Role of Transportation in the Industrial Revolution: A Comparison of England and France*. Montreal and Kingston: McGill–Queens University Press.

Taylor, P.J. (1995) 'Beyond containers: internationality, interstateness, interterritoriality', *Progress in Human Geography*, *19*(1), 1–15.

Williams, M.C. (2003) 'Words, images, enemies: securitization and international politics', *International Studies Quarterly*, *47*, 511–31.

Willke, H. (1986) 'The tragedy of the state: prolegomena to a theory of the state in polycentric society', *Archiv für Rechts und Sozialphilosophie/Archives for Philosophy of Law and Social Philosophy*, *72*(4), 455–67.

Wolff, S. (2011) 'The regional dimensions of state failure', *Review of International Studies*, *37*(3), 951–72.

Wolmar, C. (2009) *Blood, Iron and Gold: How the Railways Transformed the World*. London: Atlantic Books.

Wolmar, C. (2013) *To the Edges of the World: The Story of the Trans-Siberian Railway*. London: Atlantic Books.

2. The nature of the Global Infrastructure System

The previous chapter highlighted the close links between the state territorial system and the NIS. This National Infrastructure System (NIS) involves a mix of public and private sector actions but with the state taking a prominent role within the system as a means of enabling it to retain sovereignty over its territory. The infrastructural mandate ties state infrastructuring to this basic territorial objective. However, it is evident that infrastructures – as relational systems – can no longer confine all those relations that are key to its infrastructural mandate to the demarcated borders of the state. This creates an adaptive tension upon NIS to adjust, to capture and to manage those international flows that directly impact upon its territoriality (Keating, 2013). Conceptualised in these terms, globality within infrastructure systems is reflected in the relative ease with which international flows can move between and within NIS. This reflects not only the ability to move freely across borders but also the ability of these flows to utilise NIS to penetrate deep into state territory. The logic of state welfarism (Ruggie, 1982) depends – in part – upon the ability of the state to moderate the intensity of these flows through 'protective walls' (Genschel and Seelkopf, 2012). However, the logic of the competition state suggests that states should remove (or at the least reduce) such barriers as they seek to position themselves in a global market and capture the footloose flows of capital that move across borders.

Although states (and their respective NIS) are regarded here as the core building block of the Global Infrastructure System (GIS), the GIS is nevertheless a mixture of the territorial (that is, infrastructures that operate within the demarcated space of the state); quasi-territorial (that is, infrastructures that lie within but are not sourced or destined for that territory); and non-territorial (that is, those infrastructures beyond territorial control within the global commons). In a global system of flows (Castells, 2010), it is the interactions and interdependencies between these components that form and shape the GIS. This approach recognises that infrastructures are more than the conventional terrestrial physical assets and that international transmission can involve terrestrial and non-terrestrial movements, that global infrastructure networks have a 'non-physical' component (through

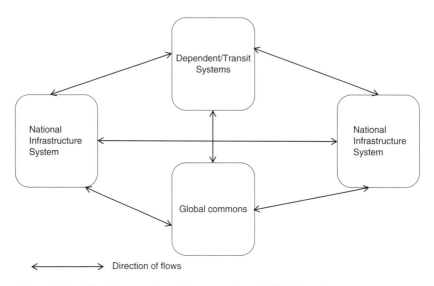

*Figure 2.1   The framework of the state-based Global Infrastructure
             System*

so-called 'soft' infrastructure systems) and include both territorial (that is,
state-based infrastructures) and non-territorial (that is, communal shipping lanes, airspace and other components of the global commons) space.
This is reflected within the GIS framework set out in Figure 2.1.

In operating as a bridge between the themes developed in Chapter 1
and the sectoral chapters that follow, this chapter explores more fully the
structure of the GIS identified in Figure 2.1. As such, the chapter initially
focuses on the adaptive tensions within the NIS generated by globality. This
involves two phases. The first outlines the case for state primacy within the
GIS, arguing that the state remains – through the infrastructuring function
– a key conditioner for the global system. This is largely viewed through the
realist lens of International Political Economy. The second phase focuses
on the adaptive tensions created within and across NIS by the process of
globality (defined here not as the end point of globalisation, as advanced
by Robertson (1992), but as a state of interaction, interdependence or
integration between national systems) and emphasises how these processes
place pressures upon these user-based systems to adapt in order to sustain
the attainment of the infrastructural mandate. After this territorial component has been explored, the issue of dependent territoriality and the role of
the global commons are examined. Whilst the territorial state dominates,
dependent territoriality and the global commons are also salient to understanding the structure and form of the system.

THE PRIMACY OF THE STATE IN THE GIS

Within the contemporary global system of territorial states, the main agent that oversees and develops infrastructure within a territory remains the state. Indeed, the Organisation for Economic Co-operation and Development (OECD, 2015) estimates that two-thirds to three-quarters of all public infrastructure investment (that is, those segments of the system which are either directly publicly funded and/or available for public use) is still undertaken by the state. As Chapter 1 argues, the infrastructural mandate (as the logic of state infrastructuring) reflects how the state organises its space through spatially fixed infrastructures to enable the state to attain its objectives (Costa et al., 2014). Even within polycentric NIS (for a review of the concept of polycentrism, see Ostrom, 2010), the state is still proactive in ensuring that non-state providers/owners of infrastructure (especially those deemed critical to the territoriality of the state – see later) support and facilitate the infrastructural mandate. Whilst this subset of the NIS is focused on private infrastructure, it remains heavily dependent upon state-funded or legitimised public infrastructure to enable end-to-end connectivity (Moteff, 2012). As such, wide area private networks can – at best – be virtually private. Moreover, the private component of the NIS also relies upon the supporting state-enabled soft infrastructure. Indeed, as mentioned in Chapter 1, much of the non-state investment in NIS occurs either with state sanction or in collaboration with the state (Stern, 2014). This reflects the co-existence of a polycentric NIS with the regulatory state to steer non-state investment towards the attainment of the state's infrastructural objectives (Majone, 1994).

Such an approach clearly takes issue with the approaches of many within the international political economy (IPE) field (such as Strange, 1996) who see polycentrism (which has emerged via the combined processes of privatisation, liberalisation and technological change) as a direct erosion of state power. The contention here is that whilst ownership, especially within developed states, has shifted towards private interests, the need for state infrastructuring and issues concerning critical infrastructures (see Chapter 1) mean the state retains a right to steer the NIS to suit its needs through regulation, legitimisation, public service obligations, residual rights and/or direct ownership (Levi-Faur, 2005). There is plenty of evidence that states are selective over who owns infrastructure, that they compel non-state owners to deliver the infrastructural mandate and that they are prepared to intervene directly in ownership when needed, especially with regard to critical infrastructure (OECD, 2008). Moreover, the privatisation of public infrastructure works where the state sees no need to own infrastructure where non-state infrastructuring offers a sustaining commercial system that does not imperil the infrastructural mandate (Brook and Irwin, 2003).

The logic of this approach is rationalised by the structure of a territorially fragmented system which interoperates and – where possible – interconnects to allow cross-border flows. The importance of NIS as the bedrock of the system is either as a source or destination of flows or as a place of transit. The state controls the system, even when the flows are over non-territorial domains due to hegemonic power within such domains (see later) and by the fact that flows over the commons require both a territorial point of embarkation and disembarkation and – where necessary – territorial transit. State primacy underscores how the efficiency of global flows depends upon national infrastructure to enable end-to-end connection, but also on state sanctioning of flows to enter a territory through state monitoring and filtering of flows through gateway infrastructures. This is complicated by spatial variations in the quality of soft infrastructure and the widely acknowledged differences between states over the quality, maturity and development of their respective NIS. Such factors condition the ability of global forces to penetrate deep into territories. Thus, although the state interacts with global forces, it remains preoccupied with strategic considerations (Jackson and James, 1993). In short, the argument that globalism overwhelms the ability of the state to manage flows through its territory and therefore undermines the power of the state finds little credence in practice (Weiss, 1998; Hay, 2004).

State primacy within the international infrastructure system finds its strongest resonance within neo-realist perspectives. Neo-realism stresses that the international system is a system of states with the former working to deliver benefits to the latter (Gilpin, 1987). As such, the interconnection between NIS occurs through the mutual benefits derived from such arrangements and where global flows add to the welfare of the state and its citizens (Dunne and Schmidt, 2005; Gilpin, 2011). This realist treatment of the GIS traces its emergence to an expression of state self-interest such that infrastructure becomes a tool of the state as it seeks to preserve and/or enhance its power within – or beyond – its borders. This approach is concerned with an abstract notion of the 'national interest' shaped by social, political and economic interests within the state. The search for consensus between these interests (as expressed within the form, structure and function of the NIS) shapes the system's development and its evolution (Walt, 2002). As the GIS has no single body responsible for shaping its development, it remains subject to state infrastructuring strategies and how these narrow, nationally focused actions shape the operation of the entire system. It is an ultimate truism that states develop NIS to serve national needs and only serve cross-border needs when it is in a state's interest to do so (Johnson and Turner, 1997, 2007).

The degree of state integration into the GIS is shaped by inconsistencies between states over relative priorities within the infrastructural mandate and by their relative capability to adapt systems to reflect these priorities (see the respective sector chapters). These inconsistencies also extend to adaption to external events and processes. According to Palan and Abbott (1996), these adaptations are driven by a constellation of international forces and by states' choice of priorities regarding flows and their impact upon any conflicts within the infrastructural mandate. The choice of strategy normally reflects one or more of the following considerations, namely the legacy of historical choices and the resilience of internal forces to drive form and change in infrastructure systems (Guzzini, 1998). However, realism cannot fully escape the criticism of social constructivists (who share the realist position of a belief in a state-centred system) that such approaches tend to treat the state as a black box with little consideration given to where the priorities within the infrastructural mandate are sourced and to how state infrastructural strategies are formed (Hurd, 2008; Adler, 2013).

GLOBALITY AND THE NATIONAL INFRASTRUCTURE SYSTEM

Whilst it has not always been explicit (see Johnson and Turner, 1997, 2007), the international dimension of infrastructure exists as a matter of practical inter-state interaction. Historically, for many states the primary focus of internationalism within the NIS has been through the creation of gateway infrastructure, which provides points of entry to NIS by non-national users and the point of exit for domestic users (Edwards et al., 2007). As globality has intensified, these practical considerations have given way to stronger adaptive tensions within NIS as states seek to manage the rising intensity and velocity of global flows which are transforming both infrastructure and the state's relationship with it (Held et al., 1999). A GIS built to serve an international system of nation states has had its deficiencies exposed as the process of globality has intensified and highlighted how states protect the integrity of their borders in the face of rising global traffic flows (Johnson and Turner, 1997). This made the focus of state infrastructuring overwhelmingly internal rather than the effective management of internal and external interfaces resulting in gateway infrastructure that was beginning to look no longer fit for purpose.

Over the past three decades, national infrastructure systems have become more globally open systems which have transformed states' relationships with infrastructure as the system adjusts to the transition from 'thin' to 'thick' globality (Keohane and Nye, 2001). The interconnections between national systems have been driven, first, by the emergence of polycentric infrastructure systems which function as an amalgam of meta-national competences and resources, with the result that the infrastructural mandate has to be realised over systems that the state no longer owns or directly controls (Rinaldi et al., 2001). This has also manifested itself in system design and configuration based on international standards, dispersed knowledge and modular structures. This adaption by states through the adoption or acceptance of international rules or norms underscores the reality that sovereignty can no longer be treated as territorially fixed and that states can influence the behaviour of other states, often through indirect chains of causation (Ruggie, 1993). Second, 'thick globality' has been driven by rising transnational traffic flows. These have intensified and embedded globality in the state's infrastructural mandate, potentially extending it beyond state borders to mitigate external risks and to create opportunities for domestic infrastructure systems sourced from infrastructures beyond its territory, both in terms another state's system or in areas that lie within the 'global commons' (see later).

This process is reflected in the adaptation of states to the emergence of spatial complexity within NIS. The spatial complexity of NIS is defined here as the idea that although infrastructures are territorially fixed, the activities that occur over them or affect their ability to act as infrastructure cannot be reducible to that point in space where they are used. Moreover, the conditions for the ability of infrastructure to act as infrastructure extend beyond the place of usage given that its effects are not spatially specific and can spread. The result of such complexity is that governance (defined here as any mode of coordination of interdependent actions, see Jessop, 1990) poses the challenge of reducing complexity because it is impossible to control all the processes, events and resultant flows that have the capability to impact on the performance of the NIS. This depends upon the identification of a subset of features of infrastructure systems that can be governed to enable the state to steer the shape and form of the NIS. The spatial complexity within NIS is a direct legacy of the coalescence of inter-relationships between technological change, globalisation and liberalisation (Graham and Marvin, 2001; Cerny, 2010; Dicken, 2011) and has driven the emergence of more structurally and functionally complex NIS (Braithwaite and Drahos, 2000; Collier and Ong, 2005). The literature on criticality within infrastructure systems (Rinaldi et al., 2001; Roberts et al., 2012), briefly explored in Chapter 1, further underlines the salience of spatial complexity where inter-system dependencies create links between

Table 2.1   Infrastructural dimension and the adaptation of infrastructure

Dimensions	Globality
Embeddedness	Networks 'sunk' into globalising activities.
Transparency	As easy to use across borders as within borders.
Reach/scope	Global activity requires corresponding networks that interconnect to enable every part of the global economy to transmit and receive traffic from any other part.
Learned as part of membership	Non-nationals should readily be able to understand the architecture of the infrastructure.
Links to conventions	Adoption of best practice of usage across territories to facilitate seamless flows of traffic.
Embodiment of standards	Facilitate seamlessness via adoption of agreed standards.
Built on installed user base	Globality is built on the changing demands of a pre-existing base of users and their changing infrastructural needs.
Visible on breakdown	Where a NIS gateway fails via capacity or transnational cascade effects (see later).

different systems that are ambiguous to the point of imperceptibility at the point of usage (Hughes, 1983). The legacy of these adaptive tensions has been underscored by the shift in the core dimensions of infrastructure identified by Bowker and Star (1999; see Table 2.1).

The global stretching of relations suggested by the maturation of modernity has made users less place-bound as they build new relations and rely less on heritage (Giddens, 1985; Beck, 2005) and where the power relations engendered within these relations can no longer be confined within borders (Taylor, 1994). The extent to which this shift in relations represents a shift in state, business and civic society relations as globality becomes the norm within intra-territorial relations is a moot point (Ohmae, 1990; Brenner, 1999; Held et al., 1999). Cameron and Palan (2004) argue that this shift in user relations reflects an ongoing discourse on the salience of globalisation and suggest that the system is being shaped by a global narrative that reinforces the notion of a scaling up of the NIS. Such narratives are often informed by debates on the competition state where infrastructure is less of a community resource and more of a national asset to aid territorial competitive positioning (Cerny, 2010). These narratives also drive a learning process within communities to create a user mind-set around globality within infrastructure systems (Marsden, 1993).

Many 'globalisation sceptics' (for example, Hirst and Thompson, 2002; Ghemawat, 2003) downplay the direct salience of globality for users by pointing out that cross-border infrastructural flows are dwarfed by domestic flows across all infrastructures. Globality is only an immediate issue for those users whose activities operate on a transnational scale, such as global logistics suppliers, energy suppliers and telecoms infrastructures' owners. Nonetheless, such reductionist approaches understate the complexity of infrastructure systems. As Sassen (2013) notes, not all processes within a territory are designed for that territory and there is plenty of anecdotal evidence indicating that the increasingly functionally and spatially complex infrastructure systems have globality buried within them to the extent that it is imperceptible to many users (Star and Bowker, 2006). This embedded globality within infrastructure systems only becomes visible to users at the point at which it shapes involuntary infrastructural relations (see later). Taylor (1994) suggests that global processes are filtered through national political and economic systems, which helps explain the opacity of these impacts on the local system.

For the state, this scaling up of user relations (and the embedded – and often imperceptible – spatial complexity) matters insofar as it impacts upon the state's infrastructural mandate. The inference from the process of globality is that there are extra-territorial determinants of the infrastructural mandate and that the state needs to act beyond its borders to enable its NIS to achieve its full territorial benefits (Van der Vleuten and Kaijser, 2005). The NIS – as territorial configurations – are under a constant process of change and are updated and reconfigured as the demands placed upon them alter (Harvey, 1982). These are shaped by interconnections between national systems as a result of meta-national competences and resources within NIS, which renders infrastructural mandate dependent – at least in part – on non-domestic resources; and by rising cross-border traffic flows that augment and/or undermine the infrastructural mandate (Badenoch and Fickers, 2010). These broad themes are reflected in Table 2.2. In the terminology of Taylor (1994), the state may be a 'leaking bordered power container', but these flows can complement, co-exist and even enhance the infrastructural mandate (see later). This argument runs counter to the hyperglobalists who suggest a conflict between the systems of global flows and the national systems that support such flows where the former erodes the infrastructural mandate. NIS are built to serve and evolve with the needs of the state. As these needs change, these systems should also evolve. As such, in assessing how the deeper integration associated with 'thick globality' affects a state's mandate, authors such as Weiss (2005) and Held and McGrew (2007) argue that globalisation does not disable the state but can complement and co-exist with state competences and that ultimately the state adapts to its changing context.

However, the GIS is not a fully open system because states retain

Table 2.2   Globality and the infrastructural mandate

Mandate Function	The indicative impact of globality
Control	Mann (1997) identified that the ability of the state to control territory has been challenged by the rise in transnational networks that supersede loyalty to the state and which can – through the utilisation of technology – be difficult to control.
Integration	The logic of the competition state suggests a need to extend the integrative role of national and sub-national infrastructure to the global system. This external integration function cascades down to all levels of intra-state infrastructure.
Security	More intensive flows (both in terms of speed and volume) crossing borders as well as new globally deployed technologies (such as information infrastructure) create new security threats. This is compounded by more diverse sources of external flows and of ownership patterns. Globality also changes the dynamics of energy and transportation systems.
Growth	As per the themes of integration, for many states their NIS needs to reflect embeddedness within the global system of flows. Growth for many states depends upon gaining access to overseas markets and resources and the NIS needs to support this.

restraints on elements of globality, in part driven by the infrastructural mandate. Globalising and opening the system may compromise this objective (OECD, 2008). As such, flows are not de-territorialised within a global network of networks but flow between multi-scalar infrastructures (see Chapter 1), with national systems connected across borders or across the global commons and variations in quality, quantity and soft infrastructure which can limit full interoperability. To some degree, these issues can be mitigated where there are historically close links between systems such as in Europe (Van der Vleuten and Kaijser, 2005). Post-9/11, many states diverted attention to effective methods of protecting critical infrastructure. The globality of the infrastructure system means that the desire to protect a territory can involve infrastructure beyond the territory that seeks protection. In other words, a state's infrastructure is vulnerable to the actions/discretion of other states based on the interconnections between states (see later).

Perrow (1984) stated that infrastructure can fail in a multitude of unpredictable ways, creating a potential conflict between globality and criticality within NIS. This conflict is created by the risk of negative feedback loops (so-called 'transnational cascades') across the GIS that can undermine the infrastructural mandate through either human-derived or natural events or processes. The existence of transnational cascades undermines the state's ability to exclude external actors, events or processes from influencing the performance of NIS. Counteracting these infrastructural cascades is problematic due to their unpredictability: first, these cascades are hybrid phenomena whose dynamics are shaped by periods of stability punctuated by discontinuities; second, their impact varies according to the state of the pre-existing network which can vary both spatially and temporally; and, third, the response of the infrastructure to discontinuities is uncertain (Rinaldi et al., 2001; OECD, 2008). Moreover, transnational cascades can also be transmitted through the perception of risk to the extent that flows are either deterred or prohibited (either by cost or legal channels) (Little, 2002). These vulnerabilities are created by twin impacts of infrastructure; that is, through acting as a transmission channel through which these cascades are transmitted into NIS or through an ongoing reliance upon external infrastructure to transmit key resources into the national econosphere, including global pipeline systems for energy security, remote server farms for the storage of mission critical data or core regional hubs that service a state's import and export markets (OECD, 2008). Dixon and Monk (2012) suggest that the impact of cascades on a state is driven by three conditions: inequality of power between states; relational sovereignty that complicates a state's capacity and the non-territorial exercise of power across space connected by flows (Agnew, 2005).

In terms of functional cascades across infrastructure, Little (2002) identifies three types of cascade. The first is a simple, linear process of transmission from one infrastructure to another through direct physical links between NIS. The second is an escalating cascade where disruption to a single piece of infrastructure escalates to generate accentuated problems in other systems. The third type of cascade is a common cause of failure in which there is a simultaneous disruption of multiple infrastructures. Transnational cascades, to some degree, have parallels in this typology but in this case the cascade effects are dependent on the degree of economic integration between states. As such, these cascade events can have bi-state (that is, a simple transmission effect between two states), multi-state (that is, transmission from one state/location to multiple locations across multiple states) and global effects (that is, where failure has a ubiquitous effect across the global economy). Table 2.3 sets out the typical transnational cascade effects which reflect system design and the role of history in creating such vulnerabilities that in some cases are due to the system not adapting to a shifting environmental context and user expectations of infrastructure (Van der Vleuten and Lagendijk, 2010).

The nature of complex infrastructure systems is such that they can fail

Table 2.3   Examples of transnational cascades

Cause	Examples of vulnerabilities
Transit rights	One state (especially, but not only, if landlocked) relies on another for transit of goods to key hubs. This is evidenced by the case of Sudan and South Sudan, where the secession of the latter from the former created co-dependencies on oil infrastructure. This is an example of dependent territoriality which is explored later.
Rogue agents	These agents can target key infrastructure through acts of piracy or terrorism that affect flows through the system (see, for example, Murphy, 2007).
Accidents	Unintended human disruption, for example anchor damage to oceanic cables. Oceanic cable damage in the Mediterranean in the late 1990s led to a 70 per cent loss of Egypt's and 60 per cent loss of India's internet capacity.
Soft infrastructure	States may have an under-developed soft infrastructure that undermines the capabilities of transmission infrastructure through forces such as corruption, bias, etc.
Capacity crunch	Unexpected bottleneck, congestion and capacity shortages within key infrastructure which – in the absence of alternatives – causes traffic flows to stall. For example, the eruption of the Icelandic volcano in 2010 which led to the cancellation of 95,000 flights across the European air space due to congested air hubs (Sammonds et al., 2010).
Depreciation	A reduction in infrastructure capability created by a failure to maintain and/or upgrade infrastructure. Transnational energy blackouts in North America and Europe/Africa (Van der Vleuten and Lagendijk, 2010) are examples of this phenomenon.
Political disputes	Divergent power relations created by ownership/access to key infrastructures and control of access to resources.
Logistical flows	Key natural or man-made constraints that limit flows through key logistical bottlenecks or through routes.
Risk in global systems	Unpredictable global events that hinder the effective functioning of transmission systems.
Principal–agent problem	Within a polycentric system, disputes can emerge between the state and the infrastructure owner over the form and function of the relevant infrastructure.
Third party export infrastructure	One state can impede another's ability to export. The XL Pipeline was proposed to allow Canada to export energy to the US (to aid its security) but this was hindered by local environmental sensitivity in north mid-western US states. The XL Pipeline was also indicative of spillover as non-national bodies were investing in another state's infrastructure to aid its exports.
Complexity cascades	These are unforeseen and unpredicted impacts across multiple states caused by a minor alteration to major infrastructure or from major alteration to minor infrastructure in another state.

in a multitude of ways, many of which are difficult to predict (Perrow, 1984). Such failures – through their impact on the infrastructural mandate (irrespective of the time frame over which the effects are evident) – represent a challenge to state power where cascade effects from the global system are difficult to isolate. This is certainly a position advanced by many complexity theorists, notably Goldin and Mariathasan (2014), who argue that such infrastructures pose a systemic risk from the international system for the state. Given such risks, there are evident incentives for states to seek greater isolation within or, at least, to renew fragmentation of the global system. However, there is a growing body of opinion within IPE that embedding the state into the global system, far from challenging state power, can actually enable it (for example, Weiss, 1998). In terms of NIS, there is little evidence that globality has decreased a state's desire to infrastructure despite the risks. Much of this has been driven not only by the logic of the competition state but also by the desire to ensure that all parts of a territory are accessible to global markets and/or value systems. Such 'global narratives' are common in state infrastructure strategies (for example, OECD, 2008). Indeed, it is commonly accepted in neo-liberal organisations such as the World Economic Forum and the OECD that states should be increasing their infrastructure spend, even against a background of widespread public sector austerity. This reinforces the view that infrastructure spending is 'good government spending' (Turnovsky, 1999). However, authors such as Flyvberg (2009) question such views given the quantity of 'bad' infrastructure that gets built. In terms of globality, the emergence of polycentric NIS means the state draws on a global pool of investment funding and know-how to both fund and shape its evolution. The need for the state to embed the NIS is evident across all the sectors studied. This is expressed most obviously in the close links between the energy security of many states and the state of the global energy system. There are evident strategies by states to ensure that – as mentioned – all parts of the territory have access to infrastructure that enables integration into the global system. Although these examples are not exhaustive, they do illustrate that there are direct incentives for states to interconnect into the global system to enable its infrastructural mandate.

***

As the bedrock of the GIS, NIS are facing up to a number of adaptive tensions created by the evolving intensity of cross-border flows. These flows reflect an increased trend towards the globalising of interactions. The legacy of this for state infrastructuring is a need to adapt the NIS to the tension formed by such pressures, notably in terms of their potential impacts upon the infrastructural mandate. For states, this means an increased focus on external facing infrastructure. However, the more tightly integrated NIS creates problems for states where there is the risk of transnational cascades that have the capability to undermine state functioning. It is with such systemic risks in mind that attention is now turned to other parts of the GIS.

GLOBAL COMMONS

With the global stretching of political, economic and social relations, the commons have become a key part of industry supply chains (Kindleberger, 1986). Although global commons do not always possess a direct physical manifestation, they are key to the operation of the global infrastructure system (Frischmann, 2005). Consequently, many states and international organisations regard the global commons as infrastructure. These commons are defined by the US Department of Defence as 'the fabric or connective tissue of the international system' (in areas such as logistics, energy and oceanic cable systems) and exhibit the following characteristics (as quoted in Aaltola et al., 2014):

1) They are not owned or controlled by any single entity (that is, no state has sovereignty or control over them) but are governed by international treaties (see Table 2.4) which define allowable uses and prohibitions.
2) Their utility as a whole is greater than individual parts.
3) States and non-state actors with the requisite technological capabilities are freely able to access and use the global commons for economic, political, scientific and cultural purposes.

So defined, these are segments of the globe that are non-territorial but which all states need to access as part of their active engagement with the global flows across infrastructure (Aaltola et al., 2014). In terms of the GIS, three areas of the commons are of direct interest: the high seas, airspace and cyberspace. The commons are open to use by states, organisations and individuals and the maintenance of these flows (and access to the commons) are core to the global system and to state mandates. However, because they are non-territorial, there is an expectation that the commons are accessible to everyone but, over the long term, they may well fall into decline because no single body takes responsibility for their upkeep (Ramel, 2014). This problem created what Hardin (1968) called the 'tragedy of the commons'. Arguably, the main problem with the global commons is that they can be a major source of disruption to global flows

Table 2.4   The global commons

Sector	Definition	Treaties
Maritime	The high seas are those areas beyond 12 miles off the coast of a state.	United Nations Charter of the Law of the Sea (UNCLOS) – signed in 1982 and effective from 1994 with 167 states (see Chapter 3).
Airspace	Those vertical components over non-territorial parts of the earth's surface and also those parts of the atmosphere above 60,000 feet.	UN International Civil Aviation Authority as established under the 1944 Chicago Convention which has 191 signatories (see Chapter 3).
Outer space	The area above the Kármán line, at an altitude of 100 km (62 miles) above sea level, is conventionally used as the start of outer space in space treaties.	Satellites regulated by a mix of bilateral, multilateral and international agreements; 1967 Outer Space Treaty
Cyberspace	This is the 'notional' environment in which communication over computer networks occurs.	A mix of national and international governance but with increased emphasis on state-based control (see Chapter 4).

across infrastructure as highlighted by events such as cyberattacks and piracy in key maritime bottlenecks.

Effective freedom to operate within the commons requires that they are secure and enable states to meet their respective mandates through these domains as the commons become increasingly key not only to the welfare enhancing effects of trade but also to security and control (Vogler, 2012). As such, the governance of the commons revolves around three key issues, namely sustained access for security and commercial reasons; protection of the commons from environmental factors that diminish their quality and securing the commons as a global public good (Jasper, 2010). The challenge of the commons for the state-based GIS is that problems between state-based users can occur over part of the Earth's surface where there is no single state control and therefore no direct responsibility for any disruption that occurs within it. The consequence has been the legitimate rise of hegemonic power within the commons as a means to secure mobility across them. It is normally the hegemon that bears the cost of this public good because to do so is in its own interest either through longer-term economic gains to itself from access or from more nuanced political gains generated by goodwill or some other form of soft power as a result of these actions. However, the commons cannot be secured in any meaningful sense and the practical governance of the commons does not refer to vast open spaces but to a few select points within the system where impeded flows can cause military or commercial harm (Ostrom et al., 1999). These choke points are defined by physical capacity relative to traffic flows in the absence of available substitutes.

Over the past seven decades, the US has led the development of shared rules for the commons designed to keep the system open for the purposes of trade and international mobility (Denmark, 2010). This was based on the development of a liberal international order to shape the management of these areas, not only to keep the system open but also to deter rogue states or agents from disrupting the system and to keep these core arteries open. According to Aaltola et al. (2014) strategising in the commons depends upon three factors:

1. Defining them as existentially important given that social and economic systems cannot function without access to the global commons;
2. Understanding of the form and nature of the vulnerabilities regarding the security of freedoms within the commons; and
3. Ensuring that action on the commons is proportionate to the threats to it.

US enforcement of the command of the commons (Posen, 2003) is carried out through the exercise of hard maritime power which requires a supporting infrastructure of military bases to exercise the necessary control. For example, the US maintains a network of military bases around core choke points in the Middle East. According to Aaltola et al. (2014), the control of the commons requires the control of three communities of practice, namely the global flow community, the security community and the hostile, disrupting community.

In light of the 2007–8 financial crisis and its legacy of austerity, the US has been seeking to share the management of the commons with key allies, notably within the context of formal military alliances such as NATO. Financial constraint by the global hegemon is compounded by a number of other factors. First, the rise of new powers. China, for example, has defined an exclusive economic zone between 12 to 200 miles from its coast and stresses that passage through this area can occur only with its assent. This sets a precedent as China is starting to challenge US dominance within the commons. This is in no small part driven by China's reliance on energy flows through these zones. Second, many states (notably the hegemonic powers) are developing access denial/area denial technologies to limit free access to the commons: this is especially true of the maritime commons, which have often been the basis for hegemonic power. Third is the increased ability of non-governmental organisations (NGO) to disrupt flows where developments such as piracy and cyber-attacks highlight that challenges to states' powers do not only emerge from the geopolitics of large states but also from smaller states and non-state actors. These threats, especially from non-state groups, are also evident within civil aviation. Fourth, there is the potential for the commons to become a battleground for states as they seek to access the mineral rights within them (for example, the rival claims over such rights within the Arctic). Such pressures could see more states taking a more concerted interest in aspects of the commons.

DEPENDENT TERRITORIALITY

Dependent territoriality is where the capability of the state to fulfil its infrastructural mandate is dependent upon another NIS. This dependence can be created from two main sources. The first is direct dependence based on flows across contiguous NIS where any disruption to the flows from the source state erodes the recipient state's infrastructural mandate. The second – and more common source of dependence – is where flows have to pass through the territory of a third party sovereign state (or states) where the transit state is neither the source nor the destination for the flow. The capability of the transit state to restrict the de-territorialisation and/or re-territorialisation of flows, as well as to affect form and volume of flows at the point of access to global system, shows it can impact upon the infra-structural mandate of either the source or destination state. Dependent ter-ritoriality demonstrates the complexity of infrastructural relations based on flows between contiguous and non-contiguous states, especially those that depend upon a transit state and the exercise of its territorial rights. There are number of dimensions to dependent territoriality in the GIS, including:

1) Dependence by a state (either the destination for or source of a flow) upon another's infrastructure due to the former's landlocked status (see Chapter 3);
2) The reliance of a state or group of states on transit routes through a third state for the purposes of logistics and movement of products in the supply chain;
3) Inadequate capacity and capability in one state leading to another state depending on another to access global flows;
4) Inadequate infrastructure in one state undermining the efficacy of another bordering state;

5) Dependence generated by the outlying location of a state away from the main transit routes to the extent that the state relies upon extra-territorial hubs to ensure flows (see Small Island Developing States (SIDS), Chapter 3).

These infrastructures highlight the potential for several developments within the broader GIS. First, flows across a state can be divorced from the attainment of an infrastructural mandate. Second, a state-based infrastructure can have an impact upon other states by operating as an international hub to the extent that their welfare can be affected by its performance. This is compounded by the potential for a free rider problem within the GIS. Third, state territoriality – in line with the perspective of Agnew (1994) – cannot be neatly confined to the demarcated borders of the state. Fourth, some key transit states push the dependent territoriality of other states to the fore of their geo-economic and/or geopolitical strategy. Fifth, the development, senescence and obsolescence of one NIS can have significant impacts on other parts of the GIS.

As highlighted in Chapter 3, landlocked states are the most evident form of dependent territoriality where the absence of a direct route into the global logistical system can represent clear vulnerability. This is not simply about the physical links to entry points into the global system but is also about the capacity and management of the entry point itself (themes explored more fully in Chapter 3). The result is that landlocked states remain vulnerable to the disruption of flows to the extent that the state's infrastructural mandate can be compromised. This vulnerability is more a feature of developing, rather than developed, landlocked states – because the latter are more tightly integrated into neighbouring infrastructure systems, which militates against any perception of isolation and facilitates access into the global system. For developing states, relations with neighbours are often less than cordial, if not outright hostile, which – in the absence of alternative links/hubs – renders the state especially vulnerable. However, much of the policy narratives for landlocked and the main type of isolated state (the SIDS – see Chapter 3) are shaped by how these states compete given their relative isolation (World Bank, 2015) and their consequent high trading costs – a problem compounded by the frequently poor state of the NIS in these locations (Arvis, 2011). This growth issue is compounded by vulnerabilities relating to economic security, and possibly control, where there is clear asymmetry of power between the state and the transit state (Gallup et al., 1999).

For developed states, the issue of dependent territoriality is sourced more from vulnerabilities within the global logistical system arising from key 'choke points' or bottlenecks (Rodrigue, 2004; Emmerson and Stevens,

2012). The main maritime channels, also including key hubs, are seen as especially problematic in time of conflict and where hegemonic action is (as mentioned earlier) commonly legitimised. These vulnerabilities have been especially evident with the spatial stretching of the global energy system (see Chapter 5). This raises not only the salience of transit through key maritime channels, especially around the Arabian Peninsula, but also that of terrestrial pipeline systems (Kong, 2010). These pipelines require multilateral legitimisation (Omonbude, 2012) where any state has the right to shift their strategic preferences which can challenge rights of transit (Kandiyoti, 2012). Again this is evident where the transit state has bargaining power that is shaped by the absence of available alternative routes. This threat to developed states is only likely to increase as energy supply chains grow more stretched and as jurisdictions become more fragmented.

These issues within dependent territoriality highlight themes identified within Chapter 1, namely the increasingly ambiguous nature of state-based territoriality, which implies that elements of the state's infrastructural mandate are externally determined. For transit states, flows through their territory that have little or no direct bearing on their own infrastructural mandate are legitimised – often by hegemonic influence – and compensated by the receipt of transit fees in exchange for free access. Issues of transit have become an especially salient theme within debates on territoriality as such rights are increasingly central to the geopolitics of the GIS. In theory, transit states represent a source of political instability in the global space of flows as they can directly alter the capacity of the system with direct consequences for the welfare of states which are either the source or the destination for flows. This reflects arguments made in Chapter 1 regarding the shifting nature of territoriality where some infrastructure systems operate in a larger operational space than can be understood purely by the state-based system. This is underpinned by the idea that infrastructural relations occur across non-contiguous spaces or where a single infrastructure has multiple destinations and span multiple layers of governance. However, in separating flows from the underlying physical infrastructure, it is evident that such meta-national systems are still heavily dependent upon the state-based system because the efficacy of such systems is contingent upon state consent and legitimisation and cannot work independently of such constraints.

It is suggested by Barysch (2008) that the political economy of dependent territoriality is shaped by factors such as the transit state's reliance upon foreign direct investment (FDI), the level of internal security, the size of the transit benefits and the availability of alternative routes. In practice, such infrastructures, most notably pipelines, tend to have a more regional than global impact with the source of the flows often being the source of disruption rather than the transit state itself. For example, the case of Russia in its dispute over the transit of gas through the Ukraine (see Larrabee, 2010). Overall, although dependent territoriality does not always create the basis for good relations between states, the prospect of rent from transit can often compensate, despite issues of geopolitics and the risk that such behaviour will only increase the perception of political risks attached to the transit state and impede ongoing and future investor relations with that state.

CONCLUSION

The framework for the GIS set out within this chapter provides a bridge for analysis between the nature of the NIS identified within Chapter 1 and the respective sectoral chapters that follow. The state-based GIS reflects how states form and shape the global system of infrastructures. The state infrastructural mandate has and is adapting to global forces. Elements of control, security, integration and prosperity are all being reshaped and redefined by the forces of globality. Nonetheless, the state infrastructural mandate remains a heavy influence on how states approach the process of interaction with other NIS as states seek to engage with international flows whilst retaining control. As this volume moves on to examine individual sectors, it is argued that state infrastructuring within a global context reflects a need to reconcile a number of potential conflicts within the state infrastructure mandate generated by global interactions. The consequence is that the GIS is often concurrently subject to forces that drive its integration and fragmentation. These forces of integration and fragmentation within the GIS reflect the multitude of forces at state level and above that are directly shaping its pattern of evolution. The increasing focus on system complexity within both infrastructure and global economic systems demonstrates that the effects of these forces of integration and fragmentation can have impacts beyond the borders of the state. Where the impact of such action has potential or actual global effects, hegemonic power is legitimised to preserve the integrity of the system.

Narratives on globality reflect the relative impact of global flows upon the state and its ability to exercise territoriality. This chapter has focused on the idea that the efficacy of these global flows depends upon the physical fixed assets located within and between states. Without these structures, the forces of globality cannot penetrate into state socio-economic and political structures. The GIS, as a means of channelling international flows, depends heavily on state-based infrastructure systems where the state – as the main exerciser of territoriality – remains the primary infrastructuring agent. This primacy reflects both the needs of the state's infrastructural mandate and the pressures for the state to adapt to global forces, both proactively and reactively, as a means of enabling, supporting or even protecting state territoriality. This is reflected within the relative forces for integration and fragmentation within the GIS which define its operation and efficacy. These forces for integration and fragmentation are dealt with on a sector-by-sector basis in the following chapters. However, the framework offered facilitates the identification of sources of integration and fragmentation within the GIS as they lie within the respective NIS and the strategies deployed both inter- and intra-territorially to secure the infrastructural mandate. Moreover, it is also evident that flows across non-territorial spaces also impact upon this process. In addition, these issues arise not only from the degree of integration of hard infrastructure but also from the extent of convergence/divergence between soft infrastructures.

REFERENCES

Aaltola, M., Vuorisalo, V. and Käpylä, M.J. (2014) *The Challenge of Global Commons and Flows for US Power: The Perils of Missing the Human Domain.* Farnham, UK: Ashgate.

Adler, E. (2013) 'Constructivism in international relations: sources, contributions, and debates', in Carlsnaes, W., Risse, T. and Simmons, B.A. (eds.), *Handbook of International Relations.* Thousand Oaks, CA: Sage, pp. 112–44.

Agnew, J. (1994) 'The territorial trap: the geographical assumptions of international relations theory', *Review of International Political Economy*, 1(1), 53–80.

Agnew, J. (2005) 'Sovereignty regimes: territoriality and state authority in contemporary world politics', *Annals of the Association of American Geographers*, 95(2), 437–61.

Arvis, J.F. (2011) *Connecting Landlocked Developing Countries to Markets: Trade Corridors in the 21st Century.* Washington, DC: World Bank Publications.

Badenoch, A. and Fickers, A. (ed.) (2010) *Materializing Europe: Transnational Infrastructures and the Project of Europe.* Basingstoke, UK: Palgrave Macmillan.

Barysch, K. (2008) *Pipelines, Politics and Power: The Future of EU–Russia Energy Relations.* London: Centre for European Reform (CER).

Beck, U. (2005) *Power in The Global Age: A New Global Political Economy.* London: Polity Press.

Bowker, G.C. and Star, S.L. (1999) *Sorting Things Out: Classification and Its Consequences. Parts II and III.* Cambridge, MA: MIT Press.

Braithwaite, J. and Drahos, P. (2000) *Global Business Regulation.* Cambridge: Cambridge University Press.

Brenner, N. (1999) 'Beyond state-centrism? Space, territoriality, and geographical scale in globalization studies', *Theory and Society*, 28, 39–78.

Brook, P.J. and Irwin, T. (eds.) (2003) *Infrastructure for poor people: public policy for private provision*, Vol. 823. Washington, DC: World Bank Publications.

Cameron, A. and Palan, R. (2004) *The Imagined Economies of Globalization.* London: Sage.

Castells, M. (2010) *End of Millennium: The Information Age: Economy, Society, and Culture*, Vol. 3, 2nd edn. Chichester, UK: Wiley Blackwell.

Cerny, P.G. (2010) 'The competition state today: from raison d'état to raison du monde', *Policy Studies*, *31*(1), 5–21.

Collier, S.J. and Ong, A. (eds.) (2005) 'Global assemblages, anthropological problems', in *Global Assemblages: Technology, Politics, and Ethics as Anthropological Problems*. Chichester, UK: Wiley Blackwell, pp. 3–21.

Costa, Á., Melo, S., Cruz, C. and Ali, A.S. (2014) 'The concept of polycentrism in infrastructure networks: an application to airports', *Procedia – Social and Behavioral Sciences*, *111*, 68–77.

Denmark, A.M. (2010) 'Managing the global commons', *The Washington Quarterly*, *33*(3), 165–82.

Dicken, P. (2011) *Global Shift: Mapping the Changing Contours of the Global Economy*, 6th edn. London: Sage.

Dixon, A.D. and Monk, A.H. (2012) 'Rethinking the sovereign in sovereign wealth funds', *Transactions of the Institute of British Geographers*, *37*(1), 104–17.

Dunne, T. and Schmidt, B.C. (2005) 'Realism', in Baylis, J. and Smith, S. (eds.), *The Globalization of World Politics*, 3rd edn. New York, NY: Oxford University Press, pp. 162–83.

Edwards, P.N., Jackson, S.J., Bowker, G.C. and Knobel, C.P. (2007) *Understanding Infrastructure: Dynamics, Tensions, and Design*. Ann Arbor, MI: DeepBlue, accessed 20 November 2016 at http://hdl.handle.net/2027.42/49353

Emmerson, C. and Stevens, P. (2012) *Maritime Choke Points and the Global Energy System: Charting a Way Forward*. London: Chatham House.

Flyvbjerg, B. (2009) 'Survival of the unfittest: why the worst infrastructure gets built —and what we can do about it', *Oxford Review of Economic Policy*, *25*(3), 344–67.

Frischmann, B.M. (2005) 'An economic theory of infrastructure and commons management', *Minnesota Law Review*, *89*, 917–1030.

Gallup, J.L., Sachs, J.D. and Mellinger, A.D. (1999) 'Geography and economic development', *International Regional Science Review*, *22*(2), 179–232.

Genschel, P. and Seelkopf, L. (2012) 'Did the competition state rise? Globalization, international tax competition, and national welfare', accessed 20 November 2016 at http://ssrn.com/abstract=2138848 or http://dx.doi.org/10.2139/ssrn.2138848

Ghemawat, P. (2003) 'Semiglobalization and International Business Strategy', *Journal of International Business Studies*, *34*(2), 138–52.

Giddens, A. (1985) *The nation-state and violence*, Vol. 2. Berkeley, CA: University of California Press.

Gilpin, R. (1987) *The Political Economy of International Relations*. Princeton, NJ: Princeton University Press.

Gilpin, R. (2011) *Global Political Economy: Understanding the International Economic Order*. Princeton, NJ: Princeton University Press.

Goldin, I. and Mariathasan, M. (2014) *The Butterfly Defect: How Globalization Creates Systemic Risks, and What to Do about It*. Princeton, NJ: Princeton University Press.

Graham, S. and Marvin, S. (2001) *Splintering Urbanism: Networked Infrastructures, Technological Mobilities and the Urban Condition*. London: Routledge.

Guzzini, S. (1998) *Realism in International Relations and International Political Economy: The Continuing Story of a Death Foretold*. London: Routledge.

Hardin, G. (1968) 'The tragedy of the commons', *Science*, *162*(3859), 1243–48.

Harvey, D. (1982) *The Limits to Capital*. Oxford: Blackwell.

Hay, C. (2004) 'Re-stating politics, re-politicising the state: neo-liberalism, economic imperatives and the rise of the competition state', *The Political Quarterly*, *75*(S1), 38–50.

Held, D. and McGrew, A. (2007) *Globalization/Anti-Globalization: Beyond the Great Divide*. London: Polity Press.

Held, D., McGrew, A., Goldblatt, D. and Perraton, J. (1999) *Global Transformations: Politics, Economics and Culture*. Cambridge: Polity Press.

Hirst, P. and Thompson, G. (2002) 'The future of globalization', *Cooperation and Conflict*, *37*(3), 247–65.

Hughes, T.P (1983) *Networks of Power: Electrification in Western Society, 1880–1930*. Baltimore, MD: Johns Hopkins University Press.

Hurd, I. (2008) 'Constructivism', in Reus-Smit, C. and Snidal, D. (eds.), *The Oxford Handbook of International Relations*. Oxford: Oxford University Press, pp. 298–316.

Jackson, R.H. and James, A. (eds.) (1993) *States in a Changing World: A Contemporary Analysis*. Clarendon Press.

Jasper, S. (ed.) (2010) *Securing Freedom in the Global Commons*. Redwood City, CA: Stanford University Press.

Jessop, B. (1990) *State Theory: Putting the Capitalist State in its Place*. Cambridge: Polity Press.

Johnson, D. and Turner, C. (1997) *Trans-European Networks: The Political Economy of Integrating Europe's Infrastructure*. Basingstoke, UK: Palgrave Macmillan.

Johnson, D. and Turner, C. (2007) *Strategy and Policy for Trans-European Networks*. Basingstoke, UK: Palgrave Macmillan.

Kandiyoti, R. (2012) *Pipelines: Flowing Oil and Crude Politics*. London: IB Tauris.

Keating, M. (2013) *Rescaling the European State: The Making of Territory and the Rise of the Meso*. Oxford: Oxford University Press.

Keohane, R.O. and Nye, J.S. (2001) *Power and Interdependence*, 3rd edn. Boston, MA: Longman.

Kindleberger, C.P. (1986) 'International public goods without international government', *The American Economic Review*, *76*(1), 1–13.

Kong, B (2010) 'The geopolitics of the Myanmar–China oil and gas pipelines', in Chow, E., Hendrix, L., Herberg, M., Itoh, S., Kong, B., Lall, M. and Stevens, P. (eds.), *Pipeline Politics in Asia: The Intersection of Demand, Energy Markets and Supply Routes*. NBR Special Report 23, Seattle, WA: National Bureau of Asian Research.

Larrabee, F.S. (2010) 'Russia, Ukraine, and Central Europe: the return of geopolitics', *Journal of International Affairs*, *63*(2), 33–52.

Levi-Faur, D. (2005) 'The global diffusion of regulatory capitalism', *Annals of the American Academy of Political and Social Science*, *598*(1), 12–32.

Little, R.G. (2002) 'Controlling cascading failure: understanding the vulnerabilities of interconnected infrastructures', *Journal of Urban Technology*, *9*(1), 109–23.

Majone, G. (1994) 'The rise of the regulatory state in Europe', *West European Politics*, *17*(3), 77–101.

Mann, M. (1997) 'Has globalization ended the rise and rise of the nation-state?' *Review of International Political Economy*, *4*(3), 472–96.

Marsden, R. (1993) 'Global monoculture, multiculture and polyculture', *Social Research*, *60*(3), 493–523.

Moteff, J.D. (2012) *Critical Infrastructure Resilience: The Evolution of Policy and Programs and Issues for Congress*. Washington, DC: Congressional Research Service.

Murphy, M. (2007) 'Piracy and UNCLOS: does international law help regional states combat piracy?', in Lehr, P. (ed.), *Violence at Sea: Piracy in the Age of Global Terrorism*. New York, NY; Abingdon, UK: Routledge, pp. 155–82.

Ohmae, K. (1990) *The Borderless World*. New York, NY: Harper Collins.

Omonbude, E.J. (2012) *Cross-Border Oil and Gas Pipelines and the Role of the Transit Country: Economics, Challenges and Solutions*. Basingstoke, UK: Palgrave Macmillan.

Organisation for Economic Co-operation and Development (OECD) (2008) *Protection of Critical Infrastructure and the Role of Investment Policies Relating to National Security*. Paris: OECD.

Organisation for Economic Co-operation and Development (OECD) (2015) *Fostering Investment in Infrastructure*. Paris: OECD.

Ostrom, E. (2010) 'Beyond markets and states: polycentric governance of complex economic systems', *Transnational Corporations Review*, *2*(2), 1–12.

Ostrom, E., Burger, J., Field, C.B., Norgaard, R.B. and Policansky, D. (1999) 'Revisiting the commons: local lessons, global challenges', *Science*, *284*(5412), 278–82.

Palan, R. and Abbott, J. (1996) *State Strategies in the Global Political Economy*. London: Pinter.

Perrow, C. (1984) *Normal Accidents: Living with High Risk Systems*. New York, NY: Basic Books.

Posen, B.R. (2003) 'Command of the commons: the military foundation of US hegemony', *International Security*, *28*(1), 5–46.

Ramel, F. (2014) 'Access to the global commons and grand strategies: a shift in global interplay', *Etude de l'IRSEM*, *30*, 1–36.

Rinaldi, S.M., Peerenboom, J.P. and Kelly, T.K. (2001) 'Identifying, understanding, and analyzing critical infrastructure interdependencies', *IEEE Control Systems*, *21*(6), 11–25.

Roberts, S., Secor, A. and Zook, M. (2012) 'Critical infrastructure: mapping the leaky plumbing of US hegemony', *Antipode*, *44*(1), 5–9.

Robertson, R. (1992) *Globalization: Social Theory and Global Culture*. London: Sage.

Rodrigue, J.P. (2004) 'Straits, passages and chokepoints: a maritime geostrategy of petroleum distribution', *Cahiers de géographie du Québec*, *48*(135), 357–74.

Ruggie, J.G. (1982) 'International regimes, transactions, and change: embedded liberalism in the postwar economic order', *International Organization*, *36*(02), 379–415.

Ruggie, J.G. (1993) 'Territoriality and beyond: problematizing modernity in international relations', *International Organization*, *47*(01), 139–74.

Sammonds, P., McGuire, B. and Edwards, S. (eds.) (2010) *Volcanic Hazard from Iceland: Analysis and Implications of the Eyjafjallajökull Eruption*. Institute for Risk and Disaster Reduction, University College London, London.

Sassen, S. (2013) 'When territory deborders territoriality', *Territory, Politics, Governance, 1*(1), 21–45.

Star, S.L. and Bowker, G.C. (2006) 'How to infrastructure', in Lievrouw, L.A. and Livingstone, S. (eds.), *Handbook of New Media: Social Shaping and Social Consequences of ICTs*. London: Sage, pp. 230–45.

Stern, J. (2014) 'The British utility regulation model: its recent history and future prospects', *Utilities Policy, 31*, 162–72.

Strange, S. (1996) *The Retreat of the State: The Diffusion of Power in the World Economy*. Cambridge: Cambridge University Press.

Taylor, P.J. (1994) 'The state as container: territoriality in the modern world-system', in Brenner, N., Jessop, M., Jessop, M. and Macleod, G. (eds.), *State/Space: A Reader*. Malden, MA: Blackwell, pp. 101–14.

Turnovsky, S.J. (1999) 'Productive government expenditure in a stochastically growing economy', *Macroeconomic Dynamics, 3*(04), 544–70.

Van der Vleuten, E. and Kaijser, A. (2005) 'Networking Europe', *History and Technology, 21*(1), 21–48.

Van der Vleuten, E. and Lagendijk, V. (2010) 'Transnational infrastructure vulnerability: the historical shaping of the 2006 European "Blackout"', *Energy Policy, 38*(4), 2042–52.

Vogler, J. (2012) 'Global commons revisited', *Global Policy, 3*(1), 61–71.

Walt, S.M. (2002) 'The enduring relevance of the realist tradition' in Katznelson, I. and Milner, H.V. (eds.), *Political Science: The State of the Discipline*. New York, NY: W.W. Norton and Company, pp. 197–230.

Weiss, L. (1998) *The Myth of the Powerless State*. Ithaca, NY: Cornell University Press.

Weiss, L. (2005) 'The state-augmenting effects of globalisation', *New Political Economy, 10*(3), 345–53.

World Bank (2015) *Development Indicators 2015*, accessed 12 September 2016 at www.worldbank.org/

3. The Global Transport Infrastructure System

The global transport infrastructure (GTI) system comprises the set of interconnected and interacting transportation infrastructures that facilitate international mobility of humanity and the transnational movement of finished, part-finished and unprocessed tangible products throughout the global economy (for a review, see Dicken, 2008). The underlying value proposition of the GTI is based on – in an ideal scenario – universal access to and global reach of infrastructure systems to enable end-to-end mobility throughout and across territories. Of all the physical infrastructures discussed in this volume, transport is arguably the most complex, not only because of its structure, which can be subdivided by type (passenger or freight), by means of conveyance (land, air or water) or by mode (road, rail, maritime, air), but also because of the interdependencies between these historically distinct sectors, especially as contemporary policy and strategy stress multi-modality (i.e. the ability to use multiple modes of transport infrastructure to attain end-to-end connectivity for a single unit of traffic flow). Ideally, the transition from one transport mode to another should be as seamless as possible with consequent implications for the evolution of transport infrastructure.

Mindful of these complexities, this chapter addresses the main forces shaping the international system and, as such, focuses upon externally facing components of national transport systems for the movement of freight and passengers. This implies, by default, an emphasis on the two sets of infrastructures that dominate these respective international flows, namely maritime and aviation infrastructures which dominate (respectively) international freight and maritime traffic. This is not to deny an international role for road and rail transport, but their reach tends to be more limited in terms of geography and of volume over longer distances. In line with the analysis in chapters 1 and 2, this implies a focus on the management of flows through national gateways and on how these infrastructures face adaptive pressures within the global system, including the forces for integration and fragmentation of the GTI.

THE NATURE OF THE GTI

The GTI is a global network of interconnected national infrastructures that enables the international mobility of passenger and freight transport. In this context, the following components are germane to the operation of the international system (Rietveld and Bruinsma, 2012).

- State-based international gateways – that is, the points at which international flows are de/re-territorialised;
- International hubs – that is, locations within a particular territory which have a role in enabling flows into multiple states;
- Transit points – that is, territory across which traffic has to flow to reach its destination but which is neither the source of nor the destination for the flow;
- Non-territorial transit points such as shipping lanes or airspace.

Historically, transport infrastructure has operated as the interface between the state and external political and economic systems (United Nations Conference on Trade and Development, UNCTAD, 2008). Indeed, in the era of the welfare state (Jessop, 2009), transport infrastructure had a central role in the monitoring, control, filtering and taxation of inter-territorial flows (Dicken et al., 2001), a role that is retained in the process of adaptation to globality and the de- and re-territorialisation of flows (Hess and Yeung, 2006; Button, 2010). Thus, such gateways remain key to state territoriality through often contradictory processes of trade facilitation, border control, market integration and state security (for a review, see Rothengatter, 2008).

International freight traffic flows are overwhelmingly – over 90 per cent of all flows by volume (Organisation for Economic Co-operation and Development, OECD/ITF, 2015a) – accounted for by maritime transport which is widely accepted as the cheapest way of moving bulky items long distances (Corbett et al., 2010). Another 1 per cent is covered by aviation. International terrestrial transport infrastructure only tends to be salient where a state is landlocked and uses these modes to connect to the main global logistical channels. This reflects the dependence of the global logistics system upon the state-based port system and global port hubs (Janelle and Beuthe, 1997). The GTI in freight has been driven by the trend towards spatially expanded industry value chains (Demetriades, 2008) that means that finished goods, semi-completed products and commodities are not always located close to the place of consumption or the final production location (Dicken and Henderson, 1999; Hummels, 2008).

Figures for international passenger movements are more difficult to obtain. Although there is plenty of evidence to show that air travel has risen with economic growth, precise figures of aggregate international passenger flows do not exist or lack reliability. Speculatively, this may be driven by high cross-border interactions in places like Europe which can be difficult to monitor. The International Air Transport Association (IATA) (2015) estimated that 6.7 billion international flights were taken in 2015, but it is unclear if this is a percentage of the total volume of transport movements, although figures from the main industrialised states suggest that the benchmark figure for the percentage of international passenger travel (as measured by crude passenger figures) undertaken by air is between two-thirds and three-quarters (OECD/ITF, 2015a).

Port Infrastructure

Ports have a multi-faceted in role in state infrastructuring. There can be little doubt that their main function is trade facilitation but it is also evident that this function is not simply about the logic of the competition state or of the efficiency with which a state can engage with international systems. Ports are also critical infrastructures – they are major points of entry to key state-enabling flows, such as energy, and damage to ports can hinder state integration into global flows, especially in relation to bulk cargos (Meersman and Van de Voorde, 2008). Moreover, the port system is also linked to security as states seek to monitor flows and to limit the flows of illicit and illegal cargoes (Jacks and Pendakur, 2010).

Ports have been the conventional gateways to most (non-landlocked) states and many cities have grown up around ports with global logistical systems largely based on inter-port flows (OECD/International Transport Forum, ITF, 2015a). Somewhat ironically, this pattern also extends to land-locked states, many of which tend to build an infrastructure system to gain access to the nearest available port infrastructure. The pressure for ports – as state-based infrastructures – to adapt to global pressures has been a constant, with many becoming focused on particular types of shipping flows (i.e. either packed cargo – cargo that is formally packed, for example, in containers) or unpacked bulk cargo (i.e. commodity cargo that is transported unpackaged in large quantities such as oil, gas, grain, iron ore, etc.) flows (Wilmsmeier et al., 2006). By 2013 (as measured by tonnage), oil and gas comprised around 30 per cent of all maritime trade, as did the five major bulk cargoes (iron ore, coal, grain, bauxite and alumina, and phosphate rock); other dry bulk cargoes (such as forest products) formed around 24 per cent; and containerised cargo 15 per cent (UNCTAD, 2014a). Thus, whilst containerisation has revolutionised the logistics of international trade (Cudahy, 2006; Levinson 2010; George, 2013), it

Table 3.1　The main global trade routes – TEUs shipped, 2013

Route	West bound	East bound	North bound	South bound	Total	Number of operating services on route
Asia–North America	7,739,000	15,386,000			23,125,000	73
Asia–North Europe	9,187,000	4,519,000			13,706,000	28
Asia–Mediterranean	4,678,000	2,061,000			6,739,000	31
Asia–Middle East	3,700,000	1,314,000			5,014,000	72
North Europe–North America	2,636,000	2,074,000			4,710,000	23
Australia–Far East			1,072,016	1,851,263	2,923,279	34
Asia–East Coast South America			621,000	1,510,000	2,131,000	
North Europe/ Mediterranean– East Coast South America			795,000	885,000	1,680,000	
North America–East Coast South America			656,000	650,000	1,306,000	26

Source:　OECD/ITF (2015a)

represents a relatively small share of world trade volume by tonnage. However, containerised cargo does represent over 50 per cent of the value of maritime trade and – by 2014 – was responsible for the movement of over 90 per cent of non-bulk cargo (UNCTAD, 2014b).

Table 3.1 identifies the world's main trade routes which reflect the largely west–east, and vice versa, direction of trade flows and the relatively minor role in world trade played by north–south flows. The major trade routes reflect the ongoing dominance of Asian, notably Chinese, ports to the world's trading system. Given Table 3.1, it is little surprise that China's ports (see Table 3.2) comprise the biggest share of the total volume of container traffic with almost one-third of total traffic compared to the next largest – the US – which has less than 10 per cent (UNCTAD, 2013). These flows are enabled by approximately 500 global liner services operating, of which nearly two-thirds are focused on these routes. There are also minor flows to Africa as well as to the west coast of Latin America. According to Frémont (2007), an east–west/north–south split has occurred in maritime transport as the larger ships emerged and focused on the east–west traffic, with the ships they replaced being redeployed on north–south routes. This forms the basis for the hub-and-spoke system that has become increasingly

Table 3.2   The world's busiest container ports

Rank	Port	Volume 2013 (million TEU)
1	Shanghai, China	33.62
2	Singapore	32.6
3	Shenzhen, China	23.28
4	Hong Kong SAR, China	22.35
5	Busan, South Korea	17.69
6	Ningbo-Zhoushan, China	17.33
7	Qingdao, China	15.52
8	Guangzhou Harbour, China	15.31
9	Jebel Ali, Dubai, United Arab Emirates	13.64
10	Tianjin, China	13.01

Source: OECD/ITF (2015a).

common in maritime networks. Thus, despite the potential for a large number of routes, the reality of commercial flows is relatively simple with the main traffic corridors linking North America, Europe and Asia/ Pacific. These routes are often defined by the need to use key transit points. These are territorial points of passage, such as the Suez Canal, the Strait of Malacca and the Panama Canal, used primarily to access key hubs as quickly and as efficiently as possible. However, these transit points also create capacity constraints and systemic risks (see later).

Increased competition between ports is pushing port capacity upwards, as is a desire for greater efficiency in the freight handling process. Terminal operating systems act as an enterprise resource planning tool with their design usually stemming from large ports (Donovan, 2004; Corbett and Winebrake, 2008). The increasingly multinational infrastructure owners who manage these ports increasingly deploy cross-port systems. A major concern of these ports is to render their facilities future proof (OECD/ ITF, 2013). Cranes, for example, were conventionally designed to serve ships that were 13-containers wide, but currently ships can be anything up to 23-containers wide and ports have to adapt their capacity or lose trade. These 'mega-ships' (see later) also require larger areas in which they can be serviced. As such, the existence of ports as competitive units within a global transport system depends upon these infrastructures not only adapting to changing technologies but also on keeping the high costs of handling bulk goods as low as possible (Hoffman and Kumar, 2010). This pushes ports towards increased scale and the adoption of the latest technology to enable them not only to lower infrastructure costs but also to reduce transhipment and administration costs. For many smaller states (as well as landlocked states), these costs can be a key factor shaping export performance (Corbett and Winebrake, 2008). This problem can be compounded if port services are also a big export earner. As a result of these costs, many states treat ports as clusters for other industries, either to limit the need to scan flows entering or leaving a territory or to limit the need for extensive hinterland infrastructure (Ducruet and Notteboom, 2012).

The increased focus on the existence of global maritime networks (like the much higher profile aviation networks) highlights the impact of network effects on the maritime system (Ducruet and Notteboom, 2012). It is also apparent that not all ports have a purely domestic focus – a hierarchy of ports is evident with some operating as hubs for a number of states, especially where landlocked states are concerned. Many argue that such processes have been driven by containerisation and its ability to generate uniformity of facilities across space (for a review, see Levinson, 2010). It is also evident that ports compete to be part of international value chains and do not operate solely as territorial gateways. In these cases, port choice is a decision of a number of factors such as costs and connectivity (UNCTAD, 2014a). Liner services have increasingly formed alliances to create network effects without the need for each operator to have universal coverage (Kaluza et al., 2010). These create a hierarchical global system for operators that are dependent upon capacity and in which the largest ships use a limited number of ports. This, in turn, creates a network of primary routes between hubs and secondary routes and between hubs and minor ports, thereby merging long distance and short sea shipping systems.

The emergence of so-called secondary/intermediate hubs has occurred alongside the rise of the major hubs. These intermediate hubs are containerised ports that focus on connecting different systems of maritime circulation and tend to be located along the key circum-maritime routes, such as Panama, Gibraltar, Suez and the Strait of Malacca (UNCTAD, 2015). Many of these ports operate on the routes between hubs on the main routes but also between north–south trade routes. The most important intermediate hub is Singapore. The rise of the intermediate hubs has generated a dual split in traffic with larger ships focused on the large hubs and vice versa. Importantly, the rise of intermediate hubs allows for the servicing of those ports that would have otherwise remained excluded from the main global trade routes.

The presumption of hub ports is that the cargo never leaves the facility and serves no hinterland. However, with rising competition between ports, there is increased focus by gateway ports on operating as a hub. This dual role has the potential to undermine the role of the pure hub. The hub ports, by their very nature, have a high degree of interconnection. The element of interconnection has been entrenched by multi-modal national and international transport infrastructures where hinterland infrastructure coevolves with the port system and where other hubs are complementary to these systems. Ports are not just points of entry but increasingly constitute contained business systems with warehousing and storage and with clusters of port-related businesses that operate as a supply point to the hinterland.

Aviation Infrastructure

Air transport has become the primary source of international passenger mobility, replacing the liner system that had reinforced port centric gateway systems. For states, the provision of air infrastructure became both an opportunity and a challenge shaped by a desire to encourage tourism as a socio-economic good with the need to regulate flows for international migration and control illicit labour mobility. Alongside the liberalisation of both aviation services and infrastructure, there was a corresponding sharp rise in international air passenger traffic which has largely been driven by tourism. This rise in traffic places pressure on infrastructure with over 100 airports operating at or close to capacity in 2014. Air travel continues to grow at a rate, according to the International Civil Aviation Organization (ICAO, 2014), of around 5 per cent per annum, with 3.1 billion passengers travelling on over 32 million flights in 2013 – up from almost zero in 1950 (IATA, 2013). These trends have proved resilient despite changes in economic and political conditions over the medium-to-long term. Air freight has grown in volume and takes an increasing proportion of trade by value despite the increased costs associated with this form of transport (Belobaba et al., 2009). As of 2014, air freight accounted for less than 10 per cent of total trade volume by tonnage but around 40 per cent by value. Three factors lie behind the increasing share of air freight in world trade. First, timely delivery has grown more valuable, both in terms of time-sensitive goods and as a strategic differentiator. Second, the cost of shipping by air has declined in both absolute and relative terms. Third, goods are becoming lighter and end users are growing wealthier. These trends are only likely to increase because of air freight's ability to reach and penetrate new markets without large-scale infrastructural investment, allowing – in the absence of sunk costs – ease of market entry and exit.

At the core of aviation infrastructure is the airport, which functions as the origin and terminus of traffic, as the point of interchange between single suppliers of services provided by alliances and as the point of interchange between two separate suppliers and points of intermodal transportation. Consequently, aviation infrastructure reflects a complex set of processes involving the mass movement of passengers (and freight). These need to be coordinated and managed to secure aviation traffic flows and to ensure they flow into and leave the global system with ease. Accordingly, the World Bank (2015a) has identified the following interlinked components within aviation infrastructure:

- Airside services such as runways, terminals beyond security controls and all facilitates enabling aircraft movement;
- Landside services – facilities associated with the movement of passenger and freight traffic to and from the aircraft and dedicated to supporting traffic within the terminal;
- Security and safety services – facilities linked with safety and security of flows; and
- Air navigation infrastructure – facilities that enable air traffic control and management within a given air space.

These components underscore the multi-functional role of airports within the state-based system by operating not only as an interface with the international system through the facilitation of mobility but also as a central element in state security, control and effective integration. As air travel has risen, so major airports have gained in salience to the maintenance of state territoriality. However, not all airports within a territory have permission to handle international flights; many have a domestic or localised focus that enables the authorities to attempt to control and monitor passenger movements through such gateways by limiting points and place of access. Moreover, airport infrastructure has in many states shifted the border of the state in from the physical edge of the territory.

The international air transport system is based on a widely recognised hierarchy of airports which operate as hubs to reach an increasingly diverse range of secondary airports whose ability to generate traffic on a point-to-point basis would leave the facility underserved. Table 3.3 identifies the world's busiest airports in terms of passenger and freight transport, all of which are hubs. The network of strategic alliances between airline operators is essential to the robustness of these hubs (Flores-Fillol and Moner-Colonques, 2007). Outside these core hubs, segmentation of the airline industry has taken place, notably with the rise of low price operators with point-to-point business models. For airlines, the hubs add value in both demand and cost terms, largely through the ability to consolidate traffic through combining different origin–destination flows on a single route. Moreover, hubs enable the averaging out of the natural peaking of demand, can generate rents and provide opportunities for mixing prices (Gillen and Morrison, 2005; Button, 2008). As Nero (1999) points out, the advantages of hubbing increase with a growing network because of the externalities and spillover effects of additional spokes.

Table 3.3   Major international air hubs, 2015

Rank	International passenger traffic	International freight
1	Dubai, AE (DXB)	Hong Kong, HK (HKG)
2	Hong Kong, HK (HKG)	Incheon, KR (ICN)
3	London, GB (LHR)	Dubai, AE (DXB)
4	Paris, FR (CDG)	Shanghai, CN (PVG)
5	Amsterdam, NL (AMS)	Taipei, TW (TPE)
6	Frankfurt, DE (FRA)	Tokyo, JP (NRT)
7	Singapore, SG (SIN)	Anchorage, AK US (ANC)
8	Incheon, KR (ICN)	Frankfurt, DE (FRA)
9	Bangkok, TH (BKK)	Miami FL, US (MIA)
10	Istanbul, TR (IST)	Singapore, SG (SIN)

Source: IATA (2015)

Table 3.4   The busiest international air routes[1]

Rank	Route	Seats
1	Hong Kong–Taipei	680,915
2	Karachi–Dubai	456,792
3	Singapore–Jakarta	442,009
4	Hong Kong–Bangkok	335,622
5	Hong-Kong–Singapore	314,422
6	London–New York	282,205
7	Tokyo–Seoul	265,230
8	Hong Kong–Manila	260,819
9	Jeddah–Cairo	259,917
10	Bangkok–Singapore	256,318

Notes: [1]Based on the total number of seats per month flown in both directions as of April 2014.

Source: IATA (2015)

As of 2015, traffic within the international system is very concentrated, with Asia demonstrating the highest rates of passenger growth. It is estimated that 20 per cent of all air traffic in Asia is on just 300 routes (IATA, 2015). Of the top 10 routes by passenger volumes, only one is inter-state (between Taipei and Hong Kong); the rest are intra-state. In Europe and the US over a third of air travel is on small intra-regional flights. The busiest international routes are reflected in Table 3.4. Of the top 50 flights per month based on seats flown, only 10 routes of the top 50 routes are international. Of the rest, 28 routes (some 70 per cent) are in Asia – further underlining Asia as the core and growing market for air travel.

The management of global airspace is core to the aviation transmission system. Although global airspace is seen as part of the global commons, there is no universal agreement on the vertical limit of airspace sovereignty. This means that – in theory – all flights flying over a territory have to gain transit rights according to the 1944 Chicago Convention, which established the rules of airspace, aircraft registration and set out the rights of signatories regarding air travel. The physical infrastructural component of such rights is created, first, by the air traffic control system deployed by states to monitor and control airspace (all flights over a territory need to be given pre-clearance) and, second, through the potential use of airports should the need arise due to re-fuelling or an emergency. The horizontal dimension of the control of airspace follows the maritime rule of 12 nautical miles from the coastline of a territory. Across airspace where there are no territorial rights, international law applies. However, with international consent, one state can assume control of this segment – as the US has done with the utilisation of its air traffic control over a large portion of the Pacific Ocean, notably those sections between the US coast and Hawaii. There are a total of 15 oceanic control centres globally which assume control over some segment of non-territorial airspace.

As part of the management of global airspace, there have been efforts to generate greater consistency in air traffic management. Whilst all states seek to control their respective airspaces, there is also desire that such demands should not impede free flows of air traffic. To some extent, these have been facilitated by the Chicago Convention, but efforts continue to be made to further align air traffic management. These are assisted by advances in in-flight technology, which have outpaced ground-based systems, with the consequent need to manage capacity better where the growth of air traffic is outpacing airport capacity and where there is a demand by states to enhance or even augment their control of terrestrial airspace. The main driver of this process has been airline efficiency but there is also an evident need for the state to maintain its ability to control vertical airspace.

Land Transit

As highlighted earlier, the main international freight and passenger movements utilise maritime and aviation modes in particular. This creates a focus in the development of the global system on the infrastructure that supports these modes which account for the bulk of traffic (Woodburn et al., 2008). However, other transnational infrastructures exist. The use of rail termini as well as road/rail corridors is common in cross-border movements where there is close proximity between source and destination, as in the US–Mexico border regions. As land-based transport is relatively expensive compared to maritime and, to a lesser extent, air transport, it is a less favoured mode unless there is close geographic proximity between producer and consumer or where a state is landlocked and where air freight is uneconomic or impractical. Accurate figures for international land-based transit trade are difficult to obtain because much of this cross-border movement is informal and unmeasured, especially in Africa. Despite such ambiguities, the World Bank (2014) estimated – as of 2014 – that 23 per cent of all international trade is by land transit. In Asia and Africa, this forms as little as 1–5 per cent of all trade; in Latin America, the equivalent figure is between 10–20 per cent and for Europe and North America between 25–35 per cent (OECD/ITF, 2015b). The vast majority of this trade both for the EU and the US is with adjacent states. Elsewhere, land transit can also be expected to rise as China expands its 'new Silk Road' into the ex-Soviet Republics of Eurasia. Whether this is for trade facilitation or for the export of Chinese know-how in infrastructure is a moot point. In the mid-2010s, the flows in both directions are limited and do not justify a need (in market terms) for the investment.

The issue for landlocked states is more salient because developing reliable corridors for the transit of goods to the key transport hubs is central to their ability to reach global trade routes. For these states, the issues focus on corridors. These are multi-modal land-based systems that cross multiple territories. The aim is to create a degree of uniformity over hard and soft infrastructures with secure transit rights for operators. This relies upon building the institutional capabilities to allow speed of transit without long border delays. In some circumstances, it might be necessary to form sub-national hubs to consolidate flows before entering the overarching network and reaching the global hub. This reflects the importance of secondary infrastructure by removing land-based bottlenecks, building cross-border connections and enabling multi-modality where appropriate. Such secondary networks have been deployed within Europe (as part of the Trans-European Network (TEN) programme) and within the US and less developed states. North American Free Trade Area (NAFTA) has four pan-regional corridors which its members are planning to upgrade; the EU has nine corridors and Africa has multiple corridors as part of its attempts to redress the liability of landlocked states (see later). For the main landlocked western European states (notably Switzerland and Austria), there is ease of access to inland waterways and to the infrastructure systems of neighbouring states. In addition, these latter states trade in high value-added products and the distance to access the major trade routes is relatively short compared to that for many less developed states.

The global transportation system is a mix of national infrastructure with an international dimension and parts of the earth's surface that are central to the transport of passengers and freight but which are outside the control of any state. However, it is the former that is the focus of this volume. It is evident that the east–west dimension (both in terms of passenger and freight traffic) of the global transport system is stronger than the north–south aspect. As such the GTS differentiates between primary (i.e. high traffic) and secondary (i.e. relatively low traffic) routes/infrastructures. The vast majority of the former are on east–west routes with further differentiation taking place between primary hubs and secondary points of access. Despite the globalising trends within the system, retention of control of the external facing aspects of the national transport system is a means of maintaining control of inward and outward flows. These gateway infrastructures are the borders of the state and territoriality requires that flows are monitored and filtered as they are de- and re-territorialised. Such preferences, on the basis of security, sustain some degree of fragmentation of the global system. However, the pressures to secure borders to control flows and manage territorial security are countered by forces that drive states to integrate their national systems into global system where the condition of a national transportation infrastructure (NTI) is widely acknowledged to be a key determinant of national competitiveness. The relative pressures on states to integrate and fragment need to be assessed.

FORCES OF INTEGRATION

Narratives of the co-evolution between globalisation and advancements in transport infrastructure have been well documented and researched (for example, Dicken, 2015). Advances in shipping and containerisation as well as the application of information and communication technologies (ICT) to port management, for example, have proved powerful factors in reshaping national transportation infrastructures as they seek to cope with a global transport system that is spatially extensive and characterised by increased velocity and volume of transnational traffic movements. This reflects the culmination of a series of factors, discussed later, that is driving the integration of national transport infrastructure systems.

Global Value Chains

Whilst globality has always been a factor in the development and organisation of NTI, the advent and growing commercial salience of global value chains have created more complex trading systems. The logic of the global production network (GPN) is to enable multinational companies (MNC) to realise value chain efficiencies by organising individual activities across states rather than organising them on a stand-alone or state-by-state basis (Coe et al., 2008). For the state, the logic of the rise of the global value chain requires the integration of domestic infrastructure systems into global systems to secure competitive advantage and to ensure that national system inefficiencies and barriers do not result in a net welfare loss (Bougheas et al., 1999). Whilst infrastructure costs are not the only factor shaping this process, they can be a deciding factor for the success of bulky products (Hess and Yeung, 2006).

Much of the argument that has influenced policy makers – which has, in turn, been influenced by the neo-liberal logic of the competition state – is that the state has an economic incentive to upgrade national infrastructure systems to enable them to benefit from the international separation of production (Gereffi et al., 2005). In international bodies such as the OECD and World Economic Forum (WEF), the narratives deployed stress that priorities within national infrastructure strategies should focus on growth objectives by enabling states to become attractive locations for investment by MNCs. The underlying logic of this argument requires an infrastructure system that enables/stimulates efficiency of circulation both within and beyond state borders. This suggests not only an incentive to upgrade infrastructure systems but also an incentive to ensure that these national systems are interoperable and integrated with the international system. The impact of territoriality on power within such networks is a moot point.

For many hyper-globalists, the trend towards such complex production networks renders states increasingly powerless in the face of the capability of MNCs to play states against each other to secure the best terms (see, for example, Ohmae, 1990). Although such arguments are simplistic, it is evident within narratives on the logic of the competition state that such complexity has had an impact on state strategy as they seek to position themselves within GPNs to enable the state to grow and prosper. This implies that both internal and external facing components of the NTI are focused towards speed of movement and mobility in and out of and around state (Levy, 2008). This trade–sovereignty trade-off has been key to hyper globalism. More pragmatic arguments suggest that the complexity arises from the state adapting to the more complex production arrangements. Whilst policy discourses are undoubtedly shaped by the narrative of the GPN and do incentivise integration, this is not solely an act of individual states as GPNs are based on polycentric national infrastructure systems (NIS; see later). Moreover, the more advanced and complex these GPNs grow, the more states seek to develop the monitoring of these processes through transnational governance arrangements, such as the US Secure Freight Initiative, to enable the monitoring of the increased trade flows and volumes (Peterson and Treat, 2008). Thus, embracing global production networks should not necessarily undermine the state capability in terms of NIS security as states have worked to re-secure gateways through international agreement. Such strategies also highlight that states are but one source of infrastructuring across borders and that all states can often do is to enable these flows (Altemöller, 2011).

The notion that the state is subservient to the forces of international capital also underplays the nature of the contemporary polycentric NIS. MNCs are also owners and developers of the NIS and have an equal incentive to develop an efficient infrastructure system (Dicken, 2015). In this context, states also work with the private sector to develop infrastructures (WEF, 2014). They attempt to build relationships with MNCs not only to capture their infrastructural know-how but also to understand their infrastructure needs more fully (OECD, 2015). In so doing, the state acts as a powerful constraint on the forms and actions of private or non-state infrastructuring through, for example, regulation on deployment of green technologies. Moreover, it is in the state's own interest to upgrade its NTI to prevent its obsolescence and senescence within the context of constantly evolving GPNs.

Trade Facilitation and the Reform of Soft Infrastructure

Connected to GPN formation and processes are measures linked to institutional reforms to aid the speed of trade flows through state gateways (Wilson et al., 2005). The underlying rationale is to accelerate the trade process by increasing the velocity with which these flows move through key infrastructures either into the hinterland or out of the state (Portugal-Perez and Wilson, 2012). Trade facilitation highlights the close link between hard and soft infrastructures where the latter can be a pivotal influence upon the performance of the former. Frequently, reform of soft infrastructure involves institutional reforms above and beyond trade measures and infrastructure investment and includes reform of border administration and the regulatory environment (WEF, 2013). The WEF (2013) identifies three aspects of border administration that can limit the free flow of goods: the efficiency of customs procedures; the efficiency of import/export procedures and the transparency of border administration (Engman, 2005). Improvements in these areas are designed to make border infrastructures work better by removing non-physical barriers to the flow of goods across borders. For businesses, trade facilitation and regulatory reform help create more secure and predictable business environments (World Trade Organization, WTO, 2015).

Trade facilitation focuses on the operational aspects of the process of international trade (WTO, 2015). Part of the process requires adaptation of formal institutional systems to cope with higher levels of flows associated with a globalisation process that is spatially extensive, operationally intense and fast. However, this process of trade facilitation has to be balanced against the need for control of borders (Engman, 2005). The logic of agreed trade facilitation procedures is that they aid security by freeing up resources from monitoring legitimate traffic towards monitoring illicit movements. According to Grainger (2008), trade facilitation is based on four main areas: the simplification and harmonisation of applicable rules and procedures; the modernisation of trade compliance systems, especially the sharing of information among key stakeholders; the management of trade and customs procedures; and institutional mechanisms to enable the implementation of trade facilitation measures. The speed with which information can be processed whilst ensuring the security of flows is key (Grainger, 2008).

In 2013, the WTO concluded an agreement on trade facilitation under the broader-based Bali Agreement. This agreement was formally agreed as an amendment to WTO protocols in November 2015. The agreement will enter into force when two-thirds of member states have completed domestic ratification. It is estimated by the WTO (2015) that – once fully implemented – the agreement will reduce trade transaction costs by around 14 per cent. As of May 2016, 84 out of 164 members had begun or completed the process of domestic ratification. In part, this relatively slow progress reflects the fact that many developed states already have active trade facilitation measures and that developing states – who are the main focus and potential beneficiaries of the agreement – often have under-developed domestic soft infrastructure systems through which these reforms should be realised.

Liberalisation of Transportation Systems

The globality of maritime and airport infrastructure has also been driven by liberalisation of services and by the rise of new business models across the sector (Button, 2010). Historically, aviation and port infrastructure were initially developed for security purposes (Forsyth, 1998). However, the rationale behind infrastructure development has shifted as new models of ownership have arrived and as states have gained confidence in the ability of polycentric infrastructure systems to enable the infrastructural mandate. Thus, despite the state taking a lower profile role within national transportation systems, the allowance of competition between and within transport infrastructure systems comes with the caveat that such acts should not undermine core critical infrastructures and the broader socio-economic objectives of territorial infrastructure. Consequently, liberalisation is often accompanied by re-regulation (ITF/OECD 2014b).

Liberalisation – through the stimulation of free trade in transport and logistical services (Nordås et al., 2006) – has further embedded national systems in global systems (as highlighted by the global strategies developed by logistics MNCs – see later) and has been an important contributing factor in the shift towards inter-modal door-to-door transport services away from the conventional port-to-port system. As embedded within the WTO's General Agreement on Trade in Services, liberalisation was also seen as a means of further stimulating trade through placing pressure on logistics costs (Adlung, 2006). This reflects, in terms of services, an under-lying logic of contestable markets given that transport services are increasingly divorced from the ownership and control of infrastructure and that the absence of the sunk costs associated with infrastructure provision allows for ease of entry and exit from markets (Fu, 2010).

In aviation, the pattern of liberalisation is uneven (Inglada et al., 2006). This pattern has been shaped by the rise of strategic airline alliances based around a network of hubs and secondary airports and by a series of bilateral agreements (by 2014, there were over 450 bilateral agreements covering 145 states) on liberalisation (IATA, 2015). This pattern has also been shaped by the frequently hesitant position of states towards liberalisation as a direct legacy of a sustained desire to offer a degree of protection to national airlines on security grounds in order to control the access of foreign aircraft and to foster military reliance on civilian airlines to supplement airlift capacity. These airline alliances are a means to circumventing this legacy system without offering any challenge to lingering concerns linked to state security. However, a distinction is made between the treatment of air freight and passenger transport in which security is more relaxed in the former than the latter. Indeed, of the 400 open skies agreements in existence, more than 100 have offered seventh freedom rights to cargo (ICAO, 2014). This enables an operator to carry freight between two foreign states without continuing onwards to service its home country. Despite this, operational restrictions remain over the use of infrastructures (such as night curfews). However, air freight cargo – according to the ICAO (2014) – is still governed by rules designed 70 years ago for passenger traffic. Where the seventh freedom rights have been extended to air freight, the effect has led to the development of private infrastructure systems locked into the NIS and based upon hub-and-spoke operations.

A direct legacy of liberalisation within air services has been the expansion of airport connectivity (ITF/OECD 2014a, 2014b). Such connectivity is fuelled by the need for both airport operators and airlines to harness network effects to support their respective traffic-based business models. The co-evolution of these factors is likely to drive the expansion or otherwise of aviation infrastructure. Globally, the expansion of connectivity has grown by 38 per cent between 2004–14 (ITF/OECD 2014a), reflecting the expansion of both hub-and-spoke and point-to-point traffic. There has also been an increased trend by airports to position themselves as hubs (Abu Dhabi, Amsterdam, Doha, Istanbul, Panama and Singapore to name only a few examples), which has shifted traffic away from US and European hubs. However, there is a fear that the dominance of hubs could see the erosion of reach and of services to secondary airports, causing either a loss of direct services or, where a hub services a nearby airport that offers higher traffic, this could leave remote or low traffic areas underserved (Fu et al., 2010). This also exposes secondary airports that have become reliant upon far away hubs (Burghouwt, 2013). There is also a widely recognised hub premium charged by airlines which increases air fares. Moreover, as airline alliances have shifted towards more formal mergers, a multi-hub strategy has emerged which enables alliance members to use multiple hubs to expand their range of traffic and the spread of markets served (Adler and Smilowitz, 2007). This creates links between these hubs as traffic is moved between them as a means of increasing aircraft utilisation rates. Within the EU, where these incumbent mergers have been most evident, the rise of the multi-hub business model is often a compromise between the firm and the regulator/state which wishes to ensure connectivity for domestic air routes to key prestige locations is sustained (ICAO, 2012).

Like civil aviation, the pattern of maritime transport liberalisation has also been mixed – some sectors, such as tankers and dry bulk shipping, have exhibited a higher degree of openness than liner shipping, for example (Parameswaran, 2004). Indeed, the former are very close to forming perfectly competitive markets. Progress under the General Agreement on Trade in Services (GATS) for liner shipping has been slow with most progress – like aviation – occurring through bilateral agreements (WTO, 2013). Where liberalisation has taken place, there is little evidence that it has had an impact on traffic as many of the goods carried would have utilised maritime channels in any case (Brooks, 2009). Although many developed states are opening up liner services (Hoffmann, and Kumar, 2010), the security objective has been a limiting factor on liberalisation in many states. Under the framework of the International Maritime Organization standards have been developed to ensure security, safety and environmental standards are not compromised (Fink et al., 2002). These have been supported by port control standards where there is concern over the footloose nature of carriers.

Transnational Transport Enterprises

The emergence of the multinational infrastructure companies (MNIC) and their management/ownership of key component of the external facing components of NIS is a key trend in the development of the GTI. These are owners of assets such as ports and airports through which flows pass rather than the generators of flows themselves. These ports and airports remain central to the strategies of states which retain the rights to legitimise both the operators and their functions and the rights to monitor and filter those flows that move beyond these facilities into the state. The rise of MNICs has been enabled by the liberalisation of facilities and/or services within these facilities and by the privatisation of state-owned infrastructure assets (UNCTAD, 2008). As the desire and ability of governments to undertake the financing of large capital projects has decreased, so MNICs have increasingly played a pivotal role in NIS and in integrating these systems into global flows.

This has been especially evident in maritime transport where liberalisations of port operations and increased competition between ports have driven port infrastructure investment. In some cases, the major shipping lines have built their own terminals to support their global presence (see Table 3.5). These ports tend to be on the main east–west routes with over 65 per cent of all terminals by all ports located within this main trading route (World Shipping Council, WSC, 2015). Only one port operator, APM, has extensive holdings on north–south routes (WSC, 2015). Given the rise of China and the consolidation of assets elsewhere, the six main port operators account for over two-thirds of all port traffic (UNCTAD, 2015). The push towards scale is driven not only by the desire for a

Table 3.5   The world's largest port multinationals

Rank	Operator	Number of locations
1	Hutchison Port Holdings	25 terminals across 15 states
2	China Merchants Holdings International	20 terminals in 3 states
3	APM Terminals	68 ports in 32 states
4	Cosco Pacific	21 terminals in 6 states
5	PSA International	26 terminals across 15 states
6	DP World	65 terminals across 32 states

Source: UNCTAD (2015)

continuous service environment but also by a belief that scale is needed to compete in the face of intense competition and the higher infrastructure costs required by the scaling up of the fleet (Frémont and Ducruet, 2005). However, the international expansion of port operators is subject to a legitimisation issue as demonstrated by the acquisition by DP World of US ports as part of its acquisition of P&O in 2006 (Cox, 2008). In this case, the security fears expressed by the US legislature led to the acquirer eventually divesting itself of this asset. Although the US government was reconciled with this ownership, political pressures within the US legislature were deciding factors in the divestment process (Graham and Marchick, 2006).

The pattern of spread of these port operators, as referred to earlier, reflects the sustained dominance of Chinese and Far Eastern ports and drives the high connectivity between these locations and the major trade routes. The Liner Shipping Connectivity Index, which measures how well a state is connected to global shipping networks, underlines this dominance (World Bank, 2015a). This is reflected in Table 3.6 which sets out a representative sample and some comparative figures. The table shows the dominance of western ports and also underlines the sheer volume of trade coming out of China. This demonstrates the hyper-connectivity of many of these states, albeit not Japan which has a connectivity index of just over 60 (World Bank, 2015a). This feeds through into those states offering high quality port infrastructure, especially noticeable in the cases of Singapore and the Netherlands, which have the highest figures for quality of port infrastructure. Locations such as Malaysia have a high connectivity score

Table 3.6   Global port infrastructure and the Liner Shipping Connectivity Index

State	Liner Shipping Connectivity Index (0–100)	Quality of port infrastructure (0=low; 7=high)
China	165	6.5
US	95.1	5.7
UK	88	5.6
Netherlands	94.2	6.8
Singapore	113.2	6.7
Malaysia	104	5.6
Korea	108.1	5.3
Germany	94	5.7
Belgium	80.7	6.4
France	75.2	5.2

Source: UNCTAD (2015)

not because of export performance but because of the role played in the trans-shipment process. This reflects the formation of container shipping networks through a series of calls on ports that often operate as hubs for those locations unable to generate sufficient traffic (Hoffman, 2012).

In contrast to ports, airports exist as more standalone assets rather than as part of an integrated global system. Airline alliances have attempted to create a global service system based on hub-and-spoke systems but there is little evidence of vertical integration between airline and airport operations (Button and Slough, 2000). Although airlines often have flagship hubs, the lack of vertical integration (often at regulatory insistence but also through sustaining market contestability) grants airlines flexibility regarding hub choice and the ability to configure and reconfigure route systems. (Graham, 2013). Airport ownership models are built on the capability to manage such assets and to generate and sustain traffic flows through these assets. Ownership of airports tends to be fragmented – many of the leading global operators are either specialist infrastructure funds or have emerged from national operators. Table 3.7 provides a snapshot of some of the leading operators which are ranked in no particular order, but trends towards the privatisation of airports and the maturing of the global investment market for infrastructure assets by investors attracted by stable long-term returns are apparent.

Airport connectivity is essential to both the state and to the airport operator. To the state, connectivity offers reach and to the operator it offers the capability to generate the traffic required for a sustainable business model (Arvis and Shepard, 2011). In 1990, US airports were the best connected, but by 2012, thousands of airports (notably across Europe and Asia) were operating as access points to the global aviation system, increasing global

Table 3.7   The world's main airport operators

Operator (nationality)	Number of airports/states
Aena (Spain)	47 airport operations in 29 states
ADP (France)	Operates or involved in operation of 30 airports across 20 states
Ferrovial (Spain)	Operators 25 airports across 8 states
Macquarie Infrastructure (Australia)	10 airports in 8 states
Schiphol Group (Netherlands)	9 airports across 6 states
Fraport (Germany)	Operates 18 airports across 12 states
AviAlliance (Germany)	Operates 6 airports across 4 states.
TAV Airports (Turkey)	10 airports across 6 states

Source: IATA (2015)

Table 3.8   The world's most connected airports

Rank	Airport (state)	Number of destinations
1	Frankfurt (Germany)	253
2	Amsterdam (Netherlands)	221
3	Paris Charles de Gaulle (France)	218
4	Atlanta (US)	200
5	Beijing (China)	190
6	Istanbul (Turkey)	185
7	Dubai (UAE)	175
8	Dallas/Fort Worth (US)	173
9	Houston (US)	168
10	Denver (US)	161

Source: IATA (2015)

connectivity by 140 per cent (IATA, 2015). This was due to the increase in the quantity and quality of indirect connections (that is, the use of hubs), a process shaped by the rise of the aforementioned airline alliances. Table 3.8 sets out the world's ten most connected airports according to the simplest measures of airport connectivity; that is, the number of destinations served as opposed to more elaborate measures that weight destinations according to their relative economic importance.

Global Governance of Flows

Narratives on globalism from both academics and policy makers claim that in a world of globalising flows (for a review, see Held et al., 1999), states will face potential conflicts within the infrastructural mandate when seeking a balance between enabling flows to enter the NIS without under-mining security. A possible solution is the development of mutually agreed security rules governing flows as they move across and between national systems. Indeed, international and inter-governmental agreements that attempt to balance the security and integration of NIS already exist in both the maritime and aviation sectors.

In the maritime sector, there is a longstanding mutual agreement between states over port security under the auspices of the UN's International Maritime Organization (IMO). As trade increased and as containerisa-tion exposed new threats, there has been an increased focus on the IMO's International ship and Port Security (ISPS) Code. This ISPS code was launched in 2004 to generate a consistent global approach to maritime security in a process that was led by the US (Goulielmos and Anastasakos,

2005). The ISPS Code imposes security-related responsibilities on governments, shipping companies and port authorities as well as offering guidelines for port and fleet operators (Bichou, 2015). Although the maritime
industry is subject to multiple security threats from terrorism, sabotage,
stowaways, illegal immigrants, asylum seekers, piracy and armed robbery
at sea, seizure, pilferage, annoyance and surprise, it is the port side (as
integral to the state infrastructural mandate) that is of concern here.

The ISPS Code requires participating ports to maintain the necessary security measures and government to pass details of the necessary
measures onto fleet operators prior to docking (Mensah, 2004). States are
also compelled to check the security of all vessels sailing under their flag.
Currently, 69 per cent of the world's ports have signed up to the Code
(IMO, 2015). However, the inability of the IMO to effectively police the
Code and the Code's inapplicability to smaller vessels that arguably represent the greater security threat are regarded as major weaknesses. The ISPS
Code's major benefits are that it has established a common baseline for
international cooperation on the issue of maritime security (Hesse, 2003)
and has improved knowledge of the main threats to maritime security. In
order to support these activities, the IMO works with the World Customs
Organisation to harmonise electronic information and to produce a har-
monised risk management approach (for a full review, see Bichou et al.,
2014). These baseline approaches within the ISPS Code form the basis for
actions by regional and national bodies in the process of reconciling trade
with state territoriality. The EU has made the code voluntary for EU states
to ensure minimum standards across the common market and has worked
to ensure minimum standards of port security. Such trends towards
regionalism run the risk fragmenting the system (see later). The problem
with the maritime security system is the absence of a hegemonic power to
enforce it and, as a result, states have a great deal of discretion over issues
of port security (Bichou, 2015). There is, for example, uncertainty as to
whether the Container Security Initiative in the US (see later) promotes or
is counterproductive for global trade.

This baseline strategy for the management of flows is also evident in
the governance of international aviation flows which are covered by agreements formed to cover the rise in air traffic in the inter-war and post-World
War Two environment. Post-9/11 these governance arrangements have
been under review especially with regard to the shortcomings identified in
the review of the attacks, which also demonstrated the incapability of the
state to shut down its territorial air space when its security is challenged
and capability to control is under threat (Milde, 2008). The 1944 Chicago
Convention and the 1963 Tokyo Convention focus on incidents on board
aircraft and not directly on airport security. These Conventions were later

supported by the 1970 Hague and Montreal Conventions that also focus on on-board events. After a terrorist bomb brought down Pan Am Flight 103 over Lockerbie in 1998, killing everyone on board and with fatalities on the ground, the ICAO offered a more facilities-based security arrangement whereby there would be agreement on the checking of flows prior to departure. However, states retain considerable discretion regarding the monitoring of flows and many OCED states have increased airport security especially in light of the increased terrorist threat and to the vulnerabilities in national airspace systems (ICAO, 2014). In short, state sovereignty of airspace remains largely intact, especially in relation to rights of traffic through airport frontiers. The Conventions, although establishing a baseline for security, also allow states considerable discretion. Given system interdependence and consensus on the desire for security, it is unlikely that any single state will act in a rogue fashion but will reserve discretionary controls only for extreme circumstances. However, power within the system is relative. Hub states have an interest in promoting adherence to the Conventions, but hegemonic states can act with greater freedom without sanction.

There have been efforts to harmonise other aspects of the air infrastructure, most notably air traffic control which requires greater coordination to ensure safe passage as aircraft transit sovereign airspace. Under the ICAO, each state is required to establish the necessary composite soft infrastructure to allow free mobility in the form of air traffic services (ATS). Whilst the ultimate role of ATS is to allow the free flow of traffic, restrictions on free flow at the point of entry at the terrestrial level are another issue. The ICAO regulation attempts to deliver an efficient flowing system over airspace with signatory states recommended to provide the necessary ATS to enable international civil aviation, but, once again, this is a baseline process (ICAO, 2014). This highlights the need to establish minimum soft infrastructure within each state to allow the flow of air traffic. Although there is no obligation to provide ATS, it is evidently in a state's interest to do so, even though the ICAO has no right of sanction, because the failure to do so would exclude a state from the global air system (Button, 2010). On a regional level, there is evidence of ATS integration between states such as the Single European Sky which offers more formal integration among national systems to cope with rising traffic (Button and Neiva, 2013). The aim is to create cross-border blocks of airspace to overcome fragmentation within the system. Given consent and coherence of principles, this represents more a pooling than a loss of sovereignty per se.

Technological Change

There has been a widespread recognition that technological change within the transport sector has coevolved with the emergence of a global transportation system (OECD/ITF, 2015b). The most evident manifestation of this is the rise of containerisation (Levinson, 2010). The impact of containerisation has been widely acknowledged: the cost of trade fell markedly across all aspects of maritime trade from the cost of loading and unloading through to insurance costs as the security of the trade process increased. These impacts were also felt in increased productivity at the points of embarkation and disembarkation and through the ease of movement into the port hinterland and into national systems (Cudahy, 2006). The impact of containerisation is increasingly extending to bulk commodities: this trend was driven in the short term by the commodity 'super cycle' which pushed up the prices of many commodities utilised by China in its rapid industrialisation. This increased the costs of bulk shipping, leading to a search for alternatives to the conventional method of transport (Notteboom and Rodrigue, 2008) – a process favoured by many states possessing vast pools of underutilised containers.

What is also evident but less explored are the adjustments needed to infrastructure generated by the shift towards containerisation, which also drives a push towards scale in maritime shipping – a trend that resulted in the rise of the mega-ship (OECD/ITF, 2015a, 2015b) and which, in turn, required widespread infrastructure investment not only in port infrastructure but also in upgrades to key international shipping channels. The Suez and Panama Canal expansions completed in 2015–16, for example, allow larger ships to use these facilities and have given rise to major investments in linked infrastructure in ports, railroads, warehouses, etc. Although this represents an adjustment challenge, it can also be a spur to global trade volumes as ports compete for traffic (Meersman and Van de Voorde, 2008). However, not all carriers have rushed for size, preferring to utilise existing space more effectively. Thus, the fine-tuning of existing fleets to generate scale within existing infrastructural constraints has been a strategy for some carriers. However, the pursuit of economies of scale in shipping is likely to limit the ability of some ports to handle the traffic generated by mega-ships. This will further embed the hub-and-spoke system with traffic from the mega-ships flowing along the main traffic lines and smaller ships being deployed on secondary routes (Imai et al., 2006).

These trends within maritime transport have been aided by the widespread adoption of information intensive infrastructures within and across the global maritime infrastructure, ostensibly as a means of promoting supply chain integration (OECD/ITF, 2015a, 2015b). This further enhances the efficiencies enabled by the containerisation process through the sequencing of loading and unloading, gate access and effective tracking, etc. Moreover, the application of these information infrastructures is a key tool in enabling the state to reconcile tighter supply chain integration with its security objectives through innovations such as e-manifests, which convey information about future shipments between authorities. Moreover, as containers can be sealed before embarkation, they are less prone to tampering (UNCTAD, 2015). Alongside this, there has been the widespread use of terminal automation strategies to allow for the fuller integration of all functions and services within the port environment, its hinterland and beyond. This has facilitated more mature inter-modalism (OECD/ITF, 2015b).

Although scale effects have not had as pronounced an effect on the major hub-and-spoke systems in the aviation sector, there has nonetheless been a need for infrastructure to respond to upgrades in the size and capacity of wide body aircraft. The spread of air travel and the rise of the hub-and-spoke system and global hubs have allowed some airlines to introduce high capacity, wide body aircraft on popular routes (OECD/ITF, 2015a). This demonstrates the trend towards economies of scale along key routes and the strategic use of such economies to reinforce the position of key hubs. These new, high capacity aircraft can carry 500–600 passengers as opposed to the 350 by the conventional workhorses of long haul travel (IATA, 2015).

FORCES OF FRAGMENTATION

If the forces of integration in the global transport system lie in those measures that have sought to remove restraints upon the global flows of freight and passengers and to which NIS have had to adjust in order to integrate into the global economic system, then the forces of fragmentation represent the physical impediments to these processes. The sources of this fragmentation do not only originate in the resistance of states to the forces of globality but also stem from strategies followed by states as they seek to balance the sometimes conflicting demands embedded within the infrastructural mandate. In some cases, the fragmentation is due to the absence of adaptability of hard or soft infrastructures to global pressures or simply to the under-development of the NIS.

Variable Soft Infrastructure

As the narrative on trade facilitation highlighted (see later), the capability of transport systems to integrate economies into the global trading system depends in no small part upon the ability and/or desire of the state to establish the necessary measures to facilitate freer cross-border mobility (Hummels, 2007). The WEF (2013) identified three generic areas as the focus of trade facilitation measures: namely the efficiency of border administration; import–export procedures and the transparency of border administration. Whilst there have been significant strides in regulatory measures to enable trade, reports from both the WEF (2013) and the WTO (2015) indicate that progress has been limited. These variable soft infrastructure systems impose barriers to global flows and highlight how NIS can be positioned to impede cross-border movements (Portugal-Perez and Wilson, 2012) and reflect how states can use gateway infrastructures to seek to improve domestic welfare through these restrictions on cross-border mobility. However, such bottlenecks are not always a measure of economic security – they can also reflect an absence of competence and/or resource by local authorities and this is an especially salient problem in developing states. The end point of these measures is that they increase transaction costs and therefore, so the argument goes, deter trade.

Grainger (2007) classifies the main categories of border control as:

1) Revenue collection, including the collection of customs duties, excise duties and other indirect taxes; payment of duties and fees; management of bonds and other financial securities;
2) Safety and security, including security and anti-smuggling controls, dangerous goods, vehicle checks, immigration and visa formalities, export licences;
3) Environment and health, including phytosanitary, veterinary and hygiene controls, health and safety measures, CITES controls, ships' waste;
4) Consumer protection, including product testing, labelling, conformity checks with marketing standards such as fruit and vegetables; and
5) Trade policy administration, including quota restrictions, refunds.

The WEF (2013) argues that inadequacies in such systems not only increase costs but also increase trade risk and delays and thus decrease trade activity. These inadequacies can take the form of both formal and informal barriers such as corruption. Indeed, the WEF (2013) estimates that trade improvements from enhancing soft infrastructure could be as much as 74 per cent of current transaction costs (for imports into

Brazil) but the efficiency gains (from the adoption of best practice for many emerging and developing states) are into double figures. This has prompted concerted action from the World Bank and other international organisations, such as the WTO, to improve these processes to promote conformity with best practice (Grainger, 2008).

Despite the perceived economic and social benefits of trade facilitation, there is growing evidence that many developed states, especially those in close proximity to developing states, are increasing the quantity and rigour of border checks. The US has imposed tougher constraints on the Mexican border primarily to stop the illicit movement of both people and goods across borders. This tightening of border checks has also been happening across the EU where states have also begun to reinforce borders (WTO, 2015). These states are seeking a trade-off between the integration of the global system with the stopping of illegal flows for which they are prepared to incur extra costs. Whilst the developed country barriers remain low compared to those in developing states, they do raise the issue of hindering trade through controlling access to the NIS as they seek to reconcile perceived conflicts within the infrastructural mandate.

Discretionary State Fragmentation

The trend towards increased border controls by many developed states highlights the increased perception (real or otherwise) of the threat to state security from the global transport system (for a review, see Lenain et al., 2002). In the post 9/11 era, the increased trade volumes associated with thick globality and with the desire for efficiency combine to place pressures on states to integrate whilst remaining secure (Mirza and Verdier, 2008). Whilst information sharing between public bodies has increased, it does not cover all contingencies regarding the security needs of the state. This has placed an emphasis on restoring the prominence of surveillance and the filtering function of gateways and has had its most evident manifestation at airports where tighter security checks on cross-border flights with tight restrictions on on-board luggage have been introduced. For large trading states vulnerable to terrorist attack, inconsistencies within the infrastructural mandate are evident (Bird, 2008). Given its experience, the US has demonstrated that it is considerably more risk averse than other states and, given its power within the international economic system, this has had implications for the global trading system. Other areas, notably the EU, have adopted a more evident balance between trade and security.

The post-9/11 security environment is being shaped by a belief that the transport system (and the extent and intensity of its globality) is an important point of vulnerability within the state-based international system (Fandl, 2004). The most evident manifestation of this has been the desire of states to reinforce border controls (Lutz and Lutz, 2006). Whilst airports were obvious targets for renewed efforts to monitor and control flows through borders, states also recognised that the spread of containerisation posed an under-recognised threat to the state security system. This was especially so within the US where the Department of Homeland Security (formed in the aftermath of the 9/11 attacks) began to focus on the security issues surrounding this segment of the GTI (Richardson, 2004). This perceived vulnerability was reinforced by the recognition that although over 9 million containers reached the US in 2002, only a small fraction was checked. Moreover, 90 per cent of these containers entered the US through the main 50 ports but only 3 per cent of this trade was carried by US operators (OECD, 2005). Fears were compounded by rising evidence of security breaches in other states and also by the fact that 17 of the ports are used by the US for major military deployments. Whilst there was arguably some degree of paranoia in this process, there were nonetheless real security issues (Nitsch and Schumacher, 2004). Controversies also arose over the ownership of both the ships and ports themselves. There was a general consensus amongst states that ownership of ships was too opaque and that this constituted a security threat. Moreover, the US grew increasingly concerned over the ownership of ports (see later).

The complexity of containerisation, whereby a single ship can carry containers with hundreds of separate owners, compounds the security dilemma, especially because not all containers bound for a destination are actually landed in that destination but arrive via a third party. For example, the US was concerned about the number of US-bound containers that were actually landed in Canada. These concerns were expressed across the OECD states, as reflected within the OECD's 2005 report (OECD, 2005) which pointed out that security threats were not necessarily located at the point of entry into the NIS but could occur further down the line through smaller operators such as inland operators and freight integrators. Indeed, across the OECD states, only an estimated 5 per cent of containers are checked (OECD, 2005). This issue was compounded by the absence of an agreed framework by states to monitor these flows.

As the global hegemonic power, the US has been proactively seeking to assert security within the GTS. In the global maritime system, the US has introduced a number of initiatives to offer better security both to flows heading for and reaching the US. The Container Security Initiative (CSI), entered into force in 2001, is the highest profile of these and involves the screening and tracking of cargo coming to the US through a series of bilateral agreements that allow the checking of US-bound cargo at the point of embarkation. The CSI focuses on those ports that send the largest volume of containers to the US. The US proposed a 100 per cent scanning of containers by 2012 (it had already implemented universal screening for air freight) but this was resisted by many states. In order to explore the feasibility of the CSI, the US launched the Secure Freight Initiative across three ports. This experience demonstrated that 100 per cent scanning is practical in low volume ports but causes severe operational difficulties in major hubs. As of 2014, the US intended to proceed with 100 per cent scanning on inbound US freight containers, thereby extending scanning to 750 ports. The EU estimates that the adoption of the proposal by EU ports would require US$588 million to be spent on infrastructure and more than US$274 million annually on operations. The net effect would be to increase the cost of transporting goods to the US by about 10 per cent (European Commission, 2010). The CSI is not about restricting flows to intentionally fragment the global maritime system, but to ensure that flows are more carefully monitored. However, the impact in terms of time and costs could amount to the same thing (Helmick, 2008).

State-driven balkanisation can also be discerned from critical infrastructure strategies (OECD, 2008; ICAO, 2011). Due to their positions as gateways to the NIS, both the main ports and airports are deemed as critical to state territoriality, with states intentionally channelling both inward and outward flows through these designated points of access. As highlighted earlier, both these gateway systems are increasingly characterised by polycentric ownership structures in which the state retains the right to influence (or even expropriate) these infrastructures should their performance or failure compromise state territoriality. Moreover, as much as the state may seek to restrict and monitor flows, it also seeks to shape the form of ownership and investment within this segment of the NIS. The OECD (2008) highlighted how discrimination arising from a legitimate security concern could fragment the system, especially where it inhibits consolidation. In the post-9/11 security environment, some states have sought to restrict forms of ownership. The most notable expression of this was the resistance of the US legislators to the ownership of US ports by Dubai on the grounds of the perceived increased security risk from Middle Eastern entities (Mostaghel, 2006).

Within civil aviation, balkanisation issues are driven less by concerns about control over flows at borders (where there is basic unanimity on the need to monitor, check and, where necessary, halt flows) and more by exemptions to transit rights (for a review, see Dempsey, 2003). The main maritime transit right treaty has almost universal access coverage, with the significant exception of the US which has recognised the treaty but not ratified it: the main objections of the US to the treaty relate mainly to its conditions on seabeds and mineral extraction rather than to rights of passage per se. However, more widespread is the non-ratification of the International Air Services Transit Agreement which grants the privilege to fly over the territory of a treaty country without landing and also to make technical stops without disembarking passengers or freight. Although 129 states have signed this agreement, notable exceptions include China, Brazil, Canada, Russia and Indonesia (ICAO, 2014). Whilst these countries do not outlaw transit, this right is not automatic and these states rely on bilateral agreements between states to agree freedoms of the air.

Bottlenecks and Choke Points

As noted earlier, the global logistical system remains vulnerable to pinch points (Emmerson and Stevens, 2012). These are territorial infrastructures (both links and hubs) that lie outside the commons and within the defined demarcated borders of a state but which are not the final destination of the flow and which cannot easily be by-passed. Importantly, these choke points have an impact beyond their locality, and even their region, and onto the global economy as a whole (Rodrigue, 2004). These choke points are normally composed of maritime infrastructures, such as the Panama and Suez Canals, but they can also include other infrastructures such as key air hubs, major oil terminals and transit passages for oceanic cable systems. These choke points are especially vulnerable in times of conflict and often rely on the exercise of hegemonic power in the form of maritime and air power to sustain flows and to ensure and secure access. However, these choke points are not only affected by inter-state conflict but also by disruptions by non-governmental bodies or rogue individuals and by the potential for human error and other accidental behaviour.

The issue is less prominent in the aviation sector but, nevertheless, it is evident that disruption to key international hubs can have cascade effects on other parts of the international air transport system (Kohl et al., 2007). These short notice events can be sourced from human and/or natural activity (Clausen, 2010). In practice, these events can be mitigated to an extent through the re-direction of traffic. This was witnessed in the disruption to the Heathrow air hub resulting from the decision of the UK authorities to close UK airspace following the 2010 eruptions of the Eyjafjallajökull volcano in Iceland. The cascade effects on European airspace led to the cancellation of over 100,000 flights (nearly half of total air traffic) during an eight-day period (Bolic and Sivcev, 2011; Budd et al., 2011).

Choke points are more of an issue in maritime transport where there is a longstanding concern over key choke points on the main east–west transit routes. Although it is the vulnerability of the energy sector to choke points (see later) which has attracted the most attention because of issues of state energy security (see Chapter 5), choke point effects inevitably spill over into containerised and other bulk commodity flows (Nincic, 2005). The dependence upon and the ease with which these routes can be disrupted, either by state or non-state actors, underscores the vulnerability of the global economic system to such shocks. For much of the twentieth century, the threat to choke points was shaped by the politics of the Cold War. This has latterly been replaced by the latent hostility to the US with the rise of the Iranian theocracy and its potential to block the Strait of Hormuz. In the twenty-first century, the threat to these choke points lies more in direct threats from piracy, collisions and instability. Nincic (2002) argues that these choke points are best seen as natural resources in the sense that they are scarce and have the potential to provoke conflict. This is, in part, due to the cost of building alternatives and of the costs encountered in detours via the Cape of Good Hope, Cape Horn, the North West Passage and the Straits of Magellan.

International law guarantees rights of transit through territorial waters under provisions of the United Nations Convention on the Law of the Sea (UNCLOS; Murphy, 2007). As the number of states with littoral zones increased in the post-war era, so did the risks to the global system. The need for reconciliation between littoral and maritime states was a direct driver behind the establishment of UNCLOS (Bateman, 2007). Littoral states retain sovereignty over this area but may not impose any measure that has the practical effect of limiting transit in those areas used for international navigation. This covers straits and other choke points such as canals. States bordering (or within which part of the straits fall) these areas can use various measures to make flows practical, such as separating out traffic (see Table 3.9). Such measures should not inhibit or

Table 3.9   The main choke points within the global transport system

Global choke points				
Eastern Mediterranean and the Persian Gulf	Eastern Pacific	Europe	Africa	The Americas
Bosphorus	Strait of Malacca	Great Belt	Mozambique	Panama Canal
Dardanelles	Sunda Strait	Kiel Canal	Channel	Cabot strait
Suez Canal	Lombok Strait	Dover Strait		Florida Straits
Strait of Hormuz	Luzon Strait	Strait of Gibraltar		Yucatan Channel
Bab-el Mandab	Singapore Strait			Windward Passage
	Makassar Strait			Mona Passage

Source: Nincic (2002)

discriminate against traffic flows or the right of transit. The acceptance of the UNCLOS rules by transit states makes it difficult for a state to use trivial regulations to impede flows. Importantly, the UNCLOS weights the system towards maintaining free flows over the rights of the sovereign state to operate unilateral control over their respective segment of the global system. However, constraints can be imposed by the sovereign state where there are concerns regarding the marine environment.

Although canals and territorial straits are both covered by UNCLOS, more specific treaties can enable states to assert sovereignty over these zones if their needs require it. For example, some states have sought to restrict flows through these zones where rising traffic can pose the risk of environmental damage or accidents. This has been the case in the Turkish management of the Bosphorus and in 1996 in Indonesia, which decided to restrict access to its islands though a series of predetermined routes that limited access to the Strait of Malacca. There have also been incidents where inter-state conflict has restricted access to these routes, including the 1956 Suez Crisis and the 1980–88 Iran–Iraq War, which posed dangers to the Strait of Hormuz. In this context, there are concerns regarding international traffic arising from an attempt by China to exert control over much of the South China Sea.

The geopolitics of energy and extra-territorial expression of power by global and regional hegemons have come to reflect the vulnerabilities represented by the transit choke points (see Chapter 5). Whilst many of these choke points can be circumvented at cost, the vulnerability of China, for example, to disruptions to energy flows through these choke points has led it to develop its 'string of pearls' strategy whereby it has been constructing new ports, mainly for civilian usage but which can also be extended for the purposes of military power (Lanteigne, 2008). These choke points and the vulnerabilities emanating from them have also been drivers for states to develop land-based strategies to avoid these choke points and to drive greater energy self-reliance. The Strait of Hormuz is seen as especially vulnerable because a third of global oil flows through this pinch point. In the cases of the Suez Canal and the Strait of Malacca, traffic can, at a cost, be diverted (Emmerson and Stevens, 2012). Threats to the main canal also derive from the failure to invest in the system to adapt to increasing volumes of trade and to the rise of the mega ship.

Piracy

Further tensions within the global system have been created by acts of piracy which are particularly prevalent in segments of territorial or non-territorial waters that are close to choke points (Chalk, 1998, 2008). The perpetrators of these acts frequently use failed or failing states to enter uncontrolled territorial waters or the high seas to seek to intercept flows. This rise of maritime piracy (Bowden et al., 2010) has occurred as the result of a combination of factors, including a sharp rise in the amount of commercial traffic that passes through key bottlenecks; poor state-based governance that allows low level piracy to continue; corruption and the spread of small arms (Nincic, 2005). The problem of managing piracy in the case of Somalia is compounded by the absence of effective state governance over its territorial waters (Hastings, 2009; Murphy, 2013) but the problem is especially acute in South East Asia which accounts for a quarter of all incidents (Emmerson and Stevens, 2012; see Table 3.10).

Maritime terrorism has also risen up the state agenda since 9/11, following increased fears that ships could be hijacked and used as weapons to

Table 3.10   The cost of maritime piracy, 2014

Region	Economic cost
Western Indian Ocean	US$2.3 billion (64 per cent borne by business), of which: • industry employed vessel protection – 56 per cent of costs (armed guards, increased speed, re-routing, security equipment); • government and civil society costs – 36 per cent of costs (naval operations, prosecutions, counter -piracy organisations); and • other industry costs – 8 per cent of costs (insurance, labour).
South East Asia	64 per cent of attacks in South East Asia: • estimated cost between US$4 and US$8 billion (no detailed breakdown of costs offered); and • insurance costs have increased by 17–20 per cent for vessel in the area.
Gulf of Guinea	US$747–US$983 million, of which: • industry employed vessel protection – 31 per cent of costs (armed guards, liaisons, Lagos escort vessels, Delta-Port escort vessels, secure zones, security equipment); • government and civil society costs – 53 per cent of costs (naval operations, prosecutions and imprisonment, counter-piracy organisations); and • other industry costs – 16 per cent of total (cargo theft, stolen goods, ransoms and associated payments, insurance, labour).

Source: Oceans Beyond Piracy (2014a, 2014b)

attack critical maritime infrastructure or could be sunk to create a blockade in shallow channels within choke points – the Malacca Strait is regarded as especially vulnerable to such attacks (Petersen and Treat, 2008; Murphy, 2013). The attacks of 9/11 highlighted the different vulnerabilities of the global infrastructure system and underscored the state vulnerabilities that emerge from the unevenness of the security checks within the maritime infrastructure system, especially in terms of containerisation and the sporadic security checks at the points of both de- and re-territorialisation. The rise of maritime terrorism also reflects many of the factors that drive piracy, namely rising traffic volumes in specific pinch points. These are compounded by the rise of water sports which offer a conduit for training and also the rise of just-in-time production systems which allow terrorists to create cascade effects through global supply chains (Walkenhorst and Dihel, 2006).

The impact of militant human activity on supply chains is more than simply one of supply constraints: the impact of terrorism and piracy can also have an impact through rising costs in areas such as insurance premiums (Murphy, 2013). It is estimated that every 1 per cent increase in costs decreases trade by around 2–3 per cent (Limao and Venables, 2001) and that additional security measures increase trade costs by around 2–3 per cent (Leonard, 2001). These effects are compounded by complex and overlapping governance systems. The threat to the multilateral trading system and to global supply chain has stimulated the exercise of military power by the US, the EU and, to a lesser extent, China (European Commission, 2010). To militate against the potential fragmentation of global value chains by states seeking to retreat behind borders, new initiatives have been launched, such as the ISPS Code which applies strict US principles of its container security initiative to 161 ports (Oceans Beyond Piracy (OBP), 2014). However, as highlighted earlier, the extent to which such measures are actually causing a fragmentation of the system is a matter of debate (Papa, 2013).

Infrastructure Under-investment

The operation of the global system (and the capability of states to secure welfare gains from it) depends upon investment in the capacity of the national infrastructure system (Held et al., 1999). The focus here is upon the state-based system and, as such, its impact upon the capability of the state to operate effectively in the global economic system. Policy discourses can be separated into two distinct themes. The first is the capability of developed states to re-infrastructure themselves through the upgrading of mature domestic systems to reflect the evolving needs of the economic system and their place within it. This is reflected in analysis from the WEF (2015) which highlighted how many developed states have lost competitiveness (as transactions costs increase) as a result of sustained under-investment within NIS. This appears to be particularly acute in the US and Germany. The second theme is the longstanding issue of the spatial variation in the availability of infrastructure between developed and developing states, especially in the difficulties of the latter in establishing basic levels of infrastructuring. The narratives of organisations such as the OECD (2011) and the WEF (2014) underscore a neo-liberal tradition of infrastructures supporting the logic of competitive interaction. As such, these narratives stress prosperity through economic integration and tend to ignore broader aspects of the state's infrastructural mandate.

The OECD – in focusing on what it terms 'strategic infrastructures' (that is, infrastructures that are external facing, such as gateways and corridors that enable imports and exports) – has argued that, given an anticipated doubling in air traffic over 15 years and a quadrupling of maritime container traffic between 2010 and 2030 (OECD, 2011), there needs to be a broad re-infrastructuring by many developed states as their key strategic infrastructures simply will not be able to cope. However, given the trends towards a polycentric system of infrastructure development, many developed states are looking towards the private sector to lead investment in these assets. However, a polycentric NIS still depends upon state involvement, either through the establishment of the necessary supporting soft infrastructure or, as is more common, by the provision of finance to enable these highly capital intensive, high sunk cost and high risk projects to be realised (OECD, 2011). Given that the emerging need for these infrastructures has coincided within an austerity consensus across many developed economies, the resources required to support sustainable public–private partnerships in infrastructure have not been forthcoming. As a result, the gap between the investment needs of strategic transport and what has actually been realised has grown. This situation has been compounded by the fact that many of the banks that offered the high risk, long-term finance required by such investments were among those most adversely affected by the financial crisis. Consequently, states have been seeking to diversify their sources of finance further and, in so doing, to alter the institutional soft infrastructure (such as customs procedures) as a means of encouraging this investment (WEF, 2014).

Many developed economy ports have adapted to the shifting technologies, such as the mega-ships mentioned earlier, but this has created a degree of concentration (OECD/IFT, 2015a, 2015b). However, there has been lack of adaption within air infrastructures, especially in Europe and the US. According to the ACI–NA (Airports Council International–North

America (ACI–NA), 2015), the US needs to invest US$15 billion per annum between 2015 and 2019 in order to upgrade existing airport capacity and to create new capacity in response to the forecast increase in traffic flows. A similar pattern is anticipated in the EU where a failure to upgrade capacity is expected to lead to significant welfare losses (IATA, 2015). The difficulties of airport investment are typified by the example of London Heathrow, the UK's main hub. Despite operating at 99 per cent of capacity, approval to upgrade the facility and/or to develop an alternative is facing fierce local resistance to the extent that any decision on this matter is unlikely to be fully implemented the mid-2020s at the earliest.

Infrastructure Adaptability

Further constraints linked to the existence of bottlenecks and choke points have emerged where state-based gateways have failed to adapt to the changing types, forms and volume of flows. As mentioned earlier, there is a push for scale in transport: this has been most evident in the maritime sector but is also apparent, to a lesser degree, within the civil aviation sector.

The process of adaptation has proven especially problematic in the maritime sector where the rise of mega-ships has not only placed pressure upon state-based maritime gateways but has also placed pressure upon main transit routes, notably the Suez and Panama Canals, to adapt. One of the main problems is that mega-ships create significant traffic peaks in port and hinterland systems which – whilst not a new area of concern – does create problems when these flows are unpredicted because of reliability issues with shipping lines. This poses the question of whether the benefits of scale are outweighed by the infrastructure costs of the rush to scale. On the main east–west sea lanes, the size of the average ship has increased by over 60 per cent between 2007 and 2014 (UNCTAD, 2014a). This raises the fear that the sustained salience of mega ships will result in increased concentration of port traffic around a series of super hubs. Another concern is that many of the key maritime choke points will be unable to cope with the rise of the mega-ships. This is especially true of the Panama Canal which, hitherto, has only been able to handle ships up to 5,000 TEU (twenty foot equivalent) – a problem when the average size of the newer generation of container ship in 2015 was 8,000 TEU and with the larger ships heading towards 18,000 TEU (OECD/ITF, 2015b). These problems for the Panama and Suez (which was constrained by the inability of two very wide ships to pass each other) Canals should be militated somewhat by planned and realised expansions. However, the Panama Canal still faces problems derived from the constraints imposed by its locks. The relative shallowness (21 metres) of the Malacca Strait poses a different constraint.

However, 24,000 TEU ships are currently designed with a draft of 16 metres, which is not expected to pose a serious problem, but the constraints imposed by the Malacca Strait could place an upper limit on future ship size (UNCTAD, 2014b).

The nature of the infrastructure problem for ports posed by mega-ships depends on the nature of the port. Inland or estuary ports have to adapt by undertaking more routine dredging of channels, but this is not clear cut because tides and ship loading also affect the required depth. Thus, in specific circumstances, ships may not be able to access port facilities. Moreover, dredging can create environmental problems. Port constraints are also apparent in physical structures such as bridges and locks and also extend to the need to alter quays and cranes. In many cases, bridges are being adapted to allow the mega-ships through. If, as the OECD antici-pates, ships continue to grow in capacity to 24,000 TEU and beyond, then there will either be a further concentration of port traffic or ports will be pressurised to spend more to update their infrastructure systems – or a mixture of both. Most ports handle an average of 7–10,000 TEU per visit but with 18,000 TEU ships they will have to deal with more freight in the same period of time. This process will intensify the trend towards fewer and bigger ships and, in turn, increase competition between ports, requiring improvements to inland infrastructure because goods may have to travel further overland to reach their final destination. The number of ships from Asia to Europe has fallen from 35 per week in 2007 to fewer than 20 in 2015 (OECD/ITF, 2016). Port authorities want traffic, and ship owners want the ship to remain in port for as short as time as possible, with the result that ports are compelled to invest in new facilities and develop strategies to increase their productivity.

In civil aviation, although the business case for new super-capacity planes has been questioned in the face of the rise of low fare, point-to-point services, nevertheless competition between hubs has spurred increased pas-senger flows and the super planes are one means of meeting additional demand. The introduction of the Airbus A380, for example, required adjustments to airport infrastructure to cope with the extra load created by these planes. For many continental hubs, such adjustments can be eco-nomically justified but for alternate airports the cost of adaptation can be prohibitive, especially when the need to accept such planes may occur only rarely, perhaps in the case of a diversion, for example. The ICAO (2014) identifies the minimum requirements for airports and the infrastructure to cope with such contingencies safely. However, Airbus argues that the A380 is targeted only at the main 80 airports, most of which would be able to cope with the demands made by the plane. Moreover, Airbus esti-mated that the cost of adapting is only 3–5 per cent of the amount that airlines must spend in any case given the upgrading needed to cope with rising traffic flows. The narrative suggests that this is a developed country problem because these planes would only be used on main east–west routes where airport capacity is more developed.

International System Outliers and Involuntary State Balkanisation

Arguably, the final main source of fragmentation within the global transport system is created by states that are outliers – either for geographical or low traffic reasons – from the international trading system and, as a result, have inadequate links to the main logistical systems which further reinforce their isolation. There are two main types of system outliers: the first are landlocked states which have no direct access to major maritime logistical hubs and the second are small island developing states (the so-called 'SIDS') which are often peripheral to the global economy.

Landlocked States

The infrastructure challenge for landlocked states varies with the degree of NIS integration with neighbouring systems. As such, the issue is of less salience for states like Switzerland and other landlocked European states, many of which have with good communications, a prominent services sector economy and which are integrated into contiguous (and semi-contiguous) European infrastructure systems. As of 2015, 43 of the 193 territorial states were landlocked (UNCTAD, 2014b). Thirty-one of these landlocked states were developing countries, 15 of which are in Africa, 12 in Asia, two in Latin America and two in Central and Eastern Europe (World Bank, 2015a). Tables 3.11 and 3.12 highlight the full list of landlocked states and the distance to nearest major ports for a selected number of these states. Over half of these landlocked states are also least developed countries. For these states in 2012, external trade comprised around 80 per cent of GDP (World Bank, 2015a) – this is higher than in many developed economies and demonstrates the need for efficient trade infrastructure. Collier (2006, 2007) estimates that approximately 40 per cent of the poorest billion of the world's population live in landlocked states and that there is a 0.7 per cent spillover for a landlocked state when its neighbour grows by 1 per cent. Moreover, some states are de facto landlocked, despite having maritime borders, because of the combined effect of most of the population living away from the littoral border and the inadequate domestic hinterland infrastructure connecting them to the ports.

The major focus of concern for many less developed landlocked states is the impact on transaction costs created arising from their relative isolation, notably with regard to access to maritime infrastructure (World Bank, 2015b). This relative isolation poses constraints upon the state's ability to compete when faced with relatively high trade costs, which also increase import prices and reduce export revenues. Of the African landlocked states, it is estimated that transport costs for these states can be as much as 77 per cent of the value of exports (UNCTAD, 2013). In addition, Gallup et al. (1999) add two further reasons that these states may be in a disadvantageous position, namely that coastal states have an incentive to undermine landlocked states and that transnational infrastructure is more difficult to arrange than internal infrastructure. Indeed, in developing states, coastal infrastructure is estimated to be up to ten times more costly to develop and manage than in developed states (UNCTAD, 2014b).

Conventional thinking was that the absence of competitiveness in landlocked states was simply a derivative of their geography and topography. However, research (for example, see Arvis et al., 2010; Arvis, 2011) increasingly suggests that it is the unreliability of the logistics system that is the greatest impediment to manufacture in landlocked states. In many less developed countries (LDC), places of manufacture and consumption can be located up to 800 km away from the nearest seaport (Uprety, 2006) which can add an extra two days' transit time. Indeed, landlocked LDCs take, on average, an extra 20 days to export than for coastal developing states – a process that is not aided by the often lengthy trade facilitation involved in such flows. Such lengthy transit times and isolation not only increase costs but also yield less turnover for transporters on their vehicles, fewer full runs and many empty return journeys. The net effect is that there is no incentive to invest in extra capacity within the system (Arvis et al., 2007). Moreover, these states are also vulnerable because they rely upon the goodwill of their neighbours, many of whom are themselves developing economies with under-developed infrastructure, to sustain access to maritime trade routes.

The Almaty Programme established by the World Bank in 2003 sought to grant states rights of transit, improve infrastructure across both dependent and transit states as well as to promote cooperation between states. However, the agreement has had limited effect – it has been poorly implemented and transport costs in dependent states have remained relatively high (Arvis, 2011). This reflects the limited power of many landlocked developing states to work against their remoteness in relation to global value chains. These problems are compounded by low internal infrastructural density with poor penetration of road, telecommunications and energy networks. In west and central Africa, for example, there are 13 major transit corridors, many of which are characterised by underdeveloped road and rail systems. In east Africa, there is much better coordination between states but aged integrated trans-national systems, such as the now defunct East African Railway Company (which handled flows to Mombasa for Kenya, Uganda, Congo, Burundi and Rwanda), have been fragmented by national systems (Arvis, 2011).

The policy narratives and practitioner discourses about landlocked states are heavily skewed by themes of competitiveness and economic growth. However, there are clearly other elements of the infrastructural mandate activated in these cases, notably economic security and – in some

Table 3.11   Distances to ports for selected landlocked developing states

State	Ports	Range (km)	Mode
Afghanistan	2	1,200–1,600	Road
Armenia	2	800–2,400	Rail, road
Azerbaijan	2	800	Rail, road
Bolivia	8	500–2,400	Road, rail, river
Botswana	4	950–1,400	Rail, road
Burkina Faso	5	1,100–1,900	Rail, road
Burundi	2	1,500–1,850	Rail, road, lake
Bhutan	1	800	Rail, road
Central African Republic	2	1,500–1,800	Rail, road
Chad	2	1,800–1,900	Rail, road
Ethiopia	3	900–1,250	Rail, road
Kyrgyzstan	4	4,500–5,200	Rail, road
Laos	3	600–750	Rail, road
Lesotho	2	500	Rail, road
Malawi	3	600–2,300	Rail, road
Mali	6	1,200–1,400	Rail, road
Mongolia	4	1,700–6,000	Rail, road
Nepal	2	1,100–1,200	Rail, road
Niger	3	900–1,200	Rail, road
Paraguay	4	1,200–1,400	Rail, road, river
Moldova	2	800	Rail, road
Rwanda	2	1,500–1,700	Rail, road, lake
Swaziland	4	250–500	Rail, road
Uganda	2	1,300–1,650	Rail, road
Uzbekistan	3	2,700	Rail, road
Tajikistan	3	1,500–2,500	Rail, road
Macedonia	1	600	Rail, road
Turkmenistan	3	4,500	Rail, road
Zambia	8	1,300–2,100	Rail, road
Zimbabwe	3	850–1,550	Rail, road

Source: UNCTAD (2013)

instances – control which can also be challenged by the powerful transit state (see the case of Sudan and its relations with South Sudan). Moreover, Gallup et al. (1999) suggest that, in some instances, coastal states may disadvantage landlocked states where there are economic or military incentives to impose restraints on these states and where infrastructure across borders is difficult to arrange. These disruptions can arise from border delays, from the initiation of transit, constraints through territoriality, local regulation and bureaucracy and even corruption.

Distance alone cannot explain fully why these states are under-developed because there are parts of China, India and Russia that are further from coastal regions but more developed. The issue appears to be one of dependence upon a transit state and therefore of control of the means of access to maritime infrastructure. Faye et al. (2004) argue that this dependence can take four forms. The first is straightforward infrastructural dependence based on the need for transit to maritime infrastructure to access global supply chains. The second is political dependence where the state of relations between the states influences the degree of access to key infrastructures. The third is dependence on peace and stability within the transit state and fourth is dependence upon the efficiency of the transit state's bureaucracy and administrative system (Hafner, 2008).

To offset these problems, conventional practice has tended towards two solutions (Uprety, 2006). The first is through the establishment of transit rights. The focal point of transit rights is the creation of transit corridors to link multi-national road and rail facilities to key hub ports, thereby lowering the time to market and costs (Kawai et al., 2011). Although, in volume terms, it is the key east–west hubs that matter, for certain states on low intensity trade routes, land-based transit systems are important

Table 3.12 Landlocked developing states

Africa	Latin America	Asia	Europe
Botswana, Burkina Faso, Burundi, Central African Republic, Chad, Ethiopia, Lesotho, Malawi, Mali, Niger, Rwanda, Swaziland, Uganda, Zambia, Zimbabwe	Bolivia, Paraguay	Mongolia, Kazakhstan, Uzbekistan, Turkmenistan, Kyrgyzstan, Nepal, Bhutan, Laos, Afghanistan, Azerbaijan, Armenia, Tajikistan	Moldova, Macedonia

Source: UNCTAD (2013)

international infrastructures. In developed economies, NTIs are a means of internal transit for these landlocked states, and these corridors are a means of rendering national systems internationally significant. The second solution attempts to create regional infrastructure systems. This has been especially evident in sub-Saharan Africa where there have been renewed attempts to upgrade and expand existing regional corridors. Such arrangements have a strong historical precedence, especially in East Africa, but political unrest, corruption and under-investment have frequently resulted in a failure of these corridors to adjust to shifting contexts.

The current strategy is reflected in the UN's Almaty Framework which very much incorporates these conventional solutions for landlocked states and which comprise a number of measures to secure transit rights and improve infrastructure, and trade facilitation measures supported by states tapping into industry best practice. The programme seeks to link reform to guaranteed transit rights, as well as promoting programmes for infrastructure enhancement of key transit routes and trade facilitation measures (Arvis, 2011). Progress has been patchy with poor implementation of agreements being partially compensated for by having the majority of landlocked capital cities connected to ports with paved infrastructure. Although port operations have improved, issues of transit and poor infrastructure across transit states remain and – as a consequence – transportation costs remain high. The improvements that have taken place have often been as a direct legacy of the commodity boom which stimulated the so-called 'Angola mode' of investment according to which investors build transit infrastructure to access coastal ports as a means of exporting commodities. However, it is widely recognised that infrastructure on its own is not enough: it has to be complemented by competition in logistical services, the absence of which is often seen as a larger problem for these states than the inadequacy of infrastructure itself.

Small Island Developing States

SIDS stand in direct contrast to landlocked states because these are, in effect, sea-locked states (see Table 3.13). However, being sea-locked is not an advantage, especially when it is combined with smallness which creates multiple vulnerabilities. In the context of the GTI, the core vulnerability of SIDS arises from their by-passing by major trade routes. The dependence of these states upon containerised imports is compounded by the fact that SIDS often face high transport costs because of the need to travel long distances with low traffic volumes created by their location outside the main east–west trade route (UNCTAD, 2013). Moreover, the location of many SIDS means they are especially vulnerable to adverse

Table 3.13   Major small island developing states (SIDS)

The major SIDS		
Caribbean	Pacific	Indian Ocean and West Africa
Anguilla, Antigua and Barbuda, Aruba, Bahamas, Barbados, Belize, British Virgin Islands, Cuba, Dominica, Dominican Republic, Grenada, Guyana, Haiti, Jamaica, Montserrat, Netherlands Antilles, Puerto Rico, Saint Kitts and Nevis, Saint Lucia, Saint Vincent and the Grenadines, Suriname, Trinidad and Tobago, US Virgin Islands	American Samoa, Cook Islands, Federated States of Micronesia, Fiji, French Polynesia, Guam, Kiribati, Marshall Islands, Nauru, New Caledonia, Niue, Northern Mariana Islands, Palau, Papua New Guinea, Samoa, Solomon Islands, Timor-Leste, Tonga, Tuvalu, Vanuatu	Bahrain, Cape Verde, Comoros, Guinea-Bissau, Maldives, Mauritius, São Tomé and Príncipe, Seychelles, Singapore

Source: UNCTAD (2014b)

weather conditions and to the hostile effects of climate change, which can further disrupt connectivity (Encontre, 1999). These states are especially reliant upon maritime trade, with more than 80 per cent of their trade being undertaken through this channel. Air transport is only used for passenger and tourism and – where relevant – island hopping (Briguglio, 1995).

SIDS are located in three main areas: the Caribbean, Indian Ocean, and West Africa and the Pacific (see Table 3.13). The positioning disadvantage for the Caribbean states is less pronounced because they are on the main east–west trade route and are close to the US, which enables them to take advantage of cabotage laws. Many SIDS are only served indirectly by the GTS – not only do they lie off the main east–west routes, but many require a big diversion from the secondary north–south routes (Armstrong and Read, 1998). The result, according to UNCTAD (2015), is that these states' transport costs are 2 per cent more than the global average as a percentage of import value. For some states (for example, the Comoros Islands), this figure is more than double the international average.

In addition to the aforementioned economies of scale, cost differences are driven by a number of factors such as imbalances (where absence of reciprocal flows means the importer has to pay for the return cost of an empty vessel), distance, competition and port characteristics. Not surprisingly, therefore, these states have poor relative connectivity to the global economy as ports cannot cope with large ships lying outside major shipping lanes. This is evidenced by their degree of dislocation from shipping lanes demonstrated by their relatively low shipping connectivity. In 2011, the best placed SIDS (Jamaica) was placed 41st in terms of global maritime connectivity. Indeed, of the 160 states assessed, SIDS occupied the bottom 10 places, with 34 of the 52 SIDS being placed in the bottom quartile (UNCTAD, 2014b). This reflects that the weighted average distance from the main global markets is 8,200 km for Caribbean SIDS and around 11, 500 for South Pacific SIDS.

The SIDs are also heavily reliant upon inter-island shipping, which can further entrench dislocation of these states, especially those within the Pacific where inter-island flows can be particularly erratic. This further compounds the vulnerability of these states to energy costs. In the Pacific, 80 per cent of all oil usage is for transport. It is also often felt that the concentration of the global freight industry has pushed up freight rates for these states, some of which, notably in Micronesia, have responded by establishing state-owned or state-controlled shipping companies. However, not all SIDS are convinced of the relevance of such measures (World Bank, 2014).

These natural and commercial disadvantages are compounded by a local maritime infrastructure that is often aged and poorly maintained. The ports are also often vulnerable to maritime accidents because many are located in shallow and/or narrow channels which can easily become obstructed. This can often place restrictions on the form and volume of traffic. Indeed, many of these states constructed infrastructure before the era of containerisation and have not since undertaken substantive investment in order to cope with the implications of this process. These problems reflect the inability of many of these states to generate the financing necessary to adapt to the changing technology of the global maritime system.

Moreover, the growing priority given to tourism and the increasing priority given to cruise ships in cargo berths also slows down the freight transmission process and can create conflicts of use. Across the SIDS, tourism in 2014 accounted for 50 per cent of GDP and 30 per cent of employment (UNCTAD, 2014b). This not only grants priority to tourism facilities in terms of infrastructure access but also requires upgrading of both maritime and civil aviation infrastructure to handle these flows efficiently. In the Caribbean, many SIDS have sought to circumvent this by establishing direct flights to key regional hubs. Nonetheless, this does not remove the need to improve maritime infrastructure to meet the needs of both the tourist and transport sectors.

The connectivity of SIDS is further challenged by their especial vulnerability to the effects of climate change and natural hazards. Many SIDS are located in areas subject to adverse meteorological or tectonic activity. The short to medium term impacts of such vulnerabilities are numerous, especially the low lying critical transport infrastructures of some SIDS that are subject to flooding, which means that the GDP impact of such events can be especially harsh as relief flows can be especially disruptive. Over the longer term, several of these states are also especially vulnerable to the impact of climate change because their frequently low-lying infrastructures are endangered by rising sea levels. The Maldives are a noteworthy but not the only example of this phenomenon.

CONCLUSION

The main drivers of the moves towards the development of a global transportation system originate in the global forces to which NIS are expected to adapt. The logic of the competition state suggests that these stimulants to cross-border flows require states to enable and facilitate the ease of flow across borders. However, there are wide discrepancies in the application of the necessary measures to assuage such pressures. States – with regard to the NTI – seem perfectly capable and willing to assert discretionary control over the core infrastructural gateways to enable or to restrict cross-border flows. Indeed, the forces for integration tend to be stronger on a regional than on a global level. The forces for integration at a global level tend to result in inter-governmental measures that offer states flexibility regarding their application. Whilst MNCs are indeed powerful forces within this segment of the GIS, there is little doubt that the dependence of global flows upon territorially fixed assets offers states the power to shape these processes. This is evident when the forces for fragmentation within the system are examined. Although there are a number of drivers in the fragmentation of global transport systems, two drivers dominate. In developed states, there appears to be a trend towards an increased preference for security within transport systems. Whilst – it appears – this is not intentionally designed to seek to limit or constrain flows, it is nonetheless an inevitable side-effect of this preference. The other main source of fragmentation is the unevenness of the development of national transportation systems within developing states, especially, but not only, in those states that are landlocked or are away from the main transport routes. The effect of these factors is that global transport flows have failed to fully embed themselves in the state-based system. Consequently, despite almost five decades of progressive globalisation, transport systems and services which fully support these trends remain elusive.

REFERENCES

Adler, N. and Smilowitz, K. (2007) 'Hub-and-spoke network alliances and mergers: price-location competition in the airline industry', *Transportation Research Part B: Methodological, 41*(4), 394–409.

Adlung, R. (2006) 'Public Services and the GATS', *Journal of International Economic Law, 9*(2), 455–85.

Airports Council International – North America (ACI–NA) (2015) Airport capital development needs 2015–2019, accessed 1 March 2016 at www.aci-na.org/

Altemöller, F. (2011) 'Towards an international regime of supply chain security: an international relations perspective', *World Customs Journal, 5*(2), 21–34.

Armstrong, H.W. and Read, R. (1998) 'Trade and growth in small states: the impact of global trade liberalisation', *The World Economy, 21*(4), 563–85.

Arvis, J.F. (2011) *Connecting Landlocked Developing Countries to Markets: Trade Corridors in the 21st Century.* Washington, DC: World Bank Publications.

Arvis, J.F. and Shepherd, B. (2011) *The Air Connectivity Index: Measuring Integration in the Global Air Transport Network.* World Bank Policy Research Working Paper Series, WPS 5722.

Arvis, J.F., Mustra, M.A., Panzer, J., Ojala, L. and Naula, T. (2007) *Connecting to Compete: Trade Logistics in the Global Economy.* Washington, DC: World Bank, accessed 13 February 2016 at www.worldbank.org/lpi

Arvis, J.F., Raballand, G. and Marteau, J.F. (2010) *The Cost of Being Landlocked: Logistics, Costs, and Supply Chain Reliability.* Washington, DC: World Bank Publications.

Bateman, S. (2007) 'UNCLOS and its limitations as the foundation for a regional maritime security regime', *Korean Journal of Defense Analysis, 19*(3), 27–56.

Belobaba, P., Odoni, A. and Barnhart, C. (eds.) (2009) *The Global Airline Industry.* Chichester, UK: John Wiley.

Bichou, K. (2015) 'The ISPS code and the cost of port compliance: an initial logistics and supply chain framework for port security assessment and management', *Port Management,* 109–37.

Bichou, K., Szyliowicz, J.S. and Zamparini, L. (eds.) (2014) *Maritime Transport Security: Issues, Challenges and National Policies.* Cheltenham, UK: Edward Elgar.

Bird, G., Blomberg, S.B. and Hess, G.D. (2008) 'International terrorism: causes, consequences and cures', *The World Economy, 31*(2), 255–74.

Bolic, T. and Sivcev, Z. (2011) 'Eruption of Eyjafjallajökull in Iceland: experience of European air traffic management', *Transportation Research Record, 2214,* 136–43.

Bougheas, S., Demetriades, P.O. and Morgenroth, E.L. (1999) 'Infrastructure, transport costs and trade', *Journal of International Economics, 47*(1), 169–89.

Bowden, A., Hurlburt, K., Aloyo, E., Marts, C. and Lee, A. (2010) *The Economic Costs of Maritime Piracy.* Broomfield, CO: One Earth Future Foundation.

Briguglio, L. (1995) 'Small island developing states and their economic vulnerabilities', *World Development*, *23*(9), 1615–32.

Brooks, M.R. (2009) *Liberalization in Maritime Transport*. Paris: OECD/ITF.

Budd, L., Griggs, S., Howarth, D. and Ison, S. (2011) 'A fiasco of volcanic proportions? Eyjafjallajökull and the closure of European airspace', *Mobilities*, *6*(1), 31–40.

Burghouwt, G. (2013) *Airport Capacity Expansion Strategies in the Era of Airline Multi-Hub Networks*. International Transport Forum Discussion Paper, No 2013–05.

Button, K. (2008) *The Impacts of Globalisation on International Air Transport Activity*. Paris: OECD.

Button, K. (2010) *Transport Economics*. Cheltenham, UK: Edward Elgar.

Button, K. and Neiva, R. (2013) 'Single European Sky and the functional airspace blocks: will they improve economic efficiency?', *Journal of Air Transport Management*, *33*, 73–80.

Button, K.J. and Stough, R. (eds.) (2000) *Air Transport Networks: Theory and Policy Implications*. Cheltenham, UK: Edward Elgar.

Chalk, P. (1998) 'Contemporary maritime piracy in Southeast Asia', *Studies in Conflict & Terrorism*, *21*(1), 87–112.

Chalk, P. (2008) *The Maritime Dimension of International Security: Terrorism, Piracy, and Challenges for the United States*, Vol. 697. Santa Monica, CA: Rand Corporation.

Clausen, J., Larsen, A., Larsen, J. and Rezanova, N.J. (2010) 'Disruption management in the airline industry – concepts, models and methods', *Computers & Operations Research*, *37*(5), 809–21.

Coe, N.M., Dicken, P. and Hess, M. (2008) 'Global production networks: realizing the potential', *Journal of Economic Geography*, *8*(3), 271–95.

Collier, P. (2006) *Africa: Geography and Growth*. Center for the Study of African Economies, Department of Economics, Oxford University, UK.

Collier, P. (2007) 'Africa's economic growth: opportunities and constraints', *African Development Review*, *19*(1), 6–25.

Corbett, J.J. and Winebrake, J.J. (2008) 'International trade and global shipping', *Handbook on Trade and the Environment*, 33–48.

Corbett, J.J., Winebrake, J., Endresen, Ø., Eide, M., Dalsøren, S., Isaksen, I.S. and Sørgård, E. (2010) 'International maritime shipping: the impact of globalisation on activity levels', in Braathens, N.-A. (ed.), *Globalisation, Transport and the Environment*. Paris: OECD, pp. 55–80.

Cox, J. (2008) 'Regulation of Foreign Direct Investment after the Dubai Ports controversy: has the US government finally figured out how to balance foreign threats to national security without alienating foreign companies', *Journal of Corporation Law*, *34*, 293–315.

Cudahy, B.J. (2006) *Box Boats: How Container Ships Changed the World*. New York, NY: Fordham University Press.

Demetriades, P.O. (2008) *Globalisation and Infrastructure Needs*. 17th International ITF/OECD Symposium on Transport Economics and Policy: Benefiting from Globalisation Transport Sector Contribution and Policy Challenges: Transport Sector Contribution and Policy Challenges. Paris: OECD.

Dempsey, P.S. (2003) 'Aviation security: the role of law in the war against terrorism', *Columbia Journal of Transnational Law*, *41*(3), 649–733.

Dicken, P. (2008) *Global Shift: Mapping the Changing Contours of the World Economy*. New York, NY: Guilford Press.

Dicken, P. (2015) *Global Shift*, 7th edn. London: Sage.

Dicken, P. and Henderson, J. (1999) *Making the Connections: Global Production Networks in Britain, East Asia and Eastern Europe*. A research proposal to the UK's Economic and Social Research Council.

Dicken, P., Kelly, P.F., Olds, K. and Yeung, H.W.-C. (2001) 'Chains and networks, territories and scales: towards a relational framework for analysing the global economy', *Global Networks*, *1*(2), 89–112.

Donovan, A. (2004) 'The impact of containerization: from Adam Smith to the 21st century', *Review of Business*, *25*(3), 10–15.

Ducruet, C. and Notteboom, T. (2012) 'The worldwide maritime network of container shipping: spatial structure and regional dynamics', *Global Networks*, *12*(3), 395–423.

Emmerson, C. and Stevens, P. (2012) *Maritime Choke Points and the Global Energy System: Charting a Way Forward*. London: Chatham House.

Encontre, P. (1999) 'The vulnerability and resilience of small island developing states in the context of globalization', *Natural Resources Forum*, *23*(3), 261–70.

Engman, M. (2005) *The Economic Impact of Trade Facilitation*. Paris: OECD.

European Commission (2010) *Secure Trade and 100% Scanning of Containers*. European Commission Staff Working Paper, SEC (2010) 131 final.

Fandl, K.J. (2004) 'Terrorism, development and trade: winning the war on terror without the war', *American University International Law Review*, *19*(3), 587–630.

Faye, M.L., McArthur, J.W., Sachs, J.D. and Snow, T. (2004) 'The challenges facing landlocked developing countries', *Journal of Human Development*, *5*(1), 31–68.

Fink, C., Mattoo, A. and Neagu, I.C. (2002) 'Trade in international maritime services: how much does policy matter?', *The World Bank Economic Review*, *16*(1), 81–108.

Flores-Fillol, R. and Moner-Colonques, R. (2007) 'Strategic formation of airline alliances', *Journal of Transport Economics and Policy*, *41*(3), 427–49.

Forsyth, P. (1998) 'The gains from the liberalisation of air transport: a review of reform', *Journal of Transport Economics and Policy*, *32*(1), 73–92.

Frémont, A. (2007) 'Global maritime networks: the case of Maersk', *Journal of Transport Geography*, *15*(6), 431–42.

Frémont, A. and Ducruet, C. (2005) 'The emergence of a mega-port from the global to the local: the case of Busan', *Tijdschrift voor Eco'nomische en Sociale Geografie*, *96*(4), 421–32.

Fu, X., Oum, T.H. and Zhang, A. (2010) 'Air transport liberalization and its impacts on airline competition and air passenger traffic', *Transportation Journal*, *49*(4), 24–41.

Gallup, J.L., Sachs, J.D. and Mellinger, A.D. (1999) 'Geography and economic development', *International Regional Science Review*, *22*(2), 179–232.

George, R. (2013) *Deep Sea and Foreign Going: Inside Shipping, the Invisible Industry that Brings You 90% of Everything*. London: Portobello Books.

Gereffi, G., Humphrey, J. and Sturgeon, T. (2005) 'The governance of global value chains', *Review of International Political Economy*, *12*(1), 78–104.

Gillen, D. and Morrison, W.G. (2005) 'Regulation, competition and network evolution in aviation', *Journal of Air Transport Management*, *11*(3), 161–74.

Goulielmos, A.M. and Anastasakos, A.A. (2005) 'Worldwide security measures for shipping, seafarers and ports: an impact assessment of ISPS code', *Disaster Prevention and Management: An International Journal*, *14*(4), 462–78.

Graham, A. (2013) *Managing Airports: An International Perspective, 4th edn.* London and New York: Routledge.

Graham, E.M. and Marchick, D. (2006) *US National Security and Foreign Direct Investment.* Washington, DC: Peterson Institute for International Economics.

Grainger, A. (2007) 'Trade facilitation: a review', *Journal of World Trade, 4*, 39–62.

Grainger, A. (2008) 'Customs and trade facilitation: from concepts to implementation', *World Customs Journal*, *2*(1), 17–30.

Hafner, G. (2008) 'Land-locked states', in Wulfrum, R. (ed.), *The Max Planck Encyclopaedia of Public International Law.* Oxford: Oxford University Press.

Hastings, J.V. (2009) 'Geographies of state failure and sophistication in maritime piracy hijackings', *Political Geography*, *28*(4), 213–23.

Held, D., McGrew, A., Goldblatt, D. and Perraton, J. (1999) *Global Transformations: Politics, Economics and Culture.* Basingstoke, UK: Palgrave Macmillan.

Helmick, J.S. (2008) 'Port and maritime security: a research perspective', *Journal of Transportation Security*, *1*(1), 15–28.

Hess, M. and Yeung, H.W.-C. (2006) 'Whither global production networks in economic geography? Past, present and future', *Environment and Planning A*, *38*(6), 1145–167.

Hesse, H.G. (2003) 'Maritime security in a multilateral context: IMO activities to enhance maritime security', *The International Journal of Marine and Coastal Law*, *18*(3), 327–40.

Hoffmann, J. (2012) 'Corridors of the sea: an investigation into liner shipping connectivity', Les Corridors de Transport, Les Océanides.

Hoffmann, J. and Kumar, S. (2010), 'Globalisation – the maritime nexus', in Grammenos, C. (ed.), *The Handbook of Maritime Economics and Business*, 2nd edn. London: Lloyd's List, p. 35–64.

Hummels, D. (2007) 'Transportation costs and international trade in the second era of globalization', *Journal of Economic Perspectives*, *21*(3), 131–54.

Hummels, D. (2008) 'Global trends in trade and transportation', in OECD, *Benefitting from Globalisation. Transport Sector Contribution and Policy Challenges.* Paris: OECD/ITF, pp. 15–36.

Imai, A., Nishimura, E., Papadimitriou, S. and Liu, M. (2006) 'The economic viability of container mega-ships', *Transportation Research Part E: Logistics and Transportation Review*, *42*(1), 21–41.

Inglada, V., Rey, B., Rodríguez-Alvarez, A. and Coto-Millan, P. (2006) 'Liberalisation and efficiency in international air transport', *Transportation Research Part A: Policy and Practice*, *40*(2), 95–105.

International Air Transport Association (IATA) (2013) *World Air Transport Statistics* (No. 50). Montréal, QC: International Air Transport Association.

International Air Transport Association (IATA) (2015) *Industry Report*, accessed 1 March 2016 at www.iata.org

International Civil Aviation Organization (ICAO) (2011) *International Aviation Security*, accessed 3 March 2016 at www.icao.org

International Civil Aviation Organization (ICAO) (2012) *Expanding Market Access for International Air Transport.* Working Paper ATConf/6-WP/13, Worldwide Air Transport Conference Sixth Meeting, Montréal, 18–22 March 2012.

International Civil Aviation Organization (ICAO) (2014) *Air Navigation Report*, accessed 6 March 2016 at www.icao.int

International Maritime Organization (IMO) (2015) *The ISPs Code,* accessed 6 March 2016 at www.imo.org

International Monetary Fund (2015) *World Economic Outlook*, accessed 12 March 2016 at www.imf.org

International Transport Forum/Organisation for Economic Co-operation and Development (2014a) *Liberalisation of Air Transport*. Paris: OECD.

International Transport Forum/Organisation for Economic Co-operation and Development (2014b) *Air Service Agreement Liberalisation and Airline Alliances.* Paris: OECD.

Jacks, D.S. and Pendakur, K. (2010) 'Global trade and the maritime transport revolution', *The Review of Economics and Statistics*, *92*(4), 745–55.

Janelle, D.G. and Beuthe, M. (1997) 'Globalization and research issues in transportation', *Journal of Transport Geography*, *5*(3), 199–206.

Jessop, B. (2009) 'From governance via governance failure and from multilevel governance to multi-scalar meta-governance', in Arts, B., Langendijk, A. and van Houtum, H. (eds.), *The Disoriented State: Shifts in Governmentality, Territoriality and Governance.* Heidelberg: Springer Verlag, pp. 79–98.

Kaluza, P., Kölzsch, A., Gastner, M.T. and Blasius, B. (2010) 'The complex network of global cargo ship movements', *Journal of the Royal Society Interface*, *7*(48), 1093–103.

Kawai, H., Hanaoka, S. and Kawasaki, T. (2011) Characteristics of international freight transport in landlocked countries. *Proceedings of Infrastructure Planning and Management*, accessed 15 March 2017 at www.ide.titech.ac.jp/~hanaoka/139. pdf

Kohl, N., Larsen, A., Larsen, J., Ross, A. and Tiourine, S. (2007) 'Airline disruption management – perspectives, experiences and outlook', *Journal of Air Transport Management*, *13*(3), 149–62.

Lanteigne, M. (2008) 'China's maritime security and the "Malacca Dilemma"', *Asian Security*, *4*(2), 143–61.

Lenain, P., Bonturi, M. and Koen, V. (2002) *The Economic Consequences of Terrorism.* Paris: OECD.

Leonard, J.S. (2001) *Impact of the September 11, 2001 Terrorist Attacks on North American Trade Flows.* Manufacturers Alliance E-Alert, Arlington, VA.

Levinson, M. (2010) *The Box: How the Shipping Container Made the World Smaller and the World Economy Bigger.* Princeton, NJ: Princeton University Press.

Levy, D.L. (2008) 'Political contestation in global production networks', *Academy of Management Review*, *33*(4), 943–63.

Limao, N. and Venables, A.J. (2001) 'Infrastructure, geographical disadvantage, transport costs, and trade', *The World Bank Economic Review*, *15*(3), 451–79.

Lutz, J.M. and Lutz, B.J. (2006) 'Terrorism as economic warfare', *Global Economy Journal*, *6*(2).

Meersman, H. and Van de Voorde, E. (2008) *Dynamic Ports within a Globalised World.* In 17th International ITF/OECD Symposium on Transport Economics and Policy: Benefiting from Globalisation Transport Sector Contribution and Policy Challenges: Transport Sector Contribution and Policy Challenges (Vol. 17, p. 321). Paris: OECD.

Mensah, T.A. (2004) 'The place of the ISPS Code in the legal international regime', *WMU Journal of Maritime Affairs*, *3*(1), 17–30.

Milde, M. (2008) *International Air Law and ICAO.* The Hague: Eleven International Publishing.

Mirza, D. and Verdier, T. (2008) 'International trade, security and transnational terrorism: theory and a survey of empirics', *Journal of Comparative Economics*, *36*(2), 179–94.

Mostaghel, D.M. (2006) 'Dubai ports world under Exon–Florio: a threat to national security or a tempest in a seaport', *Alabama Law Review*, *70*, 58–78.

Murphy, M. (2007) 'Piracy and UNCLOS: does international law help regional states combat piracy?', in Lehr, P. (ed.), *Violence at Sea: Piracy in the Age of Global Terrorism*. London: Routledge, pp. 161–63.

Murphy, M.N. (2013) *Contemporary Piracy and Maritime Terrorism: The Threat to International Security*. Abingdon, UK: Routledge.

Nero, G. (1999) 'A note on the competitive advantage of large hub-and-spoke networks', *Transportation Research Part E: Logistics and Transportation Review*, *35*(4), 225–39.

Nincic, D.J. (2002) 'Sea lane security and US maritime trade: chokepoints as scarce resources', *Globalization and Maritime Power*, 143–70.

Nincic, D.J. (2005) 'The challenge of maritime terrorism: threat identification, WMD and regime response', *Journal of Strategic Studies*, *28*(4), 619–44.

Nitsch, V. and Schumacher, D. (2004) 'Terrorism and international trade: an empirical investigation', *European Journal of Political Economy*, *20*(2), 423–33.

Nordås, H.K., Pinali, E. and Grosso, M.G. (2006) *Logistics and Time as a Trade Barrier*. Organisation for Economic Co-operation and Development Working Paper.

Notteboom, T. and Rodrigue, J.P. (2008) 'Containerisation, box logistics and global supply chains: the integration of ports and liner shipping networks', *Maritime Economics & Logistics*, *10*(1), 152–74.

Oceans Beyond Piracy (2014) *State of Maritime Piracy*, accessed 15 March 2016 at www.oceansbeyondpiracy.org/

Ohmae, K. (1990) *The Borderless World: Power and Strategy in the Interlinked Economy*. New York, NY: Harper Business.

Organisation for Economic Co-operation and Development (OECD) (2005) *Security in Maritime Transport: Risk Factors and Economic Impact*. Paris: OECD.

Organisation for Economic Co-operation and Development (OECD) (2008) *Protection of 'Critical Infrastructure' and the Role of Investment Policies Relating to National Security, May 2008*. Paris: OECD.

Organisation for Economic Co-operation and Development (OECD) (2011) *Strategic Infrastructure Needs to 2030*. Paris: OECD.

Organisation for Economic Co-operation and Development (OECD) (2015) *Implementation of the WTO Trade Facilitation Agreement: the potential impact on trade costs*, accessed 15 April 2016 at www.oecd.org

Organisation for Economic Co-operation and Development (OECD)/International Transport Forum (ITF) (2013) *ITF Transport Outlook 2013*, accessed 9 March 2016 at https://www.itf-oecd.org/

Organisation for Economic Co-operation and Development (OECD)/International Transport Forum (ITF) (2015a) *The Impact of Mega-Ships*. Paris: OECD.

Organisation for Economic Co-operation and Development (OECD)/International Transport Forum (ITF) (2015b) *ITF Transport Outlook*. Paris: OECD.

Organisation for Economic Co-operation and Development (OECD)/International Transport Forum (ITF) (2016) *ITF Transport Outlook*, accessed 2 March 2016 at www.oecd.org

Papa, P. (2013) 'US and EU strategies for maritime transport security: a comparative perspective', *Transport Policy*, *28*, 75–85.

Parameswaran, B. (2004) *The Liberalization of Maritime Transport Services: With Special Reference to the WTO/GATS Framework* (Vol. 1). Berlin, Heidelberg: Springer Verlag.

Peterson, J. and Treat, A. (2008) 'The post-9/11 global framework for cargo security', *Journal of International Commerce and Economics*, *2*, 1–30.

Portugal-Perez, A. and Wilson, J.S. (2012) 'Export performance and trade facilitation reform: hard and soft infrastructure', *World Development*, *40*(7), 1295–307.

Richardson, M. (2004) 'A time bomb for global trade: maritime-related terrorism in an age of weapons of mass destruction', *Maritime Studies*, *134*, 1–8.

Rietveld, P. and Bruinsma, F. (2012) *Is Transport Infrastructure Effective? Transport Infrastructure and Accessibility: Impacts on the Space Economy.* Berlin: Springer Verlag.

Rodrigue, J.P. (2004) 'Straits and choke points: a maritime geo-strategy of petroleum distribution', *Cahiers de Géographie du Quebec*, *48*(135), 357–74.

Rothengatter, W. (2008) *International Transport Infrastructure Trends and Plans*. 17th International ITF/OECD Symposium on Transport Economics and Policy: Benefiting from Globalisation Transport Sector Contribution and Policy Challenges: Transport Sector Contribution and Policy Challenges (Vol. 17, p. 65). Paris: OECD.

United Nations Conference on Trade and Development (UNCTAD) (2008) *World Investment Report.* Geneva: UNCTAD.

United Nations Conference on Trade and Development (UNCTAD) (2013) *Review of Maritime Transport*, accessed 5 March 2016 at www.unctad.org

United Nations Conference on Trade and Development (UNCTAD) (2014a) *Review of Maritime Transport*, accessed 24 March 2016 at www.unctad.org

United Nations Conference on Trade and Development (UNCTAD) (2014b) *Small Island Developing States: Challenges in Transport and Trade Logistics.* Note by the UNCTAD Secretariat, Geneva 24–26 November 2014.

United Nations Conference on Trade and Development (UNCTAD) (2015) *Review of Maritime Transport*, accessed 15 March 2016 at www.unctad.org

Uprety, K. (2006) *The Transit Regime for Landlocked States: International Law and Development Perspectives.* Washington, DC: World Bank Publications.

Walkenhorst, P. and Dihel, N. (2006) 'Trade impacts of increased border security concerns', *The International Trade Journal*, *20*(1), 1–31.

Wilmsmeier, G., Hoffmann, J. and Sanchez, R.J. (2006) 'The impact of port characteristics on international maritime transport costs', *Research in Transportation Economics*, *16*, 117–40.

Wilson, J.S., Mann, C.L. and Otsuki, T. (2005) 'Assessing the benefits of trade facilitation: a global perspective', *The World Economy*, *28*(6), 841–71.

Woodburn, A., Allen, J., Browne, M. and Leonardi, J. (2008) *The Impacts of Globalization on International Road and Rail Freight Transport Activity – Past Trends and Future Perspectives.* Transport Studies Department, University of Westminster, London, UK.

World Bank (2014) *Improving Trade and Transport for Landlocked Developing Countries.* Washington, DC.

World Bank (2015a) *Liner Shipping Connectivity Index,* accessed 12 April 2016 at www.worldbank.org

World Bank (2015b) *Air Transport Annual Report*, accessed 6 March 2016 at www. worldbankorg

World Economic Forum (WEF) (2013) *Enabling Trade: Valuing Growth Opportunities*, accessed 22 March 2016 at www.wef.org

World Economic Forum (WEF) (2014) *Strategic Infrastructure 2014*, accessed 22 February 2016 at www.wefforum.org

World Shipping Council (WSC) (2015) *Global Trade*, accessed 8 March 2016 at www.worldshipping.org/about-the-industry/global-trade/

World Trade Organization (WTO) (2013) *Assessing WTO Bilateral Air Services Agreement: the WTO's Air Services Agreement Projector.* Information Paper presented at the Sixth Worldwide Air Transport Conference, Montreal, March 2013, ATConf/6-IP/8, accessed 8 March 2016 at www.icao.org

World Trade Organization (WTO) (2015) *Enabling Trade Valuing Growth Opportunities*, accessed 12 March 2016 at www.wto.org

4. The Global Information Infrastructure System

Whilst the term 'Global Information Infrastructure' (GII) has fallen out of popular usage since the millennium, it remains a salient concept in exploring the emergence of the global information economy (Main, 2001; Borgman, 2003). Over time the hype surrounding such terms as the 'information superhighway' has given way to more pragmatic expressions such as the 'information society' based on the embedding of the internet throughout the global socio-economic system. As liberalisation has matured and spread (Henisz et al., 2005), the GII has evolved into a complex system based on the interoperation and integration of a network of networks, both within and between states (Organisation for Economic Co-operation and Development (OECD), 2008a, 2008b). Nonetheless, the integration of National Information Infrastructures (NII) has been accompanied by a number of political and economic caveats that render a truly ubiquitous GII based on the free and interrupted flow of traffic between any two points in geographic space elusive (Kellerman, 2002).

The state and its NII remains the core building block of the GII. However, this conceptualisation runs foul of the treatment of cyberspace as part of the global commons (Hofmokl, 2010). The conflict between the rules of a system that is both territorially bounded and a non-territorial entity goes to the heart of the evolution of the GII. To some, the innovation of the internet as a non-territorial system has given rise to institutional innovations at the global level (International Telecommunication Union (ITU), 2013). The debate is, according to Mueller (2010), between 'cyber-libertarianism' (that is, the stimulation by the internet of freedom and independence from the state) and 'realists' (that is, those who argue for the sustained role of the state in the evolution of the GII). Thus, in the formation of a GII out of NII integration, a number of conflicting forces for states are at work. These include the GII as a core platform for growth, the potential for the global system to challenge national sensitivities and divergences on issues like security and control, and new national and international digital divides exposed by the push for integration. In short, the evolution of the GII has to reflect a national as well as an international agenda (Drake, 2000).

The starting point of this chapter is that the GII represents the core underpinning architecture of the evolving global information economy (Zook, 2005) and is based not only on the integration of NIIs but also on the facilitating role in this integration process played by transnational infrastructure that traverses or occupies the 'commons' (that is, those parts of the globe beyond the power of a single state). After examining the core characteristics of the GII and its evolution, the chapter analyses the main forces of integration and fragmentation within the GII by focussing on the commercial and state-based drivers of these contrary processes.

WHAT IS THE GII?

The commonly accepted definition of the GII is of a composite entity made up of an integrated and interoperable network of networks that enable end-to-end connectivity between users across space for the purposes of the sending, transmission and receipt of all electronic traffic (Borgman, 2003). The detailed core characteristics of the ideal GII are outlined in Table 4.1. The basis of the underpinning of the network of networks lies in

Table 4.1 Characteristics of the 'ideal' Global Information Infrastructure

Characteristic	Definition
Hierarchical	Multiple national, subnational and transnational networks
Plural/modular	A complex interaction of multiple infrastructures owned by multiple owners
Globality	Universal reach across the global economy to ensure end-to-end connectivity
Access	All module providers who pass core legitimacy tests are able to connect to the GII in any given regime
Universality	All users who wish to access the GII have identifiable points of access to the system
Interoperability	All parts of the system are able to interoperate with any other part
Interconnection	All components of the system operate as a de facto single infrastructure
Quality	The system has the capability to deliver uniformity of services
Upgradability	The capability to be upgraded at any time and at given location
Freedom of traffic	The free flow of traffic across the system irrespective of its source, as long as it does not violate local norms and cultures
Non-bias/ discrimination	The GII does not offer bias or discriminate between users, providers states, etc.

the interconnection of NII systems – these NIIs represent the amalgam of all interconnected electronic information infrastructures located within the borders of any given nation state. This conception of the GII underlines – despite a common perception to the contrary – the continued importance of borders within cyberspace (OECD, 2008b). As explored later, states have the capability – although it is not always exercised – to control flows of internet traffic entering and moving around their respective territories (Kahin and Neeson, 1997).

The GII was conceived and based on a US-dominated agenda as a plurality of market-led modular infrastructures developed largely by the private sector. The system was underpinned by agreed rules on access, interoperability and interconnection that have an ability to evolve with the changing technological and commercial context (Charles and Furar, 1998; Warf, 2012). This agenda evolved via an interface between governments, multinational bodies (such as United Nations Conference on Trade and Development (UNCTAD) and the World Bank) and business to use these infrastructures as a platform for economic growth and development to ensure the evolving GII not only does not entrench existing divides but also does not create new digital segregations as a result of information infrastructure evolving unevenly across and within territories (Meisingset, 1996; Gillespie et al., 2001; Main, 2001).

In practice, the GII is an amorphous concept that, with the progression of liberalisation and technological change, has evolved into a complex infrastructure system. The interaction between telecommunications, content, IT and media industries has created a commercial information ecosystem that is above and beyond a simple physical network of networks (Dhamdhere and Dovrolis, 2011). Thus, the value creation within the GII moves beyond simple transmission and distribution of digital bits towards online interacting communities (Tapscott, 1996). This highlights the diverse interests involved in developing the GII and that it is both form and function that matter in its evolution. To focus merely on form risks understating the means through which the GII sustains itself as function reflects the traffic generated and supports the infrastructure which sustains the business models within the economic system (Corallo, 2007). This open system approach to the GII divorces the link between scale and entry, allowing firms of all sizes to operate along the creation of a digital architecture to which they add either form or functionality or a mixture of both. This process has shifted value within the GII away from the core backbone of the network towards the edge of the network and to the rise of the power of access infrastructure (so-called secondary infrastructure) as a core component of an integrated system.

The internet as the de facto GII encourages modularity as the openness and transparency of the system attracts new operators, service providers and users because they do not have to sacrifice intellectual property rights (IPR) and unique preferences in order to achieve connectivity (Berleur, 2008). However, it is important to stress that the internet is not an infrastructure as such but a virtual system of software infrastructures used for the transmission of data over networks (Ryan, 2010). The internet is a network of networks based on agreed protocols that are global in scope. Moreover, as it is based on software, the internet creates a virtual space that operates independently of physical geography. However, this virtual space is limited in actuality because the system relies on physical assets that lie within the borders of a state (Mueller and Lemstra, 2011).

The rise of the GII as a digital ecosystem also reflects a shift in governance across all sectors where – most notably in telecommunications – the state activism reflected within welfarist approaches has been replaced by the regulatory state (Levi-Faur, 2005) in which the state merely seeks to steer the development of the NII within the context of a trend towards international governance in areas of communal interest such as standards (Drake and Wilson, 2008). Governance in the GII is a multi-agent process operating across user groups, states, producer groups, non-governmental organisations and other interested parties. According to Braithwaite and Drahos (2000) state sovereignty – whilst still important – is more symbolic than real because there has been a convergence on market-based governance. This agenda reflects an historical US dominance of the system but this is eroding in the face of GII needs for cooperative frameworks (Pickard, 2007) and as the state is beginning to actively fragment the system for its own ends (see later).

A more recent trend within the GII has been the shift towards a cloud-based configuration of infrastructure based on resource sharing across space where remote resources can be accessed to complete a task (Jaeger et al., 2008). The rise of the cloud pushes the role of data storage hubs away from the desktop to large data centres (Armbrust et al., 2010). This places the need for aspects of the GII to be configured as a network of storage and computing facilities, including servers, storage systems, switches and routers. This changes the demand for infrastructure as capacity is created on demand, with users eschewing upfront commitment (Dillon et al., 2010). The reconfiguration of the GII created by these new technologies (typified by cloud computing) underlines its flexibility in the face of changing technology and user needs. Increasingly the GII is configured to facilitate two-way interaction through the layers of infrastructure.

The internet as the basis for the GII grew out the US but according to Lessig (2004) seemed to contradict the core US ideal that the economy is best managed by the division of property rights regulated by the state.

However, the internet confounded this as many of the core resources were not owned but resided within the 'global commons'. It is this commons that has driven innovation within the system and the fear is that by stifling this commons, the system will start to diminish. The nature of cyberspace as a commons was built into its development and secured the development of a complex system which has generated the innovation that has characterised the system (Hofmokl, 2010). This reflects the common conception that cyberspace, by and large, resides beyond the control of any single state.

THE STATE OF THE GII

The globality of the GII and its operations are determined by the evolution of the respective NIIs. The issue is not merely that networks are integrated and interdependent, based on the level of interactions over them, but is also about the quality of the infrastructure, both within and across territories. In short, the GII has not merely to allow connection and interoperation but the networks have to be fit for purpose. For the ITU (2013), the state of the NII is based on a three-stage process of evolution:

- Readiness – that is, does the infrastructure exist and is there universal access to it?
- Intensity – that is, what is the level of usage?
- Impact – that is, how does usage improve efficiency and effectiveness?

Arguably the most immediate barometer of the globality of the GII is the rise in international traffic (Ryan, 2010). Much of this has been driven by the increased data component of international trade arising from enabling conventional forms of cross-border interaction, the direct exchange of digital goods and through data being an increasingly core component of global supply chains. However, accurate data on the volume and value of these flows is elusive because statisticians do not measure how the services to which data is central are delivered. Whilst an increased number of services can be traded digitally, there is no clear indication as to how many of these there actually are. Moreover, there seems to be little direct link between the value and volume of data and there is ambiguity in clearly identifying where exactly value is added. This is a reflection of the fact that cross-border data is often un-priced and that its ability to drive value creation is often incidental to a firm's core value proposition.

McKinsey Global Institute (2016) have made what is perhaps the best attempt to measure these flows and have argued that global data flows have increased by over 45 times between 2004 and 2015. In comparison, the trend for financial and trade flows is flattening or actually falling. Moreover, McKinsey argue that over 35 per cent of the total value of global flows of data (as measured in terabytes per second) over the GII is made up of data flows. These global flows comprise information, searches, communications, transactions, videos and intra-company traffic. The crude data for flows of international traffic over the GII demonstrates that the international system has developed unevenly over space. For example, the international internet is composed of private cross-border links deployed by over 450 internet service providers (ISP) and 82 per cent of this cross-border bandwidth is in Europe (OECD, 2015). The traffic that flows over the system is also generated very unevenly with a 'triad of regions' (that is, Europe, Asia and North America) generating 93 per cent of all internet traffic in 2014 (Cisco, 2015). Over the past two decades, international traffic over the GII has grown on average 13 per cent annually (OECD, 2015). It fell to single figures with the global economic downturn of 2007/9, although it has since recovered. This also affected the investment of trans-national infrastructure companies (TNIC) in the GII which declined by US$15 billion in 2009 (ITU, 2015). However, such figures do not really give a full picture of the globality of the system and offer a reductionist view of the nature of this globality. Globality needs to be reflected in the sum of flows and stock of infrastructure because internal flows may also reflect an aspect of the globality of the system.

The main infrastructure of the NII is the fixed backbone and local access technologies that support the flow of and access to data between and within territories. This is mainly based on internet technologies and the deployment of the infrastructure to support the transmission of data at ever higher speeds. As the de facto GII, it is inevitable that internet networks are the focus of this analysis. However, it is not the intention to provide a further history of internet infrastructure as this has been subject to substantive research (for example, Kleinrock, 2010; Malcomson, 2015). However, the roots of the current status of internet infrastructure do lie in its history, notably in the shift in governance towards private ownership that moved the internet from a single network to one based on multiple network providers (Kesan and Shah, 2004).

The GII is a hierarchical system which, despite the existence of a number of sub-national and regional infrastructure systems, is formed mainly at the national and transnational levels. Although it is the former that forms the focus on the GII (and of this chapter), the latter remains a salient facilitator of the GII. Transnational infrastructures within the GII are based on those infrastructures that have a substantial portion of their transmitive capacity beyond the territorial domain of a state, namely the ocean cable and satellite systems which retain a national component via landing points or receiving stations. These infrastructures are subject to a mix of national and transnational rules covered by specific international treaties across the 'non-national' domains.

Transnational Information Infrastructure

Oceanic cable systems remain pivotal to the global communications system carrying some 95 per cent of international traffic (Carter et al., 2009) and over a million miles of submarine cable laid globally by 2015. Such is the importance of the global system of communications that these are designated as critical infrastructure by many states (such as Australia where 99 per cent of its data traffic flows over oceanic cable systems). The major oceans are criss-crossed by a plethora of cable systems (see www. ISCPC.org for a full list). Initially, these focussed on trans-Atlantic cables, which formed the bedrock of the system. Over time, more capacity has been deployed in Asia to reflect shifting traffic trends. It is only relatively recently that high capacity networks have started to expand into Africa, for example via the SEACOM network (Forden, 2015). However, such networks remain vulnerable to both natural and man-made disruption (such as in 2008 when there were three separate disruptions to the submarine cable system in Egypt, the Persian Gulf and the Malacca Strait), which can cause significant disruption to traffic flows.

The routes of these networks are defined by the UN Convention on the Law of the Sea (UNCLOS), which allows those deploying these systems to avoid geopolitical constraints by defining the maritime boundaries of states and the extent to which any state can control the operation of these networks. The 1884 Cable Convention defined the relationship between transnational cable systems and the integrity of state communication systems (Headrick, 1991; Headrick and Griset, 2001; Hills, 2008). These have been supported by amendments from 1958 through to 1982, which define the rights and interest of all states by ensuring that coastal states do not prejudice access to the cable system for landlocked states.

The other major transnational infrastructures are global satellite systems, which also rely on a strong national component through their reliance on NII for the terrestrial component of their operation (OECD, 2015). Introduced from the mid-1960s, the existence of satellites in various forms of orbit around the globe has been a rather latent form of transnationalism, representing merely 5 per cent of international traffic flows. As of June 2014, there were 986 satellites in orbit around the earth, of which 365 (37 per cent) were operated solely for commercial purposes and the remainder used largely for military and civil communications (Satellite Industry

Association (SIA), 2011). Although there has been a move to focus this technology on expanding broadband access, by 2010 it represented less than 10 per cent of revenues (with the majority of the rest coming from television transmission).

The attraction of satellite broadband lies in its potential to offer universal, instant communications in remote or difficult to access locations, especially in developing economies (Salin, 2000). As such, satellite technology is seen as a relatively quick method of closing the digital divide (see later) and in expanding the GII throughout less developed economies (ITU, 2011). The infrastructure required to enable this development objective depends on the nature of the orbit deployed by the satellite. The lower the orbit, the more reliable the signal but the more satellites are required to offer universal coverage. By 2011, there were 1.5 million satellite broadband subscribers, which is forecast to rise to six million by 2020, with much of this growth in Western Europe and North America (ITU, 2015). The regulation of satellite services has taken place through the ITU, which seeks to sustain access and interoperability through international agreement based upon UN declarations and treaties.

National Information Infrastructure

As mentioned, the core building block of the GII is the network of NIIs. These are the combined set of national infrastructures that transmit and distribute information around a given territory and act to define the interface between domestic users and the rest of the GII. In terms of the main public infrastructure, two elements of the complex NII are worthy of examination: the backbone (that is, the infrastructure that interconnects the modular components of the system) and local access networks (that is, the infrastructure between the end user and the nearest access point to the backbone). Although – as the OCED (2010) suggests – measuring the core internet is difficult due to the plurality of the system, by examining the development of the respective NII, these two core pieces of infrastructure do offer a fair indication of the state of the GII across states.

The divergent state of infrastructure across the global economy has been a persistent theme of public authorities at multiple levels of governance. The capacity of backbone infrastructure varies markedly: European NIIs, for example, possess – on average – eight times as much bandwidth as the average Asian NII (OECD, 2012). At the extremes, Hong Kong's bandwidth can be 60,000 times greater than that available in Nigeria (UNCTAD, 2011). Although NIIs in developing states have rapidly improving backbone infrastructures as trans-oceanic cables begin to reach them and, whilst having highly localised effects, they are also stimulating investment in backbone infrastructure in landlocked states, which are gaining better access to international backbones (UNCTAD, 2011), albeit inevitably from a low base.

It is difficult to gauge the state of an NII by the internet backbone alone. Although all sovereign territories and dependencies have some form of internet backbone, simple mileage statistics are inadequate measures as they do not reflect either the size of the state or the degree of urbanisation of the population (ITU, 2015). Consequently, the best indicator of the state of a NII is, arguably, penetration (that is, the proportion of users that are able to access the core internet backbone). Inevitably, this depends as much upon pricing and the state of local access infrastructures as upon the extensiveness of a nation's internet backbone. As such, perhaps the best proxy for the general state of an NII is simple broadband penetration, which is both a reflection of the availability of infrastructure and of user demand for such infrastructure (OECD, 2008a).

Recent (ITU, 2015) figures show that 58 states (out of 230 globally) have an internet penetration of over 50 per cent where penetration is defined as the percentage of the population using the internet. These 58 states represent 72.1 per cent of all users compared to the average world penetration of 26.6 per cent (OECD, 2015). Inevitably, those territories with high penetration rates are clustered in developed economies. Penetration rates tend to be highest in states with small clustered populations. Although broadband usage in developing economies is growing – in 2015 it was 5 per cent of the global total – much of this growth is in Asia, whilst Africa is falling further behind with a penetration rate of less than 1 per cent (ITU, 2015). Connectivity to the GII is limited in these places because there is little available backbone infrastructure upon which to build the information economy. The aggregate figures for GII by continent in Table 4.2 underline the variations in penetration and the digital divide across these locations.

Such variations are also evident when examining the local loop. A key barometer for the NII is the spread of high-speed access technologies within this segment of the national system. For one technology, the digital subscriber line (the technology that enables internet access over pre-existing copper-based infrastructure), many OECD states have universal or near universal deployment of this technology (OECD, 2015). The capabilities of the local infrastructure segment of the NII have also been enhanced by the deployment of cable technologies, which reach 93 per cent of businesses and residences in the US and 90 per cent across Europe. For the OECD (2015), such advances in local infrastructure within its members are a direct legacy of facilities competition whereby companies increasingly compete on speed and invest in infrastructure that is regarded as 'future proof'. Supplying fibre optic cable to the home is considered to

Table 4.2   Key Global Information Infrastructure indicators by region and continent in 2015 (per 100 inhabitants)

Continent/region	Fixed telephone subscriptions	Mobile cellular subscriptions	Active mobile broadband subscriptions	Fixed broadband subscriptions	Households with internet access	Individuals using the internet
Africa	1.2	73.5	17.4	0.5	10.7	20.7
Arab States	7.3	108.2	40.6	3.7	40.3	37.0
Asia and Pacific	11.3	91.6	42.3	8.9	39.0	36.9
Commonwealth of Independent States	23.1	138.1	49.7	13.6	60.1	59.9
Europe	37.3	120.6	78.2	29.6	82.1	77.6
The Americas	25.4	108.1	77.6	18.0	60.0	66.0

Source: ITU, 2015

be the ultimate future proof capability with telecommunications operators using the digital subscriber line as an interim technology.

Alongside investment in transport technologies, another key indicator of the state of the NII is the number of web hosts (that is, those devices that have an IP address). Globally, these increased ten-fold in the decade to 2010, representing an annual growth rate of 26 per cent (OECD, 2010). With the rise of the cloud as a salient form of infrastructure, attention has turned to servers as an indicator of NII. By mid-2014, there were estimated to be 46 million servers globally compared to 33 million in mid-2008. However, the rise of server farms (where server capacity is shared) means that servers can be an unreliable indicator of the internet backbone. When subdivided into secure servers (that is, those servers that are secure for the purposes of undertaking commercial transactions), evidence suggests that nearly 30 per cent are in the US alone, with the Netherlands, Denmark and Australia leading in terms of secure servers per capita. There are – as of 2015 – 3,071 server farms globally but, as Table 4.3 indicates, these are spread unevenly across the global economy, with the US containing nearly half of all data centres (see www.datacentermap.com).

Nonetheless, server farms are emerging as a key resource within NIIs and represent an increasingly salient GII resource based on the interaction between networks of server farms operating as a common resource for a large number of users across several NIIs. The geography of these server farms was initially driven by access to talent and high speed networks but as the capability of networks has spread, so these server farms have grown increasingly footloose. Facilitated by remote access capabilities, data centres can be built anywhere in the world. As users have grown more

Table 4.3   The regional spread of server farms within the Global Information Infrastructure, 2015

Region	Number of server farms	Number of states with server farms
Africa	37	7
Asia	313	14
Central America	30	9
Eastern Europe	306	20
Middle East	85	14
North America	1,622	3
Oceania	179	5
South America	67	8
Western Europe	1,031	24

Source: www.datacentermap.com, accessed 15 November 2015

cost-conscious and more aware of the environmental impact of these technologies, so the factors driving location choice have altered. Currently the top four factors are:

- Access to power (both current and future): these farms require substantial and reliable power resources, and failure of power supply can cause considerable downtime. By 2011, server farms consumed 1.5 per cent of the world's electricity.
- Cooling and climate: server farms create substantial amounts of heat, and cooling these facilities can be both expensive and difficult. This can therefore create an incentive to locate such farms in cooler climates. However, some argue that the electricity required may encourage users to locate them in warmer climates where solar power is feasible.
- Proximity to risk: as these devices are not indestructible it makes little sense to locate them in earthquake zones, areas prone to flooding, close to airports or to other sources of risk.
- Data security: privacy concerns and compliance regulations require certain types of data to be retained where it was collected or created.

Despite the potential for globality in data exchange, there is a paradox in that globality encourages locality as many firms prefer to keep data close to home. This reflects not only a desire to control aspects of the system but also the dangers of latency within the internet (that is, time delays between desired-for-access to data and the appearance of that data). At the end of 2011, there were over 2,200 server farms or data centres globally across 81 states: North America had 1,048 (48 per cent), of which 981 (or 44 per cent) were in the US; Western Europe had 705 (32 per cent), with 155 in the UK (7 per cent), 122 in Germany (6 per cent) and 101 in France (5 per cent). The whole of Africa had 22 data centres – around 1 per cent of the global total; Asia 82 (4 per cent); Central America 9 (0.5 per cent); Eastern Europe, including Russia, 198 (about 9 per cent); the Middle East 32 (just over 1 per cent) and Oceania 84 (just less than 4 per cent). This geographic spread highlights the dominance of the Europe and the US over the cloud and also that despite the potential for the global dispersion of data centres, a preference to locate locally remains (see www.datacenter.com).

The GII also comprises those devices that can be flexibly deployed – both within and across territories – to allow users to access the internet backbone. For the GII, secondary infrastructure (as we shall term access technologies) has its most evident expression in the spread of advanced mobile telecommunications devices. These represent personal infrastructure that enables users to connect to the internet irrespective of their location. The range of secondary infrastructure connected to the internet backbone has diversified from function-specific devices such as e-books and satellite navigation through to multi-function devices such as smartphones and net books. The response to the rising number of devices and of the traffic they have generated has been increased investment in primary infrastructure. As such, secondary infrastructure, as core access technologies, is a vital component of the interacting networks that form the GII. Indeed, across the OECD in 2013 there were around 500 million wireless internet users compared to 305 million for fixed line broadband (OECD, 2013).

By the end of 2014, 90 per cent of the world's population (including 80 per cent in rural areas) had access to mobile telecommunications infrastructure (UNCTAD, 2015). However, in terms of the emergence of the GII, the key barometer is the spread of third generation mobile infrastructure – the generation that allows mobile internet. By the end of 2013, 143 states were able to offer these services compared to 95 in 2007 (ITU, 2013). In more advanced states, there has been a shift towards fourth generation mobile phones based on ever more advanced broadband speeds. However, as a simple measure, mobile network growth is reaching saturation point with a penetration rate of 116 subscriptions per 100 people in developed economies and 68 per cent in developing economies. Within the OECD, 3G services have taken off as mobile telephony has matured. By the end of 2009, there were almost 300 million internet-enabled mobile devices across the OECD. The penetration rates were highest in Slovenia (100 per cent), Korea (99 per cent) and Japan (97 per cent). Across the OECD as a whole, 3G subscriptions are around 28 per cent but governments are seeking to increase its penetration via national broadband plans (OECD, 2015).

A notable trend in this aspect of the evolving GII is the spread of mobile technology across many developing states that are experiencing the fastest rates of growth for wireless internet, especially in Asia (ITU, 2012). Mobile technology is an attractive platform for these states as it can roll out access to advanced technology relatively quickly. Indeed, in some developing states, such as Morocco and South Africa, wireless internet usage has surpassed that of fixed broadband. Figure 4.1 highlights the increasing global penetration rate of smartphones – an important barometer of the rate of progress of the information economy. These aggregate figures hide a vast geographic spread in the penetration of this technology with Singapore having a penetration rate of 85 per cent, South Korea 80 per cent and Sweden 75 per cent. This contrasts with states like the Ukraine (25 per cent), Brazil (29 per cent) and Argentina (33 per cent) (ITU, 2015). Of course, such analysis precludes figures for access for Africa where the average across the continent is just 12 per cent (UNCTAD, 2015).

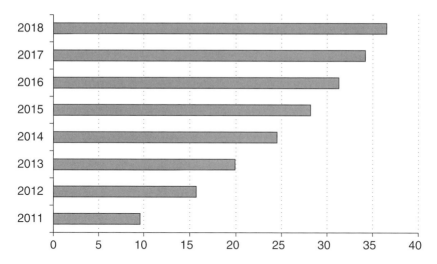

Figure 4.1   Global smartphone penetration 2011–18 (% of all users)

The other core barometer of secondary infrastructure development is the penetration of internet-enabled personal computers, which is being muddied by technological and commercial convergence with mobile devices (ITU, 2012). Nonetheless, this aspect of secondary infrastructure has variable rates of penetration across developing and developed economies. Whilst PCs were available in 1.4 billion households globally, only 0.5 billion possessed internet access, with vast discrepancies across states: for example, only 16 per cent of PCs in developing states had internet access compared to 66 per cent in developed economies (UNCTAD, 2011).

***

The state of the GII is largely dependent upon the events and processes within NIIs. The GII itself is a network of NIIs with a high degree of spatial variation in terms of infrastructural availability and capabilities. The World Economic Forum (2015) publishes a Network Readiness Index which incorporates a range of soft and hard infrastructure indicators to understand the extent to which a state has a sufficiently developed platform for the development of the information economy. The Nordic states and the 'Asian tigers' were identified as the most ready. However, there are marked differences within the EU, and Middle Eastern, Latin American and sub-Saharan African states remain the most challenged. For the OECD (2008a), such variances in universality of access to the NII are largely generated by cost. Accessibility and speed of access are key themes moving the

GII forward. Overall, the shift towards a more advanced GII is likely to happen in stages. The OECD (2015) suggests that incumbents in developed economies will be tied to existing infrastructure technologies that will lead to a gradual migration path to more advanced technologies. The first step in the evolving GII will be actions by states to prolong the life of existing infrastructure with the conversion of all IP infrastructures as the end goal.

FORCES OF INTEGRATION

Much of the early rhetoric on the evolution of the GII positioned it as an architecture that offered an aggressive advancement of global forces (for example, Cairncross, 2001). Whilst reality suggests a more sober assessment of the impact of the GII upon the state of the globalising forces of freer data flows, there can be little doubt that although there are forces within the GII that push the system towards globality, the forces of hyperglobalism are proving to be more subdued. These globalising forces (as argued later) are derived from a mix of state and non-state strategies and overwhelmingly reflect a core strategic belief in the centrality of the GII (or the state-based components of it) to the process of economic growth and/or development.

The Initial Internationalist Consensus

In the formative stages of the 'break-out' of the internet, a strong internationalist consensus emerged around a discourse that this technology, through its potential for universal reach and ubiquitous impact, was the ultimate expression of globality. Authors such as Cairncross (2001) argued that a maturing internet would naturally erode state sovereignty and necessitate the foundation of global governance systems as states are bordered and the internet is not, resulting in the latter inhibiting what the former can freely do. The argument was that variances in national laws would be rendered irrelevant by the free flow of information across borders. Popular narratives focused on the internet as an anarchic area operating in juxtaposition to a world dominated by excessive regulation that spurned innovation (Von Bernstorff, 2003). Such internationalist narratives still persist: Cavanagh (2007), Sassen (1998) and Reidenberg (2005), for example, all argue that the internet has drastically reduced state power in the face of highly permeable borders and the existence of private tunnels through which data can pass over borders. In popular narratives, the internet was the ultimate expression of a neo-liberal global system and of the futility of states to resist such pressures (Friedman, 2005).

As argued later, the hyper-globalism of the internationalists is over-stated (Corallo, 2007). The hands-off stance deployed by many states at the outset of the internet was, in practice, temporary until they began to realise the potential impact of these technologies upon state territoriality (Goldsmith and Wu, 2006). The result has been an erosion of the hyper-globalist narrative with a more pragmatic perspective which recognises that the internet can work as a powerful tool for global integration through the enablement of transnational communication and the efficiency of international transactions (Weber, 2010a) but that such processes occur within a state-based framework. Although the internet has the potential to render distance an irrelevance, it has not had the same effect on states even if they, in the desire to track and monitor harmful flows, have to work harder to ensure territorial integrity (see, for example, Yang, 2011). Those users wishing to avoid state sanction/monitoring have to work harder themselves through the creation of virtual private networks. Such pressures indicate that, as the internet has globalised, the western centric model of an internet of free exchange has been eroded as states with less democratic traditions seek to preserve domestic control and security. Nonetheless, the internet has been a powerful force in the globalising of national economic and political systems (Krasner, 2001). However, such capabilities have come up against the powerful force of state territoriality.

Economic Development Paradigm

The internationalist view has been supported by a consensus that a state's economic growth and development are closely tied into the condition of its NII and by the design of its interconnections with the global system (Chinn and Fairlie, 2007). For developed economies (especially mature, low growth economies), the stimulation of the onset of the global information economy has operated as a core platform for industrial competitiveness strategies (see, for example, European Commission, 2014). For emerging and developing economies, these processes offer the opportunity for accelerated development (World Bank, 2016). Consequently, state infrastructural mandates have been heavily influenced by the concept of achieving prosperity through information infrastructure – a reflection of the power of the narrative provided by the logic of the Schumpeterian competition state (Jessop, 2002). This is based on the presumption that there is value to be delivered to the competitive position of states through the wider use of information across a broader range of activities. There is therefore a belief in the greater efficiency of social and economic systems through the wider use of information technologies (Czernich et al., 2011). This promotes not only efficiency in existing tasks but also creates new

opportunities. Thus, the logic supports the normal efficiency of circulation that usually accompanies the wider deployment of technologies and
the increased information intensity of tasks. In addition, the shift is about
adding to the skills base and new industries (UNCTAD, 2011, 2015).

This GII-growth/development consensus has been driven by a
US-led liberal hegemony (especially during the initial stages of the GII
development) which emphasises that the information economy has to
be driven by NII plurality and an open trading system in information
technology and services (OECD, 2008b).This is typified by the policy
guidance and market-based governance advocated by international organisations such as the World Bank, UNCTAD and the Global Information
Infrastructure Commission (GIIC) which offered support to NIIs on
the basis of a commitment to plural ownership and an adherence to the
liberal consensus embodied within the World Trade Organization (WTO)
agreements of Basic Telecommunications and ICTs (see later). In practice, the pro-growth consensus embedded within government information
economy/society strategies was a mixture of public and private actions to
ensure that the GII's evolution did not reinforce the digital divide and that
NIIs were set on a path for self-sustaining critical mass (see OECD, 2008a).
This position underpins much of the analysis from market-led bodies, such
as the World Economic Forum, which see the development of the GII as
market-led with the state operating to generate and manage the underpinning soft infrastructure or acting as a catalyst to stimulate market-led
development (Röller and Waverman, 2001).

Meta/Macro-Level Consensus via WTO GII-Related Agreements

Reflecting the US GII hegemony, the integration of the NII into a global
system was driven by an international consensus on the role of market
forces as the main driver of this process (Henisz et al., 2005; Levi-Faur,
2005). This consensus reflected an expectation that network effects would
drive the development of the GII and that this would be stimulated by
the impact of liberalisation and the anticipated by-products of product
innovation and cost efficiencies. Progressively, across both developed and
developing states, services (and later infrastructure) have been liberalised
following the acceptance by many states that investment in the NII is
beyond the capability of the state alone (Henisz et al., 2005). As networks
expanded and interconnected and as new technologies demonstrated
increased functionality, so NIIs would demonstrate a virtuous cycle of
development. This liberal trajectory for the development a global network
of NIIs had its most evident manifestation in the WTO Agreement in
Basic Telecommunications (Bronckers and Larouche, 2008). By 2012, 108

states had signed up to the agreement signifying an expanding consensus on the role of market-based governance over telecommunications infrastructure (WTO, 2012). Of these 108, 99 have agreed to extend the process beyond the minimum (ITU, 2015).

The WTO Agreement on Trade in IT sits alongside the telecommunications services agreement and is also pivotal to the development of the GII. By 2014, the agreement covered 70 states and 97 per cent of the world trade in IT products (WTO, 2015). The agreement commits states to completely eliminate trade restrictions on trade in this class of products, with developing states being given – as with the telecommunications agreement – a prolonged time to adopt these measures (Clark and Wallstein, 2006). Whilst not an immediate concern, an inevitable by-product of allowing freer trade in IT would be to allow the freer and easier movement of secondary infrastructure across borders. Global trade in ICT tripled in the period between 1996 and 2010 (OECD, 2010) with the main thrust of the growth of ICT trade in the spread of computer technology across the globe (Greenstein and McDevitt, 2011).

For the World Bank (2016), the core issue is to achieve a managed process of competition that allows free access to NII whilst preserving the incentive to invest in infrastructure. This is especially salient as newer mobile and cable technologies are expected to eat into the traffic load of the core public networks. However, upgrading to allow ubiquitous fibre infrastructure is difficult due to industry economics and regulatory uncertainty (for a review, see UNCTAD, 2011). There is, to some degree, a policy choice to be made in balancing desire for investment with competition when allowing terms of exclusivity for infrastructure developers as information infrastructure underpins other activities (Guermazi, 2008). Such a balancing act offers partial explanation for the uneven implementation of the WTO Agreement in Basic Telecommunications where access to and control of infrastructure remains a core issue of concern, especially regarding bottlenecks or monopolistic components that inhibit end-to-end connectivity. The ITU (2013) notes in its assessment of the regulation that fixed-line service openings are in contrast to mobile services in terms of market opening. As a result, the ITU argues there is a degree of widening between developing and developed states in the quality of the underpinning telecommunications infrastructure.

Global Communications Multinational Companies

The onset of the liberalisation of services and infrastructure was accompanied by the activities of those telecommunications operators that built their business models on the transnational supply of telecommunication services, either through their own infrastructure or via leased capacity (Sarker et al., 1999). Often through mixing and matching their own activities with those of third parties, these operators have been able to build a uniform service environment to match the bespoke requirements of users (Jakopin, 2008). In the formative period of liberalisation, such service environments were created by operator-based alliances. However, as service liberalisation has been accompanied by widespread facilities competition, so operators have both built their own infrastructure and used third party networks (dependent on the need for infrastructure control within any given territory). This market has been fed by the desire to meet the communications needs of multinational companies (MNC) and also by operators seeking to generate synergy across a multi-market presence (ITU, 2012a). The rise of these businesses was driven by a mix of home market maturity, rent seeking and technological change.

In the market for global communications services, there is an in-built tendency towards network extensiveness because network externalities are a core differentiator within this market segment (Katz and Shapiro, 1994; UNCTAD, 2011). However, given the commoditisation of network capacity within the major markets of the GII, this does not necessitate the ownership of infrastructure because an active wholesale market enables virtual operators to exist by building value propositions that mix and match capacity to customer requirements facilitated by the uniformity of services across multiple locations (Peppard and Rylander, 2006). Inevitably, investment is focused on developing infrastructure in those locations where demand for these services is highest – in developed economies. Outside these economies, there has been investment in those emerging locations, such as Latin America (UNCTAD, 2011). These were often linked to investment in mobile infrastructure and reflected the fact the over two-thirds of telecommunications foreign direct investment (FDI) is greenfield investment (UNCTAD, 2015).

As global communications businesses expanded their operations, they invested heavily in information infrastructure and marketed their services aggressively in order to sustain their traffic-based business models. This indicates a model in which infrastructure investment runs ahead of traffic and requires innovation to generate the necessary traffic. This evidently became an issue at the peak of the dot com boom when substantial investment in capacity ran way ahead of traffic estimates (ITU, 2015). This overcapacity eroded the business models of some providers and undermined the financial position of many others who built substantial global networks (OECD, 2015). Moreover, as a result of these investments, TNICs had an incentive to push the liberalisation agenda as a means of sustaining growth and of securing returns on investment.

The Rise of the Global Virtual Value Chain

As globalisation has matured alongside more advanced information infrastructures, so the latter have become central to the former through trade enablement and through the integration of international value chains. With the maturity of corporate information systems, the production process has become informationised to form what Rayport and Sviokla (1995) term the 'virtual value chain' in which the flow of complete and semi-complete tangibles across borders is accompanied by a flow of intangibles in the form of information and knowledge exchange (for a review, see Dicken, 2015). At each stage of the value creation process, information is created which needs to be gathered and distributed across the firm. This invokes the creation of a non-national market space where information flows for the purpose of value creation and where information infrastructure has altered the notion of value creation (Rayport and Sviokla, 1995).

The legacy of the virtual value chain is a virtuous cycle between information infrastructure and increased information and knowledge flows across borders, with many of the larger multi-national operations establishing virtually private telecommunications systems (Peppard and Rylander, 2006). This traffic is expected to increase as cloud computing becomes more widely adopted by corporate IT departments (Armbrust et al., 2010). This has been driven by the cost of developing their own IT infrastructure and having key hubs that lie idle and are inefficient in their handling of inter- and intra-corporate traffic. This virtual network of networks relies on the commoditisation of capacity and liberal conditions across the GII to allow bespoke global information infrastructure to be offered (Gershon, 2013). As the market for corporate telecommunications has matured and the competition between providers increased, so the options (both in product design and choice) have grown and with them the capability for users to have customised infrastructure. This trend has been accentuated by the rise of virtual products and the existence and creation of the market space where products are created more by flows of information and the combination of digital bits. Thus, value creation for all businesses will be shaped by the interchange of digital bits across space to varying degrees (Tapscott, 1996).

Transnational Governance

Perhaps the greatest advance in the creation of the GII has been the emergence of a global governance system to oversee interoperability through agreed international standards (ITU, 2012). These standards are largely industry-led and are a reflection of US hegemony of the GII in its formative phase (for an early overview, see Drake and Wilson, 2008). This US-led self-regulatory system was seen to benefit the emergence of the GII, stimulating innovation. Mueller (2010) argues that there were two main watersheds in the development of internet governance. The first was the creation of the Internet Corporation for Assigned Names and Numbers (ICANN) in 1998; the second was the multilateral World Summit on the Information Society between 2002 and 2005. The former was non-governmental but US-led, whilst the latter was governmental and very much a response to perceived US dominance.

Other important organisations are the ITU and the Internet Engineering Task Force (IETF) (Drake, 2008). The ITU has been the foundation of GII governance but its influence has waned as liberalisation has evolved. It is an offshoot of the United Nations and represents the interests of states in the evolving GII. The ITU works with private sector bodies such as the IETF to create an integrated system. However, given the interests of different states in pushing their agenda in the information economy, different bodies have emerged. Over time, the IETF has replaced a lot of the work done by the ITU and is a non-formal; non-state organisation. Its industry standards are underpinned by core principles, namely that they must be open and non-proprietal, that they are end-to-end, that they are simple and scalable, and that information regarding their form is easily available. The ITU and IETF represent two distinct aspects of standardisation. The IETF creates standards for new products whereas the ITU maintains and upgrades existing standards. As technology has matured, however, the former's focus is increasingly becoming similar to the latter. Although there are attempts to coordinate their work, the efforts of these bodies can overlap.

Many states regard the internet as the de facto global telecommunications system and want it to be run accordingly. As such, these states wish to see internet governance brought formally within the ITU treaty, but western states are resistant to this. Moreover, many states are growing resistant to US dominance of the standards setting system, especially as the number of users outside the US grows (see later). This issue has become especially salient as cyberspace begins to morph into the global commons (see, for example, Murphy, 2010). In reflection of the asymmetry of power within the system and of the strong regional and national players that remain a key part of the system, there has been a streamlining of the standardisation process via the Global Standards Collaboration (GSC). The GSC is a collaboration agreement between the US, the main Far East and European standards bodies and the ITU to speed the decision making and standards formation process through enhanced collaboration between the main producers and users of fixed telecommunication systems.

Industry-Led Regulation and Innovation

Governance, according to Drezner (2004), reflects state interests and is a mix of public and private sector action that seeks to build a consensus on the rules, conventions and protocols guiding activity in the information infrastructure. Increasingly, state-based actions within this governance partnership are largely reduced to 'steering' other actors towards attaining desired outcomes (Braithwaite and Drahos, 2000). The Internet Governance Foundation sees the governance issue as being based on three issues, namely standardisation (see earlier); resource allocation such as spectrum allocation, domain names, etc.; and policy formulation, enforcement and dispute resolution to allow the development of norms, rules and procedures that govern the conduct of all agents linked to the infrastructure. The resource allocation function is based on managing the IP address and domain name spaces and is mainly managed through ICANN – an industry-led initiative which allocates space on infrastructure and whose work is supported by other non-state actors at national, transnational and international levels (Marsden, 2000).

The policy aspect of governance involves a multitude of bodies at national, regional and international levels to promote different aspects of the GII (for a review, see James, 2001). These bodies include the ITU (to govern standards); the World Intellectual Property Organization (WIPO) to protect intellectual property; the WTO to establish the conditions for world trade; and regional bodies such as the European Union, the OECD, the G8 and the G20. This range reflects the fact that, as traffic has evolved, it has generated more malign elements and has resulted in more state intervention (see later). The salient question is whether the governance developed for the internet when it was in its infancy remains appropriate in its more mature stages (Palfrey, 2010). The governance agenda has largely followed the preferences of developed states (Weiser, 2009). Developing states would prefer laxer standards as a means of accelerating the transfer of technology (Bygrave and Bing, 2009). As a result, the IPR regimes under the WIPO have been strengthened and WTO sanctions in intellectual property (IP)-related issues have been enhanced and, in the eyes of some, the threat of WTO sections has been a powerful factor in reducing copyright theft.

FORCES OF FRAGMENTATION

As the GII has matured, so the extreme internationalist perspective has been gradually eroded by a more pragmatic perspective according to which the virtual world more fully mirrors the physical, state-based systems. However, this is not to dismiss the globalising impact of the GII – states are beginning to assert control over flows as they catch up with the territorial implications of the internet and are responding to the unpredictable nature of the impact of global information flows on state territoriality. Consequently, as the system has matured the GII has begun to represent national preferences in the content and treatment of flows – a reflection of how states comprehend the intimacy between the GII and the infrastructural mandate (Reynolds, 2009). The main barriers identified later reflect inter-state differences on a number of GII issues that, if not fragmenting what was at its birth a global system, are limiting its ability to fully evolve into a global system. These state-based differences are also compounded by commercial actions that offer incentives to move towards a more fragmented system. These core sources of fragmentation are dealt with in turn through state-based sources that dominate the following analysis. The technical sources of fragmentation are ignored within the political economy approach developed here, but interested readers should see Drake et al. (2016) for a summary of these issues.

Non-State Drivers of Fragmentation

That commerce might be an active contributor to the fragmentation of the GII might seem counter-intuitive given the nature of the forces for integration outlined earlier and the fact that these forces originate mainly from the exercise of market pressures and commercial practices by technology companies. As much as it might seem that commerce will want to integrate NIIs, nonetheless commercially based forces for fragmentation do exist. The actions of businesses within specific markets often have the effect of splintering systems, either at the service or the infrastructure level. Although acknowledging that these forces of fragmentation might not be as strong as state-based forces, Drake et al. (2016) nevertheless identify four commercial sources of fragmentation (alongside the issue of piracy mentioned in more detail later). These are:

- Peering and standardisation: this is where firms (especially incumbents) seek to shift the terms and form of NII interconnection and interoperability in their favour. This is compounded by a concern that competing standards could emerge creating differing blocs that commit to different technologies based on different proprietary standards that have the effect of fragmenting the evolving GII.
- Network neutrality: this is where network operators actively discriminate between types of traffic (as defined by type and form of

user, content, application or mode) to the extent that these actions fragment the GII through disruptions to the flow of traffic that impede user interaction.

- Walled gardens: these are part of the internet ecosystem that are not universally available because the application/service owner has total control over this segment of cyberspace. Whilst this has a clear commercial logic for the operators, many of the constraints are sources of fragmentation by design because movement across these walls is limited as users are encouraged to operate exclusively within the confines of the walls.
- Geo-localisation and geo-blocking: these are GII capabilities that discriminate by location of user where the users are either limited to localised content or are denied access to specific forms of content due to their location. These can reflect state action to limit cultural incursion by undesirable flows but can also be deployed by private operators seeking to protect intellectual property rights. Overall, the net effect of either action is to limit accessibility to content by particular users, which has the effect of fragmenting the GII.

When looked at in its entirety, it is evident that the openness of the GII has potential to work against commercial concerns involved in the development of the GII. These emergent commercial drivers of fragmentation can reflect the desire of incumbents to protect their position. However, they can also reflect the desire of commerce to ensure a fair return for their assets and that the internet as a 'free for all' can work against this. This has had its most evident expression in the area of digital piracy and the protection of IPR. This is dealt within in more depth later.

Piracy

The GII has evolved around a 'content is king' consensus that the value of the system is based on what is delivered over it and to whom (Dinwoodie and Dreyfuss, 2009). In a market-driven system, business model sustainability is driven by the ability of this content to generate revenue flows, both direct and indirectly. Although the development of a GII enables digital content to be moved easily throughout the system, it also opens channels for piracy as this content can be endlessly replicated and globally distributed and, in so doing, undermine the revenue streams upon which content-based business models are sustained (May, 2006). It is widely believed, albeit not proven, that the failure to secure valuable content and limit digital piracy could deter the generation and submission of 'valuable' content to GII-based environments (Ang, 2008). The danger is that such infringements of IP, by undermining the exclusive rights of owners to exploit their creations, can undermine the market for information/ knowledge creation that underpins the GII (Chaudhry et al., 2011). In 2011, the software industry estimated that its losses due to piracy were US$50bn, the movie business US$6.1bn and music industry US$5bn (OECD, 2013). The problem of piracy is compounded by cyberlockers that allow users to share content that is uploaded to the cloud and which are often beyond the reach of the authorities and illegal streaming services that operate via mobile devices.

Although there is a consensus on the desirability of the protection of IP across the GII, enforcement across the system has been inconsistent (Hamelick, 2008). This reflects historical differences between states on various issues, including the moral rights of IPR, the fair use of IP (that is, how much can be used without permission), the duration of copyright, the protection of data, rights relating to sound recordings, the exhaustion of rights, work for hire arrangements, the avoidance of encryption technologies, and ISP liability for pirated content. Not surprisingly, IPR is driven by richer states who are content creators, whilst developing states tend to prefer laxer standards as a way of promoting technology transfer (May, 2008). Importantly, the resolution of digital piracy does not merely lie in legislation/regulation but also in the configuration of business models where there is a trade-off for those engaging in piracy that will entice them to move towards subscription models or some other form of payment.

Transnational governance of IP over the GII has been justified by the increasing spatial complexity of IP exchange. It is entirely feasible, for example, that content owned by someone in one state can be uploaded in another, downloaded in a third via a website whose servers are in a fourth, which is operated by a party that is basically untraceable. Since 1995, there has been a shift towards global governance within the IP system via the Trade-Related Intellectual Property Agreement (TRIPS), which is overseen by the WTO. TRIPS is operated in support of and with the cooperation of WIPO (Dinwoodie and Dreyfuss, 2009). Despite TRIPS, the main platform for action lies in the WIPO treaties, which are enforced by action through the WTO. Reciprocity is the mainstay of the WIPO system, with TRIPS adding 'national treatment' and 'most favoured nation' clauses to the governance of IPR (Pager, 2006). The latter applies the law to all states whereas the former forbids states from allowing piracy of overseas IPR through the protection of nationals. TRIPS also made IPR subject to the dispute settlement mechanism. This was enhanced by the WIPO Copyright Treaty and its Treaty on Performances and Phonograms (both of which came into force in 2002), which have impacted on the ability of software to circumvent these controls. To support this process, the WIPO has also acted in a consultative role to spread effective governance of IPR within states without a culture of such protection. This imposes costs of adaptation upon less developed economies (Deere, 2008).

Across the GII, there is an emerging consensus based on holding intermediaries responsible for piracy. States are seeking to control these intermediaries by stopping (as the US proposes) domiciled businesses doing business with the offending sites. This places a responsibility upon the intermediary to deny access to the site or, at least, make it much harder to access (OECD, 2015). Such denial of access requests can be onerous and could give the rights holder a lot of power and be a front for censorship, with ardent users able to bypass such controls. Indeed, there is little evidence to suggest that past efforts have had any tangible effect on levels of piracy – the tendency has been that, as soon as one website closes, another sets up in their place. Another response is to require ISPs to threaten the downloader with cessation of services (ITU, 2015). However, this may be difficult to implement where users share a connection, and experience has shown that whilst such threats have a short term impact, in the long term users still download illegally. In seeking to protect IP, many states have also created safe harbours which explicitly protect intermediaries, such as search engines and social networks, from user actions. In some cases, companies have simply moved to states with laxer jurisdictions (Drezner, 2004).

For increasingly content-driven economies, rendering the GII as a positive force in the process of value creation is central to the infrastructural mandate. As the internet is positioned at the centre of growth strategies, the drive to facilitate the monetisation of content is key to creating a virtuous cycle of network development. For other states, access to pirated content may offer limited advantages, even if they are gained illicitly. Others have argued that piracy might actually offer benefits to firms through circumventing unfair controls, offsetting deadweight loss and putting pressure upon industry to innovate in relation to their models to disincentivise piracy (Dahlander and Gann, 2010). In addition, the risk of piracy could also make companies implement effective corporate cyber-security systems. This perversely portrays piracy as a social good if it stimulates innovation and helps overcome the problem that content industries have not changed their business models fast enough to cope with technological change.

State 'Splintering' of the GII

Underpinning many of the fragmentary forces within the GII is the increasing proactivity of states in the management of data flows that cross into their territory. In other words, although the widespread development of NIIs that interact with the global system can aid growth and promote economic and social integration, they can also present a challenge to state control and security. In short, the almost utopian instincts of the internationalist look impossibly idealistic given the pattern of development of the GII over the past two decades (Ananthaswamy, 2011). Although state borders are not as easily recognisable in an online environment and consist of a mix of public and private resources, there can be little doubt that territoriality is important in the GII and that cyberspace as a part of the global commons is vastly overstated for the following reasons:

- The GII requires a physical structure within the border of a state.
- The GII needs a governance system that belongs somewhere.
- The GII needs a legal system to govern the financial relationships across cyberspace.
- Internet content in the GII is subject to real world laws.
- The GII requires that states need to be in cyberspace to assert territoriality.
- The rules that oversee cyberspace need sovereign legitimacy.

In the absence of an international agreement on the governance of the GII, the state is the natural agent to ensure these changes, even if it is through bilateral or multilateral agreement. Global norms are not only difficult to establish; they are also difficult to enforce. Any attempt at a global treaty has proven difficult to date (Millard et al., 2015). The closest proxy to such a treaty is the Council of Europe Treaty on Cyber Crime which is open for signature by all parties (Clough, 2012). However, the absence of adoption reveals that although there is a consensus on the need to control cybercrime, sovereignty issues limit international agreement. State action is the norm, with states signing up to bilateral treaties to push forward system governance (Jiang, 2014).

It is both unrealistic and idealistic to argue that the state should be absent from the GII. As Goldsmith and Wu (2006) argue, the state will continue to be present within the GII because of:

1) the continuing cultural and linguistic diversity of humanity, which the internet will not harmonise and which requires a degree of recognition and reassertion;
2) the proven capability of states to deploy the technology that controls flows within and into and out of the state; and
3) the proven capability of states to deploy national laws in cyberspace.

It has become evident that as the GII evolves it is splintering in the manner envisaged by Graham and Marvin (2001), whereby social divisions within and across territories are reinforced by the effective splintering of information infrastructure through the imposition of walls, not only along national lines but also via private walled gardens that isolate private systems and by commercial discrimination against content by network providers (see earlier).

The contemporary policy discourses on GII balkanization are about both the top-down management of the system and also the aspirations of individuals for the internet to reflect their own cultures in the face of a fear of cultural homogeneity driven by systems with a dominant narrative. In short, GII balkanisation is a reflection of the physical world which contains different languages and content preferences and confirms that place remains important in the GII. These forces indicate that NIIs are embedded in all aspects of state activity and underscore the intimate link between the state infrastructural mandate and control over the NII, both inter-and intra-territorially (Deibert and Crete-Nishihata, 2012). The rise of cyber power and the accompanying security threats, as well as challenging state control through the globally embedded NII, tie the capability of the state to the management of its information infrastructure (see later). The challenge for the state is to keep abreast of technologies and to monitor flows that run contrary to its infrastructural mandate. The capability of users to deploy false flag technology and virtual private networks to circumvent state control and the increasing threat from cyber-attacks highlights the challenges for state territoriality posed by the GII. These pressures legitimise the imposition of state controls and – where necessary – borders around the internet to prevent security breaches from external sources. The state control of the internet often reflects national preferences, the technological advancement of the state and a desire to enforce its national laws in an online environment (Schultz, 2008). However, Mueller (2010) argues that despite this attempt by states to reassert control over information infrastructure the positive effects of globality within governance systems should not be understated. The network effects within the GII and those arising from the connections of an NII to the GII remain strong.

Most states have a guarded attitude to globality. Where it is tolerated, it is on condition that such flows do not undermine security and/or control (Franzese, 2009). This extends beyond limits placed on 'offensive' content to those flows that can challenge political control or security (see later). Many western liberal democracies do not apply the formal firewalls deployed by the more autocratic states but regulate access through cost and the application of pressure to ISPs. Thus, whilst many see explicit controls as anathema to their basic values, the use of implicit controls is a key function of the infrastructural mandates of all states (Schiller, 2011). These pressures have grown in the post-9/11 environment, in which many of these states are discussing explicitly the use of kill switches to shut down targeted websites. These trends reflect a sustained erosion of US hegemony of the GII. Eichensehr (2015) argues that a bi-polar debate is occurring over the governance of the cyber system. Russia and China want the state to be sovereign in the cyber system, whereas the western liberal democracies are in favour of a polycentric system in which the state is merely one player.

The year 2012 was arguably a watershed for internet governance because the World Conference on International Communications – which sought to rewrite the remit of the ITU – saw a gap emerge between states on their role in the GII (ITU, 2015). A group of states led by China, Russia and several Arab states sought to bring the internet under the remit of the ITU in a bid to gain a consensus for more formal borders within the GII. These states wanted to expand the definition of a telecommunication operating agency to include a broader range of entities such as Google, amongst others (Rioux and Fontaine-Skronski, 2015). This was linked to issues of net neutrality (see earlier), where many of the less developed states felt that larger users of their networks should contribute something to its upgrade. This move was resisted by the liberal states who felt that it would undermine the core founding principles of the internet. Nonetheless, these proposals were an attempt to reverse the degree of globality within the system by limiting the form, quality and content of international traffic flows (Hill, 2014). This would be done under the guise of security concerns and for the protection of national citizens accessing the NII. To others, however, the measures were a restatement of the globality of the system by moving its governance away from dominance by the US (and agencies based there) towards a broader set of states with a direct interest in how the system evolves. The US and other developed states wanted to defend what is termed its 'dynamic governance' model based on cooperation between civil society, global technical bodies and the private sector (Bradshaw et al., 2015). The agreed treaty impinged on this model by:

- Mandating coordination on security, which it is feared may evolve into formally legitimising surveillance of global traffic.
- Committing states to defend against spam: to some, this is unnecessary because competence already exists to deal with this and this commitment could be used as a censorship tool.
- Calling upon states to play an increased role in internet governance and to ensure the stability, continuity and security of the existing networks.

● Changing the treaty, which offers up new ambiguities that allow for a new set of telecommunications entities to fall under state jurisdiction.

Given the refusal of a number of key states (such as the US) to sign the Treaty, the outcome could be a multi-form of governance for the internet. Eighty-nine states agreed to the Treaty changes and eighty did not, resulting in a divergent soft infrastructure for the GII with different rules for the GII between territories (ITU, 2015). However, governments are but one set of actors within the internet ecosystem: civil society groups, the private sector, as well as academics and engineers, have always been prominent within the system. As such, internet governance is not like conventional diplomacy (Hofmann, 2016). Moreover, many would argue that the contents of the Treaty do not amount to much and certainly do not represent the 'Trojan horse' as claimed by many. In short, the ITU does not have as much power within the GII as claimed by its detractors. There is a need for realism within the governance system, rather than fear of the ITU, with the engagement of all states in a liberal and open consensus on internet management (DeNardis, 2012).

However, the trend towards the balkanisation of the internet appears to be becoming more widespread. There is pressure from more states to disconnect from the US hegemonic structures that characterise the GII and to develop their own governance structures for their own segment of the system (Van Eeten and Mueller, 2012). Again, this is a reaction to what is regarded as an abuse of hegemonic power by the US under the guise of the National Security Agency and the Snowden revelations. The US not only contravened laws in the global cyber commons but also acted without consent to serve its own, rather than global, interests. The idea that a balkanised internet is better for the state's mandate than an open but US-dominated system seems to be gaining traction with the EU, Brazil, China, Russia, Turkey, Indonesia and India, all of whom are appearing hesitant to support an international regime. This is in addition to regimes that openly utilise NIIs as state tools. However, the US has also contributed to the fragmentation of the system, not only through the reaction of other states but also as a result of discriminating between users in terms of geo-location and the differential treatment of data, notably according to whether users are US citizen or not (DeNardis, 2012).

Overall, an erosion of the internationalist consensus between those states who want to avoid a top-down government controlled approach to internet governance and those states (mainly developing and communist or former communist states) who wish to see greatly enhanced state controls is emerging. Many were especially hostile to the continuation of

US dominance of the system via ICANN and the creation of a new inter-governmental body. Although these views did not prevail at the World Summit on the Information Society, a balance was struck to support a decentralised, plural, open approach to the internet and the creation of the Internet Governance Forum.

The main sources of state-based fragmentation (namely, security, privacy and the digital divide) are mentioned in more detail later. However, it is worth mentioning several other methods utilised by states in their attempts to assert a higher degree of control over cyberspace as a means of assert-ing control and securing their infrastructural mandate. These alternative sources of fragmentation (as identified by DeNardis, 2012; Hill, 2012; Drake et al., 2016) include:

- Content and censorship: the state attempts to influence the content delivered to local users where such content allegedly threatens system stability, contravenes local laws and cultures, and where there could be a threat to the state's ability to sustain territorial control. This may involve the state monitoring and, where necessary, blocking external flows into the NIS targeted at specific user groups. These measures directly overlap with security issues. According to DeNardis (2011), this process is often delegated by government requests to providers or intermediaries to restrict content, either under national law or through a private adjudication of a government request (see later).
- E-commerce and trade: where states seek to restrict what can be traded and accessed over the NII as a means of protecting local busi-nesses. This has led to the charge of 'digital protectionism' (Drake et al., 2016) when users are blocked access to major platforms and devices necessary for effective engagement in the GII.
- Data localization: this occurs when states limit the movement, storage and/or processing of data within specified territories with the result that national businesses have to either process, store and/or keep data and consequent flows within limited geographic confines. These restrictions can apply to both public and private infrastruc-tures and represent the terms of operation within a given territory. This can often involve sensitive information but, nonetheless, the net effect is to block certain data flows out of a territory and therefore create new forms of fragmentation.
- Intelligent policy enforcement: this is based on the examination of inbound and outbound traffic flows to and from a state, as well as flows within it, which it also has the ability to alter. In some states (as mentioned), direct state-based firewalls are applied to restrict specific flows that can hinder state control/security. In other cases,

more informal monitoring of flows is common. These are linked to what DeNardis (2014) terms 'denial of service attacks', where the state proactively hinders flows to internal threats.

- 'Kill switch': these are key infrastructure points where governments have the opportunity to disrupt communication flows. States can order infrastructure owners to shut down networks in the short term while the state regains control and/or militates against the threats to the system posed by the infected infrastructure.
- Erosion of internationalism: states (as mentioned earlier) are seeking to develop alternative processes to the common core system of web addressing developed by ICANN, which runs the risk that parts of the global system could be separated from other parts. This is a result of the strong pressures on core internet standards as more states seek to resist formalisation of US hegemonic control of the GII. This has been compounded by the increasing frequency of the breakdown of transit agreements through the rise of methods such as the erosion of net neutrality (see earlier).

Inevitably, these sources of fragmentation overlap with the main themes embedded within state-based sources of fragmentation, namely security and privacy – discussion of which follows.

Security

As the GII has matured and the interactions between NIIs have increased, so the implications for national security from globally integrated information infrastructures have grown in strategic salience (Clemente, 2013). The focus on security reflects the NII's status as a source of state vulnerability, both as state cyber power grows and as the private segments of the NII become increasingly vulnerable to cyber attack (Nye, 2011). State security is tied intimately into the security of the NII, as well as into other components of the NIS and critical infrastructures. This includes military and economic assets, such as banks whose systems have become open to attack from the very digital systems that enable them (Gray, 2013) and whose failure could undermine, at least in part, state functionality. These military and civilian concerns have been a driver of internet balkanisation process (see later). As the internet penetrates deep into a state's civic society, as well as into state and business structures, so the capability for a state to exercise infrastructural power in a malign fashion grows (Betz and Stevens, 2011). The core problem is the combination of open networks and the rapid development of powerful software and devices that take advantage of them (Klimburg, 2011). This has created advanced and persistent threats, the highest profile of which was the Stuxnet virus that hindered Iran's nuclear programme. It was widely believed that this was developed by the US and/or Israeli governments, but China and Russia are also potential perpetrators (Farwell and Rohozinski, 2011).

For these reasons, states frequently retain the rights to control access to technology, networks and content should the resultant globality work to undermine the state's core functions. Although some might argue that such trends justify international governance, the diversity of states and their demands means that borders operate as the most effective filter (Kramer et al., 2009). In the last resort, most states have access to a kill switch to turn off the internet within their territories should security be so severely challenged. By 2015, over 30 states engaged in internet filtering. Although all of these were authoritarian states, many liberal democratic states reserve the rights to control flows should state control or security be compromised (Open Net Initiative, 2015). Moreover, many states retain the right to monitor traffic. There is a clear suggestion of isomorphic pressures spreading the norms of cyber control (Deibert and Crete-Nishihata, 2012): a process driven by not by a central treaty but through a mix of bilateral, inter-state channels. These pressures are being enhanced by self-control within civil society and the treatment of cyber security as a private good.

Attacks on these systems from the 'global commons' of cyberspace can render international governance irrelevant given that many powerful states use this asset to test the security systems of other states (Murphy, 2010). This has been borne out by the number of security threats from hacking. The danger is that the desire to protect can introduce bias into the system as states seek to defend their NII from external threats and attacks. NIIs are particularly vulnerable where there are key bottlenecks or hubs within the system, such as a reliance on undersea cables or a limited number of server farms, or where poor governance in parts of the GII allows cyber attacks to proliferate unchecked (Libicki, 2007). A major problem in promoting international cooperation is that few states want to agree rules and many are beneficiaries of this method of warfare (Flournoy and Brimley, 2009). Moreover, there are widely divergent views on what such an agreement should look like and there are problems in actually working out where an attack originated.

The challenge for a state seeking to control infrastructure it does not own is not to deter investment that advances the capabilities of its own infrastructure by being too stringent in rule formation. In other words, there is a risk that threats to national security fragment the global system by eroding the value of openness. The result is the erection of walls within the internet that inhibit free movement of traffic and limit control in places. States have already introduced 'firewalls' into the system that impose tight controls on internet links, monitoring links and making many sites and services unavailable. In addition, companies are also fragmenting the system by building the aforementioned 'walled gardens' (Paterson, 2012). The fear is that these, in combination with other factors, could fragment the internet and create a series of propriety islands that work against the interoperability of the GII as closed systems within it become more common (Nakamura and Chow-White, 2011).

Although cyber security can be treated as a private good, the fact that it is lacking reflects an absence of value attached to achieving a GII or, at the very least, that it is not a strategic priority. However, its adoption within critical infrastructure systems renders it a public good (McKnight and Bailey, 1998). In many cases, states now take the lead in both ensuring public systems are sound and ensuring that private concerns are aware of the risk (Deibert and Crete-Nishihata, 2012). There has also been a trend for the state to become increasingly proactive regarding the public good aspects of security. In the formative period of the GII under US hegemony, it was intended that the market would lead security. However, as the internet has permeated deeper into state socio-economic structures, this is viewed by many states as inadequate and subject to market failure (Drissel, 2006). As a result, many states – even more liberal states – have grown increasingly proactive in governing the security aspects of NIIs and how they feed into security more generally (Open Net Initiative, 2015). This has become evident, not only with the increased narrative of cyber power but also with the vulnerabilities of the military architecture to cyber attacks and other such devices that can seek to turn a state's NII on itself, thereby undermining its infrastructural mandate.

The rise of cyber power has highlighted in terms of control and security how the state is being challenged by the increased supply of information (Nye, 2011). The state is powerful within the cyber system, but there are evident challenges to it from the rise of new cyber power, especially within the private sector that collects information. The state seeks to control information through sanctioning key channels but preservation of cyber power can fragment the system (DeNardis, 2009). The cost of cyber power is considerably less than the ability to project power in the domains. Governments exert cyber power over their territories by controlling access to the internet. The immediate response of some states to the Arab Spring was to blackout the internet. Kuehl (2009, p. 24) defines cyber power as the 'ability to use cyberspace to create advantages and to influence events in all operational environments and across the instruments of power', reflecting the need to exert influence over land, sea, air, space and, evidently, cyberspace. Normally these tools of power are solely linked to the state, but it is evident that this cyber power extends to non-state actors, especially as barriers to entry are low and network effects enable extensive reach without the need for large investment exist.

According to Rowland et al. (2014a), cyber entities have three components: an ideology, a body politic and an infrastructure. As cyber systems mature, states can use these systems to exert power both internally and externally to their borders. It is through this domain that informational power will be used. However, these cyber systems are also open to abuse through non-state entities for the purposes of eroding the welfare of local populations. Events like WikiLeaks have demonstrated how the activity of the state in the information age is subject to scrutiny and how the state is under pressure to keep its information infrastructure up to speed to enable it to cope with sophisticated cyber attacks. The result is that states will erect new barriers, both internally and externally, to counter these threats. This cyber power can work both for and against the state. It was evident in the example of the Arab Spring where the use of cyber resources posed a challenge to the state. These represent new challenges as scale does not seem to matter in imposing a challenge to the state (Rowland et al., 2014b).

The capability of cyber power to undermine control is also evident where it mobilises local threats to the state system. For these reasons, states may seek to reassert control because the cyber system can facilitate challenges to state supremacy within a region. The Arab Spring was a wake-up call for many states that witnessed at first-hand the ability of social media or the GII to turn against the power elites within a state (DeNardis, 2012). This helps explain the impetus behind state efforts to control these forces. Moreover, the exposure of state activity in the WikiLeaks scandal also highlighted how a torch can be shone into all areas of a state's activities against its wishes. Such resistance to intrusion of state activities has underpinned resistance by many states (such as China and Russia, as well as many developing states) to the Council of Europe Framework on Cybersecurity as a formal agreement for cyber security, with these states feeling that it seeks too many intrusions into national sovereignty.

Privacy

The issue of privacy involves a conflict between issues of access and quality in the development of the GII, where the desire for a fit-for-purpose quality system that drives value creation can contradict the private rights of an individual in infrastructure usage (OECD, 2010). There is a belief that, if left to markets, privacy will be eroded (Rust et al., 2002; Chadwick, 2006). This has been reinforced by the political rhetoric surrounding 'Big Data' (Mayer-Schönberger and Cukier, 2013). Privacy has three main areas: the storage of personal data on personal devices; snooping software; and the collection of data for marketing/commercial purposes (Schwartz, 1999). For many businesses, value is generated by the ability to collect user information as a precursor to 'mining' it for commercial gain. The concern is whether this process is voluntary on the part of the user or whether it is an infringement on their personal rights (Chadwick, 2006). Alternatively, it can be argued the autonomy of users over data usage is overstated because most remain unsophisticated (Farrell, 2008). Nonetheless, it is widely accepted that to use ignorance as a justification for unethical activities is unwarranted (Dutta et al., 2011). The right of privacy in the GII is a function of the user's right to control information about themselves and how it is used once volunteered. As technology evolves, this right becomes harder to enforce (Newman, 2008). The problem is compounded by the transnational nature of data traffic, whereby data flows to regimes that differ in their attitude to privacy (Bennett and Raab, 2006).

The increasing salience of security in the online environment has forced a revision in the importance of user privacy by states (see Chadwick and Howard, 2010). Their challenge is to strike a balance between the development of a GII based on users' rights of privacy and its efforts to sustain the integrity and security of its borders and of the activity that goes on within them (Weber, 2010b). The danger is that the strictness of these laws may impede the creation of the GII by acting as a de facto trade barrier through limiting the free flow of services across borders (DeNardis, 2011). There is also a potential clash between privacy and the protection of IPR as a user's right to surf unscrutinised can conflict with the desire of rights' owners to track who is unlawfully using their IP and when and where they are doing it. The danger is that privacy violations deter usage and lead to fragmentation of the GII (OECD, 2015).

Managing these rights across regimes, some of which prefer direct regulation and others self-regulation, is a major source of international disputes (ITU, 2015). Privacy was seen as a natural right at the time of the foundation of the internet, but this view has been eroded somewhat as threats to the system and the links to security have become more explicit. That states will monitor flows is of little surprise but this has come into prominence as the security apparatus of the state attempts to counter the illegal activity which has transferred to an online environment (Schwartz, 1999). The challenge is to balance globality with national preferences in the GII. Often the resolution of these issues can only be through international cooperation (OECD, 2015). Attitudes to privacy are embedded in the cultural context/heritage of a given state (Nissenbaum, 2009). The response also reflects the tendencies of states to directly control or allow for self-regulation. The result has been protracted disputes over the most effective forms of governance and the degree of control or compulsion required to secure the credibility of these flows (for a review, see Farrell, 2006).

In the US, the notion of freedom from state intervention is embedded within the social system whereas in the EU these rights have to be guaranteed by the state (Birnhack, 2008). Consequently, the US opted for a self-regulatory system, as did the EU provided they complied with its regulation on data privacy. This was the so-called 'safe harbour' compromise which came into effect in 2000. The implementation of the EU's Data Protection Directive prohibited the export of EU data where there was inadequate protection. This forced some states to adjust their own laws. The US sought to persuade its MNCs to adopt a voluntary code that conformed to EU rules (Long and Quek, 2002). However, EU and US rules remain rival standards because the safe harbour rules remain voluntary (Law, 2015). The EU took the lead on internet privacy with its formal directive on privacy, which has spilled over into other national domains as traffic flows across borders have increased (Kobrin, 2004). The EU's data directive has proved especially salient in shaping the privacy debate between states, especially so in middle income states which have felt compelled to follow the EU's proposal. In 2012, the US government signalled a stronger stance on privacy, albeit not outright legal control. This was a consequence of breaches of privacy commitments by Facebook and Google. The US still wants to avoid outright regulation for fear of stifling innovation. The legacy of divergence in privacy rules creates discrimination where states fragment the system or create barriers to the free flow of traffic around the system (Newman, 2008).

The trend towards the divergence of the treatment of privacy within the GII is also apparent in the reaction of states outside the US to the snooping activities of the US security agencies into their activities, which has been to pass stronger data protection laws to limit the activities of bodies such as the National Security Agency. Under the EU–US Safe Harbour Agreement, more than 4,000 technology companies can transfer data collected in Europe and send it back – wholesale – to the US (Schwartz, 2013). However, parts of the EU institutional system argue that this agreement is illegal because the protection of privacy is turning out to be lower than was agreed in the US, where there is a failure to protect EU citizens from indiscriminate, widespread surveillance. If the EU follows through with this argument, US technology companies will be forced to create parallel storage systems within the EU – in effect ending the Safe Harbour Agreement (Swire, 2015). As data transfer underpins almost all trade in the global economy, this would increase transaction costs and hinder the efficiency of a global system of digital flows. This would be replaced by national systems with varying rules. Although the US has attempted to be more open, this breach of trust has not satisfied many states (Schwartz and Solove, 2014).

The Digital Divide

As a source of state-based fragmentation in the GII, the digital divide is less about the strategic intent of the state to assert control and more about the generic absence of the capability to offer an effective conduit for global flows throughout a state's territory. Whilst a strategic intent to deny service and to limit access as a means of control cannot be ruled out, digital divides more often emerge as the result of the unevenness of economic development, especially within a market-driven system.

Whilst there is an emerging consensus on the role of the information economy in economic growth and development, as mentioned earlier, there remains a digital divide, both within and across NIIs, that results in the GII developing unevenly both within and across states (ITU, 2007). In a market-based system, such unevenness is generated by wide spatial variances in actual and anticipated traffic flows, which drive information infrastructure investment (OECD, 2015; UNCTAD, 2015). The fear is that the unevenness of access to the GII reinforces digital divisions and patterns of economic growth and development created by a vicious cycle of underdevelopment of the local NII (Chinn and Fairlie, 2007). The universality of the GII does not require the even development of information infrastructure, merely that access is open to all – a feature that is key to ensuring the end-to-end connectivity that is the cornerstone of the system (Guillén and Suárez, 2005).

Evidence presented to the World Economic Forum (2015) highlights the nature of the digital divide: the gap is greatest between developed economies and those in sub-Saharan Africa. The main indicators of this gap are in terms of infrastructure quality and accessibility to content. In short, the large technical systems that are required of infrastructure are almost non-existent in extreme cases. The digital divide reflects power asymmetries within the GII whose development remains largely shaped by the wealthier information-intensive states. Thus, little value is lost where underdevelopment of the NII merely reflects an absence of requirement or need. Consequently, there is a debate to be had as to how big a source of fragmentation within the GII such digital divides actually are because they can often reflect a gap between the social needs and economic demands of the different parts of the system. Such divergences create evident differentiations in policy terms between the idealised GII (identified in Table 4.1) and the broader-based information society (Chinn and Fairlie, 2007).

Despite such perspectives, it is inevitable that the traffic-based business models that underpin the GII will underserve 'information poor' regions, leading to the reinforcement of existing divides. Often such divides – certainly at the national level – are linked to variances in liberalisation and openness to global forces. Indeed, Drake and Wilson (2008) refer to the notion of 'Washington Consensus' in the development of the GII. Whilst there has been 'Angola Mode' investment in 'information poor regions', these have often been strategic on behalf of the donor and are not always carried out with the interests of the host to the fore. Although there are evidently inter-state differentials in the relative development of NIIs, there are also intra-state divergences and the possibility of the state limiting full integration of all social and economic groupings into the NII and the GII as a means of sustaining territorial control and of inhibiting opposition.

CONCLUSION

Arguably, of all the forms of economic infrastructure examined within this book, the GII demonstrates the greatest retrenchment of state power. In part this has been a reactive strategy by states that were slow to appreciate fully how the evolution of internet-based technologies represents a clear challenge to state territoriality. Initially, much of the reining in of global flows has occurred in more autocratic states where control over these flows represents an extension of state power. However, this has also occurred to an extent in many liberal democratic states where cyber systems have been a conduit for external non-governmental bodies to challenge both state security and control. It is evident that all states filter traffic and retain the right to operate a kill switch in extreme situations when state security is threatened. However, despite these growing challenges to the market-led development of the GII, there can be little doubt that private bodies remain major players. In practice, the splintering of the GII emerges from the state seeking to apply the same rules to online global flows as apply to other sectors.

REFERENCES

Ananthaswamy, A. (2011) 'Age of the splinternet', *New Scientist*, *211*(2821), 42–5.
Ang, P.H. (2008) 'International regulation of internet content possibilities and limits', in Drake, W.J. and Wilson III, E.J. (eds.), *Governing Global Electronic Networks: International Perspectives on Policy and Power.* Cambridge, MA: MIT Press, pp. 305–31.

Armbrust, M., Fox, A., Griffith, R., Joseph, A.D., Katz, R., Konwinski, A. and Zaharia, M. (2010) 'A view of cloud computing', *Communications of the ACM*, *53*(4), 50–8.

Bennett, C.J. and Raab, C.D. (2006) *The Governance of Privacy: Policy Instruments in Global Perspective*. Cambridge, MA: MIT Press.

Berleur, J. (2008) '15 years of ways of internet governance: towards a new agenda for action', in Avgerou, C., Smith, M. and Van der Besselaar, P. (eds.), *Social Dimensions of Information and Communication Technology Policy*. New York, NY: Springer, pp. 255–74.

Betz, D. and Stevens, T. (2011) *Cyberspace and the State: Toward a Strategy for Cyber-Power*. London: The International Institute for Strategic Studies.

Birnhack, M.D. (2008) 'The EU data protection directive: an engine of a global regime', *Computer Law and Security Review*, *24*(6), 508–20.

Borgman, C.L. (2003) *From Gutenberg to the Global Information Infrastructure: Access to Information in the Networked World*. Cambridge, MA: MIT Press.

Bradshaw, S., DeNardis, L., Hampson, F.O., Jardine, E. and Raymond, M. (2015) *The Emergence of Contention in Global Internet Governance*. London: Royal Institute of International Affairs.

Braithwaite, J. and Drahos, P. (2000) *Global Business Regulation*. Cambridge: Cambridge University Press.

Bronckers, M. and Larouche, P. (2008) 'A review of the WTO regime for telecommunications services', in Alexander, K. and Andenas, M. (eds.), *The World Trade Organization and Trade in Services*. Leiden, The Netherlands: Martinus Nijhoff Publishers, pp. 319–79.

Bygrave, L.A. and Bing, J. (eds.) (2009) *Internet Governance: Infrastructure and Institutions*. Oxford: Oxford University Press.

Cairncross, F. (2001) *The Death of Distance: How the Communications Revolution Is Changing Our Lives*. Boston, MA: Harvard Business School Press.

Carter, L., Burnett, D., Drew, S., Marle, G., Hagadorn, L., Bartlett-McNeil, D. and Irvine, N. (2009) *Submarine Cables and the Oceans: Connecting the World*. UNEP–WCMC Biodiversity Series No. 31. ICPC/UNEP/UNEP–WCMC.

Cavanagh, A. (2007) *Sociology in the Age of the Internet*. Maidenhead, UK: McGraw-Hill Education.

Chadwick, A. (2006) *Internet Politics: States, Citizens, and New Communication Technologies*. Cary, NC: Oxford University Press.

Chadwick, A. and Howard, P.N. (eds.) (2010) *Routledge Handbook of Internet Politics*. Abingdon, UK: Routledge.

Charles, C.A. and Furar, L.E. (1998) *Building the Global Information Economy: A Roadmap from the Global Information Infrastructure Commission*. Washington, DC: Center for Strategic and International Studies.

Chaudhry, P.E., Chaudhry, S.S., Stumpf, S.A. and Sudler, H. (2011) 'Piracy in cyber space: consumer complicity, pirates and enterprise enforcement', *Enterprise Information Systems*, *5*(2), 255–71.

Chinn, M. and Fairlie, R. (2007) 'The determinants of the global digital divide: a cross-country analysis of computer and internet penetration', *Oxford Economic Papers*, *59*(1), 16–44.

Cisco (2015) *The Cisco VNI data traffic forecast*, accessed 2015 at www.cisco.com

Clark, G.R.G. and Wallstein, S.J. (2006) 'Has the Internet increased trade? Developed and developing country evidence', *Economic Enquiry*, *44*(3), 465–84.

Clemente, D. (2013) *Cyber Security and Global Interdependence: What Is Critical?* London: Royal Institute of International Affairs.

Clough, J. (2012) 'The Council of Europe Convention on Cybercrime: defining "crime" in a digital world', *Criminal Law Forum*, *23*(4), 363–91.

Corallo, A., Passiante, G. and Prencipe, A. (eds.) (2007) *The Digital Business Ecosystem*. Cheltenham, UK: Edward Elgar.

Czernich, N., Falck, O., Kretschmer, T. and Woessmann, L. (2011) 'Broadband infrastructure and economic growth', *Economic Journal*, *121*(552), 505–32.

Dahlander, L. and Gann, D.M. (2010) 'How open is innovation?', *Research Policy*, *39*(6), 699–709.

Deere, C. (2008) *The Implementation Game: The TRIPS Agreement and the Global Politics of Intellectual Property Reform in Developing Countries*. Oxford: Oxford University Press.

Deibert, R.J. and Crete-Nishihata, M. (2012) 'Global governance and the spread of cyberspace controls', *Global Governance*, *18*(3), 339–61.

DeNardis, L. (2009) *Protocol Politics: The Globalization of Internet Governance*. Cambridge, MA: MIT Press.

DeNardis, L. (ed.) (2011) *Opening Standards: The Global Politics of Interoperability.* Cambridge, MA: MIT Press.

DeNardis, L. (2012) 'Hidden levers of Internet control: an infrastructure-based theory of internet governance', *Information, Communication and Society*, *15*(5), 720–38.

DeNardis, L. (2014) *The Global War for Internet Governance*. New Haven, CT: Yale University Press.

Dhamdhere, A. and Dovrolis, C. (2011) 'Twelve years in the evolution of the internet ecosystem', *IEEE/ACM Transactions on Networking*, *19*(5), 1420–33.

Dicken, P. (2015) *Global Shift: Mapping the Changing Contours of the World Economy*. London: Guilford.

Dillon, T., Wu, C. and Chang, E. (2010) Cloud computing: issues and challenges in *Advanced Information Networking and Applications (AINA), 24th IEEE International Conference*, 27–33.

Dinwoodie, G.B. and Dreyfuss, R.C. (2009) 'Designing a global intellectual property system responsive to change: the WTO, WIPO, and beyond', *Houston Law Review*, *46*, 1187–234.

Drake, W.J. (2000) 'The rise and decline of the international telecommunications regime', *Regulating the Global Information Society*, 124–77.

Drake, W.J. (2008) 'Introduction: the distributed architecture of network global governance', in Drake, W.J. and Wilson III, E.J. (eds.), *Governing Global Electronic Networks: International Perspectives on Policy and Power*. Cambridge, MA: MIT Press, pp. 1–80.

Drake, W.J. and Wilson, E.J. (eds.) (2008) *Governing Global Electronic Networks: International Perspectives on Policy and Power.* Cambridge, MA: MIT Press.

Drake, W.J, Cerf, V. and Kleinwachter, W. (2016) *Internet Fragmentation: An Overview*. World Economic Forum, Future of the Internet White Paper, accessed 2015 at www.wef.org

Drezner, D.W. (*2004*) 'The global governance of the internet: bringing the state back in', *Political Science Quarterly*, *119*(3), 477–98.

Drissel, D. (2006) 'Internet governance in a multipolar world: challenging American hegemony', Cambridge *Review of International Affairs*, *19*(1), 105–20.

Dutta, S., Dutton, W.H. and Law, G. (2011) *The New Internet World: A Global*

Perspective on Freedom of Expression, Privacy, Trust and Security Online. INSEAD Working Paper, No 2011/89/TOM.

Eichensehr, K.E. (2015) 'Cyber-law of nations', *Georgetown Law Journal*, *103*(2), 317–80.

European Commission (2014) *The European Competitiveness Report.* Commission Staff Working Document SWD(2014)277 final.

Farrell, H. (2006) 'Regulating information flows: states, private actors and e-commerce', *Annual Review of Political Science*, *9*, 353–74.

Farrell, H. (2008) 'Privacy in the digital age states: private actors, and hybrid arrangements', in Drake, W.J. and Wilson III, E.J. (eds.), *Governing Global Electronic Networks: International Perspectives on Policy and Power.* Cambridge, MA: MIT Press, pp. 375–400.

Farwell, J.P. and Rohozinski, R. (2011) 'Stuxnet and the future of cyber war', *Survival*, *53*(1), 23–40.

Flournoy, M. and Brimley, S. (2009) 'The contested commons', *US Naval Institute, Proceedings*, *135*, 7.

Forden, E. (2015) *The Undersea Cable Boom in Sub-Saharan Africa.* Office of Industries USITC Executive Briefing on Trade.

Franzese, P.W. (2009) 'Sovereignty in cyberspace: can it exist?', *Air Force Law Review*, *64*, 1–42.

Friedman, T.L. (2005) *The World Is Flat: A Brief History of the Twenty-First Century.* Basingstoke, UK: Macmillan.

Gershon, R. (2013) *Media, Telecommunications and Business Strategy.* New York, NY: Routledge.

Gillespie, A., Richardson, R. and Cornford, J. (2001) 'Regional development and the new economy', *EIB Papers*, *6*(1), 109–31.

Goldsmith, J. and Wu, T. (2006) *Who Controls the Internet? Illusions of a Borderless World.* Oxford: Oxford University Press.

Graham, S. and Marvin, S. (2001) *Splintering Urbanism: Networked Infrastructures, Technological Mobilities and the Urban Condition.* London: Routledge.

Gray, C.S. (2013) *Making Strategic Sense of Cyber Power: Why The Sky Is Not Falling.* Strategic Studies Institute, Carlisle Barracks, PA: US Army War College Press.

Greenstein, S. and McDevitt, R. (2011) 'The broadband bonus: estimating broadband internet's economic value', *Telecommunications Policy*, 35(7), 617–32.

Guermazi, B. (2008) 'The GATS Agreement on basic telecommunications: a developing country perspective', in Drake, W.J. and Wilson III, E.J. (eds.), *Governing Global Electronic Networks: International Perspectives on Policy and Power.* Cambridge, MA: MIT Press, pp. 187.

Guillén, M.F. and Suárez, S.L. (2005) 'Explaining the global digital divide: economic, political and sociological drivers of cross-national Internet use', *Social Forces*, 84(2), 681–708.

Hamelink, C.J. (2008) 'The global governance of mass media content countries', in Drake, W.J. and Wilson III, E.J. (eds.), *Governing Global Electronic Networks: International Perspectives on Policy and Power.* Cambridge, MA: MIT Press, pp. 275–74.

Headrick, D. (1991) *The Invisible Weapon: Telecommunications and International Politics 1851–1945.* Oxford: Oxford University Press.

Headrick, D. and Griset, P. (2001) 'Submarine telegraph cables: business and politics, 1838–1939', *Business History Review*, *75*, 543–78.

Henisz, W.J., Zelner, B.A. and Guillén, M.F. (2005) 'The worldwide diffusion of market-oriented infrastructure reform, 1977–1999', *American Sociological Review*, *70*(6), 871–97.

Hill, J.F. (2012) *Internet Fragmentation: Highlighting the Major Technical, Governance and Diplomatic Challenges for US Policy Makers*. Cambridge, MA: Berkman Center Research Paper.

Hill, R. (2014) *The New International Telecommunication Regulations and the Internet: a Commentary and Legislative History*. New York, NY: Springer.

Hills, J. (2008) *Telecommunications and Empire*. Champaign, IL: University of Illinois Press.

Hofmann, J. (2016) 'Multi-stakeholderism in internet governance: putting a fiction into practice', *Journal of Cyber Policy*, *1*(1), 29–49.

Hofmokl, J. (2010) 'The Internet commons: towards an eclectic theoretical framework', *International Journal of the Commons*, *4*(1), 226–50.

International Telecommunication Union (ITU) (2007) *Bridging the Digital Divide*. World Information Society Report 2007. Geneva: ITU.

International Telecommunication Union (ITU) (2011) *Measuring the Information Society*, accessed 12 November 2015 at www.itu.net

International Telecommunication Union (ITU) (2012) *Measuring The Information Society*, accessed 12 November 2015 at www.itu.int

International Telecommunication Union (ITU) (2013) *Trends in Telecommunications Regulatory Reform,* accessed 2015 at www.itu.int

International Telecommunication Union (ITU) (2015) *Trends in Telecommunications Regulatory Reform,* accessed 2015 at www.itu.int

Jaeger, P.T., Lin, J. and Grimes, J.M. (2008) 'Cloud computing and information policy: computing in a policy cloud?', *Journal of Information Technology and Politics*, *5*(3), 269–83.

Jakopin, N.M. (2008) 'Internationalisation in the telecommunications services industry: Literature review and research agenda', *Telecommunications Policy*, *32*(8), 531–544.

James, J. (2001) 'The global information infrastructure revisited', *Third World Quarterly, 22*(5), 813–22.

Jessop, R.D. (2002) *The Future of the Capitalist State*. London: Polity Press.

Jiang, M. (2014) 'Internet sovereignty: a new paradigm of internet governance', in Haerens, M. and Zott, L.M. (eds.)*, Internet Censorship*. Farmington Hills, MI: Greenhaven Press, pp. 23–8.

Kahin, B. and Neeson, C. (1997) *Borders in Cyberspace: Information Policy and the Global Information Infrastructure*. Cambridge, MA: MIT Press.

Katz, M.L. and Shapiro, C. (1994) 'Systems competition and network effects', *Journal of Economic Perspectives*, *8*(2), 93–115.

Kellerman, A. (2002) *The Internet on Earth: A Geography of Information*. Chichester, UK: Wiley and Sons.

Kesan, J.P. and Shah, R.C. (2004) 'Deconstructing code', *Yale Journal of Law and Technology*, *6*, 277–389.

Kleinrock, L. (2010) 'An early history of the internet', *Communications Magazine IEEE*, *48*(8), 26–36.

Klimburg, A. (2011) 'Mobilising cyber power', *Survival*, *53*(1), 41–60.

Kobrin, S.J. (2004) 'Safe harbours are hard to find: the trans-Atlantic data privacy dispute, territorial jurisdiction and global governance', *Review of International Studies*, *30*(1), 111–31.

Kramer, F.D., Starr, S.H. and Wentz, L. (2009) *Cyber Power and National Security.* Dulles, VA: Potomac Books.

Krasner, S.D. (2001) 'Abiding sovereignty', *International Political Science Review*, *22*(3), 229–51.

Kuehl, D.T. (2009) 'From cyberspace to cyberpower: defining the problem', in Kramer, F., Starr, S. and Wentz, L. (eds.), *Cyber Power and National Security.* Dulles, VA: Potomac Books, pp. 24–42.

Law, P. (2015) 'Legal problems in data management: global approach to data privacy: safe harbor', *John Marshall Journal of Information Technology and Privacy Law*, *31*(4), 633–9.

Lessig, L. (2004) *Free Culture: How Big Media Uses Technology and the Law to Lock Down Culture and Control Creativity.* New York, NY: Penguin Press.

Levi-Faur, D. (2005) 'The global diffusion of regulatory capitalism', *Annals of the American Academy of Political and Social Sciences*, *598*, 12–32.

Libicki, M.C. (2007) *Conquest in Cyberspace: National Security and Information Warfare.* Cambridge: Cambridge University Press.

Long, W.J. and Quek, M.P. (2002) 'Personal data privacy protection in an age of globalization: the US–EU safe harbor compromise', *Journal of European Public Policy*, *9*(3), 325–44.

Main, L. (2001) 'The global information infrastructure: empowerment or imperialism?', *Third World Quarterly*, *22*(1), 83–97.

Malcomson, S. (2015) *Splinternet: How Geopolitics and Commerce Are Fragmenting the World Wide Web.* London: OR Books.

Marsden, C. (ed.) (2000) *Regulating the Global Information Society*. London: Routledge.

May, C. (2006) 'The World Intellectual Property Organization', *New Political Economy*, *11*(3), 435–45.

May, C. (2008) 'Intellectual property rights, capacity building, and "informational development" in developing countries', in Drake, W.J. and Wilson III, E.J. (eds.), *Governing Global Electronic Networks: International Perspectives on Policy and Power.* Cambridge, MA: MIT Press, pp. 401–26.

Mayer-Schönberger, V. and Cukier, K. (2013) *Big Data: A Revolution That Will Transform How We Live, Work, and Think.* Boston, MA: Houghton Mifflin Harcourt.

McKinsey Global Institute (2016) *Digital Globalisation: The New Era of Global Flows*, accessed 2016 at www.mgi.org

McKnight, L.W. and Bailey, J.P. (1998) *Internet Economics.* Cambridge, MA: MIT Press.

Meisingset, A. (1996) 'Global information infrastructure', *Telektronikk*, *92*(1), 92–5.

Millard, C., Kuner, C., Cate, F., Svantesson, D. and Lynskey, O. (2015) 'Internet Balkanization gathers pace: is privacy the real driver?', *International Data Privacy Law*, *5*(1), 1–2.

Mueller, M.L. (2010) *Networks and States: The Global Politics of Internet Governance*. Cambridge, MA*:* MIT Press.

Mueller, M.L. and Lemstra, W. (2011) 'Liberalization and the Internet', in Künneke, R.W. and Finger, M. (eds.), *International Handbook of Network Industries.* Cheltenham, UK: Edward Elgar, pp. 144–61.

Murphy, T. (2010) 'Security challenges in the 21st century global commons', *Yale Journal of International Affairs*, *5*(2) 28–43.

Nakamura, L. and Chow-White, P. (eds.) (2011) *Race After the Internet*. London: Routledge.

Newman, A. (2008) *Protectors of Privacy: Regulating Personal Data in the Global Economy*. Ithaca, NY: Cornell University Press.

Nissenbaum, H. (2009) *Privacy in Context: Technology, Policy, and the Integrity of Social Life*. Redwood, CA: Stanford University Press.

Nye, J. (2011) 'Power and national security in cyberspace', *America's Cyber Future: Security and Prosperity in the Information Age*, *2*, 5–23.

Open Net Initiative (2015) ONI data, accessed May 2016 at https://opennet.net/research/data

Organisation for Economic Co-operation and Development (OECD) (2008a) *Broadband Growth and Policies in OECD Countries*. Paris: OECD.

Organisation for Economic Co-operation and Development (OECD) (2008b) *Broadband and the Economy, Ministerial Background Report*. DSTI/ICCP/IE(2007)3/FINAL. Paris: OECD.

Organisation for Economic Co-operation and Development (OECD) (2010) *The Evolving Privacy Landscape: 30 Years After the OECD Privacy Guidelines*. DSTI/ICCP/REG(2010)6/FINAL. Paris: OECD.

Organisation for Economic Co-operation and Development (OECD) (2012) *Internet Economy Outlook*, accessed 13 December 2015 at www.oecd.org

Organisation for Economic Co-operation and Development (OECD) (2013) *Communications Outlook*. Paris: OECD.

Organisation for Economic Co-operation and Development (OECD) (2015) *Digital Economy Outlook*. Paris: OECD.

Pager, S.A. (2006) 'TRIPS: a link too far? A proposal for procedural restraints on regulatory linkage in the WTO', *Marquette Intellectual Property Law Review*, *10*(2), 215–71.

Palfrey, J. (2010) 'Four phases of internet regulation', *Social Research*, *77*(3), 981–96.

Paterson, N. (2012) 'Walled gardens: the new shape of the public Internet', *Proceedings of the 2012 iConference*, 97–104.

Peppard, J. and Rylander, A. (2006) 'From value chain to value network: insights for mobile operators', *European Management Journal*, *24*(2), 128–41.

Pickard, V. (2007) 'Neoliberal visions and revisions in global communications policy from NWICO to WSIS', *Journal of Communication Inquiry*, *31*(2), 118–39.

Rayport, J.F. and Sviokla, J.J. (1995) 'Exploiting the virtual value chain', *Harvard Business Review*, November–December issue, 75–85.

Reidenberg, J.R. (2005) 'Technology and internet jurisdiction', *University of Pennsylvania Law Review*, 1951–74.

Reynolds, T. (2009) *The Role of communication Infrastructure Investment in economic Recovery*. OECD Digital Economy Papers, No. 154. Paris: OECD Publishing.

Rioux, M. and Fontaine-Skronski, K. (2015) 'Conceptualizing institutional changes in a world of great transformations: from the old telecommunications regime to the new global internet governance', in Rioux, M. and Fontaine-Skronski, K. (eds.), *Global Governance Facing Structural Changes: New Institutional Trajectories for Digital and Transnational Capitalism*. New York, NY: Palgrave Macmillan US, pp. 59–78.

Röller, L. and Waverman, L. (2001) 'Telecommunications infrastructure and economic development: a simultaneous approach', *The American Economic Review*, *91*(4), 909–23.

Rowland, J., Rice, M. and Shenoi, S. (2014a) 'The anatomy of a cyber power', *International Journal of Critical Infrastructure Protection*, *7*(1), 3–11.

Rowland, J., Rice, M. and Shenoi, S. (2014b) 'Whither cyberpower?', *International Journal of Critical Infrastructure Protection*, *7*(2), 124–37.

Rust, R.T., Kannan, P.K. and Peng, N. (2002) 'The customer economics of internet privacy', *Journal of the Academy of Marketing Science*, *30*(4), 455–64.

Ryan, J. (2010) *A History of the Internet and the Digital Future*. London: Reaktion Books.

Salin, P.A. (2000) *Satellite Communications Regulations in the Early 21st Century: Changes for a New Era*. Zuidpoolsingel, The Netherlands: Kluwer Law International.

Sarkar, M.B., Cavusgil, S.T. and Aulakh, P.S. (1999) 'International expansion of telecommunication carriers: the influence of market structure, network characteristics, and entry imperfections', *Journal of International Business Studies*, *30*(2), 361–81.

Sassen, S. (1998) 'On the internet and sovereignty', *Indiana Journal of Global Legal Studies*, *5*(2), 545–59.

Satellite Industry Association (SIA) (2011) *The Satellite Market,* accessed 2015 at www.sia.org

Schiller, D. (2011) 'Power under pressure: digital capitalism in crisis', *International Journal of Communication*, *5*(18), 924–41.

Schultz, T. (2008) 'Carving up the Internet: jurisdiction, legal orders, and the private/public international law interface', *European Journal of International Law*, *19*(4), 799–839.

Schwartz, P.M. (1999) 'Internet privacy and the state', *Connecticut Law Review,* *32*, 815–859.

Schwartz, P.M. (2013) 'The EU–US privacy collision: a turn to institutions and procedures', *Harvard Law Review*, *126*(7), 1966–2009.

Schwartz, P.M. and Solove, D.J. (2014) 'Reconciling personal information in the United States and European Union, *California Law Review*, *102*(4), 877–916.

Swire, P. (2015) 'US surveillance law, safe harbor, and reforms since 2013', Georgia Tech Scheller College of Business Research Paper, No. 36.

Tapscott, D. (1996) *'The Digital Economy: Promise and Peril in the Age of Networked Intelligence*. New York, NY: McGraw-Hill.

United Nations Conference on Trade and Development (UNCTAD) (2011) *Information Economy Report 2011: ICTs as an Enabler for Private Sector Development*. Geneva: UN Publications.

United Nations Conference on Trade and Development (UNCTAD) (2015) *Information Economy Report 2015: Unlocking the Potential of E-Commerce for Developing Countries*. Geneva: UN Publications.

Van Eeten, M.J. and Mueller, M. (2012) 'Where is the governance in internet governance?', *New Media and Society*, *15*(5), 720–36.

Von Bernstorff, J. (2003) 'Democratic global Internet regulation? Governance networks, international law and the shadow of hegemony', *European Law Journal*, *9*(4), 511–26.

Warf, B. (2012) *Global Geographies of the Internet*. London: Springer.

Weber, R.H. (2010a) 'New sovereignty concepts in the age of internet', *Journal of Internet Law*, *14*(8), 12–20.

Weber, R.H. (2010b) 'Internet of things – new security and privacy challenges', *Computer Law and Security Review*, *26*(1), 23–30.

Weiser, P.J. (2009) 'Future of internet regulation', *UC Davis Law Review*, *43*, 529–90.

World Bank (2016) *World Development Report 2016: Digital Dividends*. Washington, DC: World Bank Publications.

World Economic Forum (2015) *Global Information Technology Report*, accessed 2015 at www.wef.org

World Trade Organization (WTO) (2012) *Services Database*, accessed 2015 at www.wto.org

World Trade Organization (WTO) (2015) *Information Technology Agreement: Implementation Update*, accessed 2015 at www.wto.org

Yang, G. (2011) *The Power of the Internet in China*. New York, NY: Columbia University Press.

Zook, M. (2005) *The Geography of the Internet Industry: Venture Capital, Dot-Coms and Local Knowledge*. Oxford: Blackwell.

5. The Global Energy System

Securing a reliable and plentiful supply of energy is key to state power. Intra-territoriality facilitates the interconnection of local systems to create national energy systems, thereby ensuring that uneven distribution of energy resources does not undermine the core strategies of the state. Since the 1950s, there has been a continuation of this scaling up process towards the establishment of global energy systems in a manner which closely links energy systems and their security to scale. The desire of the state to participate in an international energy system stems from the need to create security of flows around a system in which the risk is from barriers to circulation not from the circulation itself. Thus, depending on its energy balance, the state builds a national energy infrastructure system (that is, the physical infrastructure required for producing, transforming, transmitting, distributing and storing energy) which is designed to secure sufficient resources to enable the operation of the state based on a mix of indigenous and imported resources. This has parallels with transport where bottlenecks and barriers can also pose a threat to the sustenance of global flows.

The following analysis focuses upon the development of the infrastructure needed to support the transmission of primary energy sources (that is, those energy sources that have not been subjected to any conversion or transformation process). In this context, the infrastructures supporting the supply of three types of energy – oil, gas and coal – are considered. Those infrastructures that have been developed to support cross-border electricity transmission (which is done sporadically on bi-lateral bases with congruent territories) are not included within this analysis of the global energy system (GES). As befits the theme of global systems, this chapter focuses on those energy infrastructures that support or enable the production and transmission of energy along the industry value chain across international borders, through transit territories where appropriate, to the point of entry into national energy systems and final consumption. The chapter first examines how the relevant infrastructures have evolved and then examines the forces for integration and fragmentation within the GES.

THE GLOBAL ENERGY INFRASTRUCTURE SYSTEM

For many centuries, energy systems were mainly locally based. Although limited cross-border trade based mainly on the interaction between contiguous systems did occur, this characteristic remained largely unchanged until the 1950s according to Hafele and Sassin (1977). Pre-GES, the security of energy supply was based on indigenous resources, but as economies have grown and domestic resources have declined, both in absolute and relative terms, states have looked beyond their borders for other energy supplies and, with this, the need for infrastructure to service this need has increased.

At the core of the contemporary GES is the transmission of the main forms of energy production: coal, gas and oil. As reflected in Figure 5.1, these three main forms of energy account for over 80 per cent of total global energy supply. These are the three main fuels at the core of the transmission of international energy flows. As such, the focus on the infrastructure to support the GES is based around that developed to enable international transmission of flows across these three main fuels.

A contemporary common feature of the three primary energy resources discussed in this chapter is the mismatch between the main location of energy production and the main locations of energy consumption. Oil became the first commercial fuel to be traded internationally in large

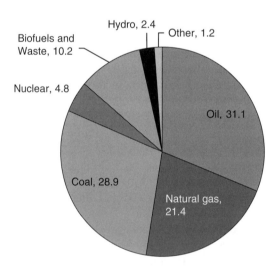

Source: IEA (2014a).

Figure 5.1   Total global energy supply by fuel, 2014

quantities, mainly by the so-called 'seven sisters', a group of US and European multinational oil companies which dominated the international oil industry for many years. The internationalisation of oil trade was followed by that of gas and has latterly become more important for coal given its declining production in traditional producing areas in Europe as a result of cost and environmental factors. Coal consumption, although in decline in Europe, persists and, as such, necessitates imports, often over long distances, and thus the existence of coal import infrastructure. Moreover, the growing economic role of emerging markets, some of which have relatively extensive indigenous energy supplies, but many of which do not, has boosted international energy demand and accentuated the mismatch between production and consumption for all three fuels and created new needs for international energy infrastructure.

Inevitably such change introduces vulnerabilities and uncertainties into the strategies of states as they seek to access sufficient energy at prices that do not undermine state power and/or capabilities. Expressed in these terms, the need for states to look abroad for secure and reliable sources of energy represents a second-best scenario compared to a national energy system based solely on indigenous production. As of 2015, the global trade in primary energy was worth about US$2.3 trillion per annum or 16 per cent of all international trade (World Trade Organization (WTO), 2016). Indeed, over the period 1996–2015, the international trade in energy exhibited an annual growth rate of 12 per cent per annum. Measured in pure dollar terms, the trade in energy rose eight-fold over this period, although this is driven in part by rises in energy prices (WTO, 2015).

The emergence of the GES (through the internationalisation of national energy systems, the scaling up of energy infrastructures and the consequent transnational flows of energy) came to strategic prominence during the 1973–4 oil crisis. Since this crisis (and in the aftermath of consequent crises), the global energy system based on the international movement of primary energy supplies has become a key factor shaping geopolitical and geo-economic strategies as they seek to enable this transmission of energy from points of high production to high consumption. The events of 1973 have left a lasting impact upon western states and exposed their vulnerability to cartelised supply of major energy inputs to which they have responded by engaging with the GES and diversifying their suppliers. However, the growing gap between indigenous energy supply and the reduced capacity to meet demand with this supply have resulted in growing reliance on imported energy in Europe in particular, despite increased energy efficiency and lower energy intensity.

In some Organisation for Economic Co-operation and Development (OECD) members, however, energy production in 2014 was the highest it had been for over 25 years, leading to falling imports and rising exports. However, these figures were heavily skewed by the US, Australia and Canada. Whilst the latter two have been major energy exporters for decades, the US, after several years of rising imports stemming from falling indigenous energy production, became a net energy exporter once more, largely as a result of rapid exploitation of shale oil and gas. Thus, whilst there is a positive energy trade balance for the OECD as a whole, the aggregate picture masks big differences between states. For the OECD as a whole, energy self-sufficiency in 2014 was around 78 per cent, with North American members registering 99 per cent self-sufficiency (International Energy Agency (IEA), 2015b). However, in Europe, where production has fallen, energy self-sufficiency has fallen to below 60 per cent and is expected to fall to 40 per cent by 2020 (BP, 2016a). Historically Oceania has also had relatively low levels of self-sufficiency, averaging around 40 per cent (IEA, 2015a). Whilst OECD states have shifted towards more renewable forms of energy, their strong reliance on hydrocarbons remains: for example, 60 per cent of all electricity generated in OECD states is based on hydrocarbons. Supply problems have been compounded by demand in the rest of the world which has shown a high degree of resilience (largely driven by sustained Chinese consumption), despite lower rates of economic growth since 2008 (World Energy Council (WEC), 2015a).

At the regional level, a growing energy gap between energy exporters and importers is anticipated between 1990 and 2035. Figures from BP (2016a) indicate that exporters will increase their energy surplus from around 1 billion tonnes of oil equivalent (btoe) in 1990 to around 3 btoe in 2035, which is roughly balanced by the net energy deficit of importing states. These relative deficits and surpluses underline the vulnerabilities and sources of instability within the GES stemming from the oscillation of energy import prices and from the response of importing states through energy efficiency programmes, diversification of international supplies and the stimulation of indigenous supplies.

The GES has been core to meeting the needs of the evolving global economy where the combination of economic growth, development, shifting demographics, industrialisation and income growth have seen global energy consumption increase by 157 per cent – from 104 million barrels of oil equivalent per day (mboe/d) in 1970 to 268 mboe/d in 2013 (BP, 2016a). The most marked change in energy balances has been in emerging and developing states, where energy demand increased by almost 500 per cent between 1970 and 2013. By 2035, BP (2016a) estimates that Asia will account for 70 per cent of inter-regional imports of energy (BP, 2016b). Overall, the import dependency of Asia is expected to rise to 27 per cent in 2035 (a figure which understates the import dependency – notably in east

Asia – due to high oil exports in the Middle East) with much of this rise being accounted for by rising oil consumption, with imports to the region in 2035 being as large as the entirety of the Organization of the Petroleum Exporting Countries' (OPEC) production in 2015 (BP, 2016a).

This growth in energy demand is expected to continue up to 2035, with rising consumption driven by India, China, Africa, the Middle East and Southeast Asia. It is estimated that China and India will have to increase their energy consumption by 150 and 100 per cent, respectively, by 2020 simply to sustain current growth rates (IEA, 2015b). The great unknowable factor for the GES is how it will be transformed given that major energy consumers such as China and the OECD states are looking to decouple economic growth from rising energy usage. However, although China will remain the single biggest energy consumer, India will exhibit the highest energy growth in energy demand. In 2015, it was only 6 per cent of global energy consumption despite being the seventh largest economy (although it ranks third when gross domestic product (GDP) is measured by purchasing power parity (PPP)) and having one-sixth of the world's population (BP, 2016a).

Developed (that is, OECD) economy demand has increased 69 per cent over the period 1970–2013 due to the above active energy strategies (IEA, 2015a), although towards the latter part of this period, the OECD states have sought to curtail demand growth as they adapt to the combined impact of shifting demography and the desire for greater efficiency. The IEA (2015a) estimates that by 2040 the energy consumption of the EU will fall by 15 per cent, Japan by 12 per cent and the US by 3 per cent. Overall, these long-term energy consumption trends will remain fairly stable across the OECD, with no major demand spikes anticipated given that these states have the long-term strategic objective of decoupling economic growth from energy consumption. Indeed, energy intensity (that is, total primary energy consumption per unit of gross domestic product) has declined across the OECD, with the largest falls occurring in heavy and manufacturing industry (IEA, 2015b). Across the OECD, energy self-sufficiency (that is, domestic production as a percentage of total demand) has risen to 78 per cent, with that of North America approaching 99 per cent (IEA, 2015a). Although OECD energy production and exports are at a historical high and imports at their lowest for over a decade, this has been mainly driven by North American oil and gas and Australian coal. Europe and Japan are expected to experience persistent energy deficits in the future, underlying why these states are at the nexus of much of the emerging infrastructure of the GES. Indeed, the IEA (2015b) estimates that OECD Europe and OECD Asia Pacific have self-sufficiency rates of 58 per cent and 56 per cent respectively. Between 1971 and 2013, the

OECD's relative importance in world energy production has declined with its share in world total primary energy supply (TPES) falling from 60 per cent to 39 per cent (IEA, 2015b).

These spatial variances, which form the basis of the GES, are shaped by an increasingly consensual view that energy security is a common responsibility for the leading industrialised states and that no state should undermine the security of any other state (G8 Communique, 2014), although figures for the investment needed in infrastructure can vary widely and are subject to swings in commodity prices. However, what is commercially viable in terms of this infrastructure is also highly variable. This was highlighted in 2015–16 when many commercial investors mothballed or cancelled infrastructure investment following falls in energy prices. Nonetheless, the GES relies on the development of infrastructure that enables trade in energy. The IEA, in its 2014 Annual Investment Outlook (IEA, 2014b), estimated that the GES needs investment between US$48 to US$53 trillion up to 2035 (IEA, 2014b). This is total investment needed to supply the world's rising energy demand and those measures designed to generate energy efficiency. Of this, US$7 trillion is needed to aid the transmission and distribution of energy, which will be mainly focused on emerging and developing economies, notably Asia. The vast majority of the required investment is focused on domestic facing infrastructure, namely power plants (WEC, 2015a).

Oil Infrastructure

Oil remains the cornerstone of the GES. According to the IEA (2016), 53 per cent of world TPES was sourced from oil in 1973. By 2014, although oil had fallen to around 36 per cent of TPES, it was still the single biggest contributor to primary energy supply. The share of oil is forecast to fall to just over 30 per cent by 2035 as states switch to gas and renewables (BP, 2016b) in search of lower greenhouse gas emissions. Nevertheless, oil consumption is expected to grow by around 1 per cent per year between 2015 and 2035. This trend is driven by two factors. First, oil demand will be buoyed by emerging economies, particularly China and India. Second, although oil has been substituted in many sectors, this substitution has been confined to a few, more niche applications in the transport sector, especially for motor vehicles which, as other end-uses have declined, have become a relatively more important outlet for oil. In the longer term, technological and economic factors may result in greater substitutability in transport applications.

The major oil consuming and producing regions in 2014 are set out in Figures 5.2 and 5.3. Juxtaposition of these two figures highlights the

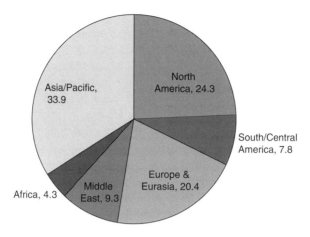

Source: BP (2016b)

Figure 5.2   Global oil consumption by region, 2014

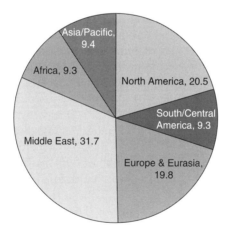

Source: BP (2016b)

Figure 5.3   Global oil production by region, 2014

mismatch in supply and demand alluded to earlier. Notably, the Asia and Pacific region in 2014 accounted for one-third of world oil consumption but produced less than one-tenth of the world's oil, whereas almost exactly the reverse is true of the Middle East. The aggregate figures for Europe and Eurasia imply that oil demand and supply are almost in balance. However, these aggregate figures mask the dominance of oil production in the former Soviet Union and the decline of indigenous oil production in the rest of Europe. This trend has heightened the supply security concerns of European states in recent years. The Americas is the one region where the oil supply–demand mismatch has diminished. This is largely because of developments in the US where oil production increased by over one million barrels a day (mb/d) for three consecutive years between 2012 and 2015, thereby reversing the trend of increasing US energy import dependency and returning the US its former status of a net oil exporter.

In terms of the GES, the role of oil infrastructure is defined as those infrastructures that enable and support the transmission of oil (both crude and refined) across long distances between the producers, refiners (which are usually located near the point of production or consumption) and consumers (Organization of the Petroleum Exporting Countries (OPEC), 2015b). Oil in its crude or newly extracted form needs to be moved to refineries and delivered to points of distribution and consumption. Unlike other hydrocarbons, the majority of oil produced is exported – that is, 60 per cent of all oil produced in 2015. The transmission of this trade is split between maritime and pipeline systems, with 62 per cent travelling by sea and 38 per cent transported through pipelines (IEA, 2015a). A small amount is moved via road/rail but this is largely over shorter distances.

The volume and direction of inter-state movement of oil are affected by a number of factors including the production and quality of crude and non-crude streams; demand levels; product quality specifications; refinery configurations; policy-driven trade barriers or incentives; capacity availability and the economics of transport infrastructure (such as ports, tankers, pipelines and railways); ownership interests; term contracts; price levels/differentials; and geopolitics (Energy Information Administration (EIA), 2014). In terms of interregional movements (set out in Table 5.1), the major origin of oil transmission is the Middle East – the source of 35 per cent of all exports of crude oil which, in this case, is mainly moved through maritime transmission channels. The major transmitters of oil by pipeline are the inter-regional flows within North America and Europe/ Eurasia. In North America, one-third of US, 95 per cent of Canadian and 65 per cent of Mexican oil flows through pipelines. Elsewhere over three-quarters of oil from the former Soviet Union (FSU) utilises pipeline systems (IEA, 2015b).

The international oil port system, of which a small percentage of ports also operate as the focus of refining activities and as regional hubs for the re-export of refined products, lies at the heart of the long distance international transmission of oil and has shaped the configuration of the main maritime oil transportation routes (OPEC, 2015a, 2015b). There are currently 113 oil ports (that is, ports across the world that have the physical,

Table 5.1   Oil trade movements, 2015

Imports		Exports	
State/region	Per cent	State/region	Per cent
US	16.3	US	7.2
Europe	22.2	Canada	6.2
Japan	7.6	Mexico	2.3
Rest of World	53.9	South & Central America	6.9
		Europe	4.0
		Former Soviet Union	15.7
		Middle East	34.8
		North Africa	3.1
		West Africa	7.8
		Asia-Pacific	11.0
		Rest of the World	0.8
World	100	World	100

Source: BP (2016a).

deep-water characteristics and capability to handle large tanker traffic) and the spread of these ports follows the pattern of international oil trade (Global Energy Observatory (GEO), 2015b). Clear regional/national hubs, such as Rotterdam in Europe and Qingdao in China, exist within the network. In relation to production, which is more concentrated than consumption, ports tend to be concentrated around the Persian Gulf, with further concentration in the Mediterranean. In terms of numbers, the US, China and Japan have the most oil ports (EIA, 2014).

Although less important than maritime transport in terms of flows, oil pipeline infrastructure is essential to the international transportation of oil. Such pipelines tend to be used for short–medium distance transmission and are the method of choice when overland oil transportation is the only realistic option. In many cases, especially in the Middle East, these pipelines are used as an intermediate transport between the wellhead and the maritime infrastructure. When used for transmission, pipelines are lucrative to operate (especially compared to gas) because they carry a higher energy per unit of volume. The main international pipelines in the oil component of the GES are noted in Table 5.2.

Alongside the oil pipeline and maritime systems, the other key component of oil infrastructure in the GES is the refinery system, which processes crude oil into products for end-use. The biggest producer of refined products is the US which accounts for nearly 20 per cent of total global refining capacity followed by China with about 15 per cent. The leading

Table 5.2   Major cross-border oil pipelines, 2015

Continent	Source	Destination	Number
North America	Canada	United States	5
	United States	Canada	1
Africa	Algeria	Tunisia	2
Asia	Myanmar	India	1
	Kazakhstan	China	1
	Russia	China	1
	Kazakhstan	China	1
	Kazakhstan	Iran	1
	Kazakhstan	Pakistan	1
	Russia	China	1
Middle East	Iraq	Syria	1
	Iraq	Israel	1
	Iraq	Turkey	1
	Iraq	Saudi Arabia	1
	Kuwait	Saudi Arabia	1
Former Soviet Union	Azerbaijan	Georgia	2
	Azerbaijan	Turkey	1
	Azerbaijan	Russia	2
	Belarus	Ukraine	1
	Kazakhstan	Russia	4
	Russia	Azerbaijan	1
	Russia	Kazakhstan	1
	Ukraine	Russia	2
	Uzbekistan	Tajikistan	1
	Ukraine	Czech Republic	1
	Ukraine	Hungary	1
	Ukraine	Poland	1
	Russia	Germany	1
	Russia	Latvia	1
	Russia	Lithuania	1
	Russia	Uzbekistan	1
Europe	Bulgaria	Albania	1
	Croatia	Serbia	1
	Greece	FYROM	1
	Slovakia	Croatia	1
	France	Germany	2
	France	Switzerland	1
	Netherlands	Belgium	1
	Czech Republic	Germany	1
	Italy	Germany	2
	Netherlands	Germany	1
	Italy	Switzerland	1

Table 5.2   (continued)

Continent	Source	Destination	Number
	Norway	United Kingdom	1
Latin America	Bolivia	Argentina	1
	Bolivia	Chile	1

Source: GEO (2015a)

product exporters are Russia, the US and India (IEA, 2015a, 2015b). Nearly half of the total refining capacity lies within the OECD (down from over two-thirds in 1973), with Asia witnessing the biggest rise with rises from 5.8 per cent of global refining capacity in 1973 to nearly a quarter in 2014 (IEA, 2015b). Oil refineries are central to the international system as many refined products are re-exported and refineries frequently operate as multi-state hubs. Although producing regions may favour refining in their territory to potentially gain greater value-added, sector economics (notably the lower transport costs for crude relative to refined oil) suggest that it is often preferable to locate this infrastructure in consuming regions. This preference can be altered by factors such as construction costs which can outweigh benefits from lower transport costs. However, in order to secure supplies of refined products, consumers will often seek to internalise this aspect of the industry value chain.

Gas Infrastructure

Gas is becoming an increasingly important component of the global energy mix and forecast to be on par with oil and coal over the medium to long term (IEA, 2015a). In the ten years to 2014, gas consumption globally increased at 3.4 per cent per annum and by 2015 accounted for nearly a quarter of overall energy consumption (IEA, 2015a). This growing role for gas within the GES has been driven by a combination of factors, including its relative abundance, its environmental advantages compared with other fossil fuels, and also the flexibility and adaptability that make it a valuable component of a gradually decarbonising electricity and energy system (International Gas Union (IGU), 2015). However, these advantages are compromised by the disadvantage that it is costly to transport (relative to energy density) and that its versatility makes it easy to replace (EIA, 2014). Most of the increased demand is from emerging economies (notably China and India and, to a lesser extent, the Middle East) where increasing consumption has been driven by industry. In the OECD, the contribution

Table 5.3   Major gas producing countries, 2014

State	Production (billion cubic metres)	Share
United States	730	20.7
Russian Federation	644	18.3
Islamic Republic of Iran	169	4.8
Canada	162	4.6
Qatar	160	4.5
People's Republic of China	130	3.7
Norway	113	3.2
Turkmenistan	87	2.5
Saudi Arabia	84	2.4
Algeria	80	2.3
Rest of the world	1,165	33.0
World	3,524	100.0

Source: IEA (2015a)

of gas to total energy usage has risen from a fifth to over a quarter – the major driver of this demand is from power generation where it has largely replaced oil and is competing with coal (BP, 2016a). Gas imports as a share of total consumption are expected to rise towards 80 per cent by 2035 in Europe and 50 per cent in China. Meanwhile, the US is expected to become a net exporter of gas (IEA, 2015a).

Table 5.3 sets out the world's main producers of gas, a list which is headed by the US. The world's major gas reserves are concentrated in the Middle East and Europe/Eurasia, which together account for nearly three-quarters of proven reserves (BP, 2016a). Overall 30 per cent of all gas produced is exported – up from virtually zero in the early 1970s. This gas is transported either through pipelines as natural gas or through maritime channels in liquefied natural gas (LNG) carriers. By 2014, the split between the two modes of transport was 66 per cent by pipeline and 34 per cent by LNG carrier (IGU, 2015). It is forecast that by 2035 volumes transported by sea will have overtaken those transported by pipeline (BP, 2016b).

Due to the costs of infrastructure development and transmission, gas trade remains overwhelmingly intra-regional, with only 20 per cent traded beyond the regions where it is sourced (IGU, 2015). However, this pattern is changing with the rapid growth in the market for LNG and also, to some extent, the construction of very long distance gas pipelines. Over a third of international LNG movements comes from Qatar alone, with Malaysia and Australia contributing around 10 per cent each and Nigeria around 8

Table 5.4 International gas trade by region, billion cubic metres

Region	Imports		Exports	
	Pipelines	Liquefied natural gas	Pipelines	Liquefied natural gas
North America	116.9	11.6	116.9	0.4
South and Central America	17.8	21.4	17.8	25.1
Europe and Eurasia	435.7	52.1	435.9	28.1
Middle East	27.2	5.4	29.7	130.9
Africa	8.5	0	34.3	48.5
Asia-Pacific	57.8	242.7	29.5	100.5
Total World	663.9	333.3	663.9	333.3

Source: BP (2016a)

per cent (IEA, 2015a). Table 5.4 highlights the breakdown by type for both imports and exports by region.

The process of natural gas production and transmission is more expensive than for crude oil, requiring longer lead times, higher safety standards and bigger longer term financial commitments (Dieckhöner et al., 2013). Moreover, gas infrastructure transports gas to a specific point rather than to a more general distribution and processing point (IGU, 2015), necessitating long-term contracts for suppliers. The need for continuity of flow also means that gas transmission is more difficult. The recent shift towards gas transport by LNG carrier over long distances illustrates this.

Due to this, pipelines are a more economic option over short distances (that is, less than 2,000 miles). Transmission by gas pipeline is based on contiguous or semi-contiguous territoriality (that is, where transit is possible). The main gas pipelines are indicated in Table 5.5. The major pipeline routes originate in the FSU, which accounts for almost 40 per cent of the volume of pipeline-traded gas, and run between Canada and the US, carrying 10 per cent of all pipeline-traded gas (BP, 2016a). Other major international pipeline gas exporters include Norway, Algeria, Bolivia and Qatar. Europe is the main recipient of pipeline transmitted gas, with it representing nearly 55 per cent of all pipeline-based gas transmissions (BP, 2015).

Although gas pipelines will continue to remain important, especially over connectable land masses, LNG shipments (IGU, 2015) are becoming a major mode of inter-continental natural gas trade. In 2014, total LNG trade was 241.1 million tonnes (the second largest ever, peaking in the aftermath of the Fukushima crisis) (IGU, 2015). Such movements also utilise stranded resources and facilitate the supply of isolated markets.

Table 5.5 International gas pipelines

Continent	Source	Destination	Number
North America	Canada	United States	10
	United States	Canada	2
	Mexico	United States	1
Africa	Algeria	Italy	2
	Algeria	Morocco	1
	Algeria	Spain	1
	Algeria	Tunisia	1
	Egypt	Jordan	1
	Libya	Italy	1
	Libya	Tunisia	1
	Morocco	Spain	1
	Nigeria	Algeria	1
	Ghana	Cote d'Ivoire	1
	Nigeria	Ghana	1
Asia	Indonesia	Singapore	1
	Malaysia	Philippines	1
	Malaysia	Singapore	1
	Myanmar	China	1
	Myanmar	Thailand	2
	Thailand	Malaysia	1
	Afghanistan	Uzbekistan	1
	Bangladesh	India	1
	Russia	China	1
	Turkmenistan	Pakistan	1
Oceania	Papua New Guinea	Australia	1
Middle East	Iran	India	1
	Iraq	Kuwait	1
	Jordan	Syria	1
	Qatar	Oman	1
	Saudi Arabia	Bahrain	1
	Saudi Arabia	Lebanon	1
Former Soviet	Azerbaijan	Kazakhstan	1
Union	Azerbaijan	Turkey	2
	Azerbaijan	Russia	1
	Belarus	Poland	1
	Belarus	Russia	1
	Kazakhstan	Turkmenistan	1
	Russia	Estonia	1
	Russia	Hungary	1
	Russia	Germany	1
	Russia	Latvia	1

Table 5.5 (continued)

Continent	Source	Destination	Number
	Russia	Turkey	1
	Russia	Ukraine	6
	Tajikistan	Russia	1
	Turkmenistan	Turkey	1
	Turkmenistan	Uzbekistan	1
	Ukraine	Germany	2
	Uzbekistan	Kazakhstan	1
	Uzbekistan	Russia	1
Europe	Bulgaria	Turkey	1
	Bulgaria	Ukraine	1
	Croatia	Slovenia	1
	Hungary	Ukraine	1
	Italy	Greece	1
	Italy	Slovenia	1
	Italy	Bosnia	1
	Serbia	Hungary	1
	Turkey	Austria	1
	Turkey	Greece	2
	France	Spain	1
	Netherlands	France	3
	Netherlands	United Kingdom	1
	United Kingdom	Belgium	2
	Lithuania	Latvia	1
	Austria	Germany	1
	Czech Republic	Germany	1
	Germany	Denmark	2
	Netherlands	Germany	1
	Netherlands	Italy	2
	Norway	Germany	1
	Austria	Italy	1
	Denmark	Sweden	1
	Norway	United Kingdom	2
	Spain	Portugal	1
	United Kingdom	Ireland	1
South/Central	Argentina	Brazil	2
America	Argentina	Chile	4
	Argentina	Uruguay	1
	Barbados	Martinique	1
	Bolivia	Argentina	1
	Bolivia	Brazil	3
	Brazil	Argentina	1

Table 5.5   (continued)

Continent	Source	Destination	Number
South/Central America	Chile	Argentina	1
	Martinique	Guadeloupe	1
	Peru	Chile	1
	Venezuela	Brazil	1
	Trinidad and Tobago	Barbados	1

Source: GEO (2015b)

LNG trade involves the liquefaction of the gas at its point of departure to reduce its volume and the regasification of the product at the destination port. This enhances trade flexibility for both gas exporters and importers rather than a reliance solely on pipelines which fix routes between the importer and exporter. When LNG trade is possible, exporters can send their product to any location with a gasification plant and, conversely, importers can receive their gas from any location with a liquefaction plant. The trend towards increased LNG trade has necessitated large infrastructure investment in terms of liquefaction and gasification plants, LNG tankers and receiving and storage terminals (see later). In addition, some investment has taken place in floating liquefaction platforms, currently largely peripheral but growing in importance with 16 active terminals in 11 countries – floating LNG (FLNG) capacity is around 10 per cent of normal liquefaction capacity (IGU, 2015).

The number of states with LNG import facilities has expanded significantly. Between 2008 and 2013 11 states became LNG importers for the first time. By 2015, 33 states had LNG import terminals: this expansion is attributable, in part, to state efforts to improve energy security (IEA, 2015a) and changes in the economics of LNG. This expansion has diversified the geographic spread of LNG importing countries, but Asia remains the dominant LNG importer, possessing about half of global LNG import capacity. In 2015 Japan and South Korea were the two largest importers of LNG, together constituting over half the total market for LNG and meeting their entire gas demand from LNG imports. Other states tend to use LNG to balance regional supply and demand, as in Europe, or to meet demand where gas comprises a relatively small proportion of total demand as is the case in Taiwan, Puerto Rico, Dominican Republic and Chile. The expansion in the number of gas receiving terminals in the five years to 2015 was also mainly driven by Asian markets, but new terminals have also come online in Brazil, Indonesia, Lithuania, Jordan, Egypt, Pakistan and Poland, while Chile, Kuwait, Singapore, and again Brazil have finalised expansions at existing LNG import facilities. The total number of active regasification terminals at the end of 2014 reached 101 (IGU, 2015). This number is expected to increase to at least 120 by 2020. Capacity at the 20 largest LNG storage terminals accounts for 41 per cent of the world's total with 14 of these terminals located in South Korea and Japan. Overall, the IEA (2015a) forecasts that international trade in LNG will expand by over 46 per cent between 2015 and 2040 (EIA, 2014).

Nearly two-thirds of the world's LNG production capacity is held in just five countries: Qatar, Indonesia, Australia, Malaysia and Nigeria. Qatar alone holds 26 per cent of the total. Overall, just 19 states possess infrastructure for the export of LNG. Much of the growth in exports trade has been and will continue to be driven by Australia, which in 2015 was in the process of undertaking substantial investment in its LNG exporting facilities to increase its exporting capacity by over 50 per cent by 2020. Increase in capacity is also evident in the US and Canada. Furthermore, Africa is anticipated to become more involved in LNG exporting. Much of this increased LNG export capacity will serve growing gas demand in Asia.

A key trend since 2011 has been the re-export of LNG, especially from Europe where weak gas demand has encouraged shipping LNG to more lucrative end markets in Latin America and the Asia-Pacific region. Spain is by far the largest re-exporter – all its regasification terminals are equipped with re-export infrastructure and, of the world's 19 re-export terminals in nine states, six of them are in Spain (IGU, 2015).

Coal Infrastructure

Between 1971 and 2013, the share of coal in total global primary energy consumption remained steady at around a third, falling by only two percentage points over the period. However, aggregate figures mask major regional shifts in coal consumption. Notably, coal's share of primary energy consumption in the OECD has fallen from nearly 11 per cent in 1971 to less than 4 per cent in 2014, whereas coal consumption and production has risen sharply in China and, to a lesser extent, in other parts of Asia. This upturn in Chinese production has been especially marked since 1990 and really took off after 2005, highlighting how growth within this region has been fuelled by coal consumption. By 2014, China accounted for nearly half of total global production of coal compared to 13.6 per cent in 1973 (IEA, 2015b). Over the same period, the OECD's share of global coal production fell from nearly 56 per cent to just over 25 per cent.

BP (2016b) estimates that coal's share of TPES is expected to fall to around 25 per cent by 2035. For many developed and emerging economies coal has constituted the main source of indigenous fuel. However, because

Table 5.6   International trade in coal

Exports		Imports	
State	Million tonnes	State	Million tonnes
Indonesia	409	China	286
Australia	375	India	238
Russia	130	Japan	188
Colombia	80	South Korea	131
United States	78	Taiwan	67
South Africa	75	Germany	56
Kazakhstan	29	United Kingdom	40
Canada	27	Turkey	30
Mongolia	19	Malaysia	23
North Korea	15	Thailand	21
Others	18	Others	215

Source: VBIK (2015)

of shifts in the composition of economic growth, the rise of alternative fuels and also environmental factors many states are seeking to reduce their consumption of coal – the most polluting hydrocarbon – and to diversify their sources of energy supply (Schernikau, 2010). For many states, however, coal remains a bedrock of national energy systems and in 2014 remained responsible for generating over 41 per cent of world electricity (up from 38.3 per cent in 1971) (IEA, 2015b). China dominates coal-fired power generation, accounting for as much as 43 per cent of the global total, with output that is nearly two-and-half times greater than the world's second highest producer of electricity generated by coal – the US.

When compared to oil and gas, international trade in coal is relatively small – in 2014, only 18 per cent of hard coal production was internationally traded (IEA, 2015a). This relatively low level of international trade in coal is explained by the inevitably high transportation costs of such a relatively bulky material. Indeed, logistics costs account for 80–90 per cent of the delivered price of coal (EIA, 2016). Nonetheless, a relatively open market for coal exists in which the US operates as a large swing supplier (Schernikau, 2010). The vast majority of this trade is seaborne where coal is sold into the export market normally at the load port or delivered to a destination port. Thus much of the infrastructure to support the global trade in coal is maritime (Verein der Kohlenimporteure (VBIK), 2015). The rise in the coal trade was driven by the aftermath of the 1973 oil crisis as states sought alternative sources of fuel. Overall, of the nearly 20 per cent of coal produced that is internationally traded, over 90 per cent is traded

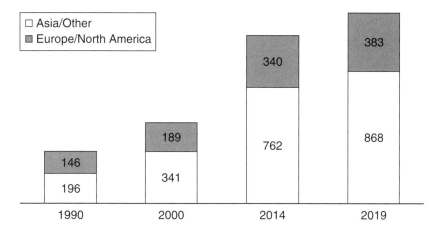

Source: VBIK (2015)

Figure 5.4   Seaborne hard coal trade by importing region (millions of tonnes of coal equivalent, mtce)

through maritime transmission channels. As of 2014, coal comprised 14 per cent of the total maritime transport flows (IEA, 2015a). Figures 5.4 and 5.5 demonstrate both the main sources of coal imports (between 1990 and 2019) and the dominance of maritime transmission of these imports.

A big change within the international coal trade over the past decade has been the emergence of China as a major coal importer where the main driver of imports is coal for heat generation (Schernikau, 2010). China's share of global shipments of coal was around 20 per cent which was up from 2 per cent in 2005 (IEA, 2015b). However, the Chinese demand for coal imports is falling as industrial production slows and as efforts to protect domestic coal sources begin to take effect. In 2012 only around 17 per cent of coal was traded, with the market dominated by a few players.

However, it is evident (see Table 5.6) that the main focus of international coal trade is in Asia and much less on the erstwhile dominant European market. Indeed, China has become the major influence on international coal prices. However, Europe is gaining share of global consumption because the price of coal fell and price of oil rose in the 2011/12 period: this trend has not been radically altered by the 'oil drop' after 2014 when the global market for coal was flooded by cheap US exports. The rising demand for coal by China has fuelled much infrastructure development to facilitate the movement of coal into this market. However, many high quality mines with low cost resources have been depleted, with the result that exporters have to move to locations that are dislocated from main

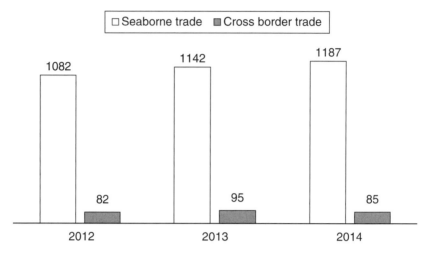

Source: VBIK (2015)

Figure 5.5 *World hard coal trade (millions of tonnes of coal equivalent, mtce)*

export terminals. This problem has been especially acute for Australia where coal exports have been hit by a shortage of rail and port capacity.

The great unknown is how China manages the transition away from coal and the impact that this has on the coal system. Since 2011, it has been a net coal importer. On its own, China now represents a quarter of all the market for imported coal, reflecting not merely its rising demand for energy but also of the inadequacies of internal transport that led to users in the south-eastern coastal regions importing coal rather than sourcing internally (Cornot-Gandolphe, 2014). However, it is evident that China has spent vast amounts on the internal transport system, with improvements in the transmission of coal a major driver in this process. This improved allocation within the state suggests that the need for external facing infrastructure will be more limited, although the Chinese government is still keen for high quality coals to be imported.

The main infrastructure supporting the international transmission and distribution of coal is an international port system. As of 2015, there were nearly 200 major coal terminals dedicated to the import and/or export of coal. Nearly 90 per cent of these coal ports are located within just eight states (mainly focused on the Asia-Pacific region), with nearly three-quarters focused just on five states. Table 5.7 indicates the geographic spread of these ports and covers both current and proposed terminals as

Table 5.7 Geographic spread of coal port infrastructure in the global energy system

State	Number of coal ports	Import/Export
Indonesia	41	All export focused
India	35	All import focused
United States	33	19 export focused; 5 import focused; 2 cover both exports and imports and 8 are domestic only
China	25	All import focused
Australia	21	All export focused
Germany	13	All import focused
Columbia	12	11 export focused; 1 import focused
Canada	7	6 export focused; 1 import focused.

Source: www.sourcewatch.org/index.php/Coal_terminals, accessed 5 March 2016

of December 2015. Although not all the ports report capacity, it is evident that the largest capacities exist around China and Australia. Indonesia and India may have the largest number of ports, but the largest ports lie in China (the Port of Qinhuangdao is the single largest coal port) and Australia (which has three of the top five ports by capacity). Alongside this dominance by the large players within the global coal market, there is a significant tail of smaller coal ports across the globe. Nonetheless the key theme in this port infrastructure is the pursuit of scale to help militate against the high logistics costs endured by the international trade of this commodity (VBIK, 2015).

THE STATE AND ENERGY SECURITY

Ultimately state engagement with the GES is driven by the need to obtain secure supplies of energy where indigenous production is unable to meet its energy requirements (Hall, 1992). Winzer (2012, p. 36) offers a rather conventional definition based on 'the continuity of energy supplies relative to demand'. Such a definition suggests that security is not about a point in time, nor is it a fixed amount of energy supply. However, Barrett et al. (2010, p. 6) claim '. . .security is not determined by supplies alone, but by the immediate balance between supply and demand and the longer term trade-off between more energy security and environmental considerations'. Instead, these authors place an emphasis on the criticality of energy services which underpin territoriality. Kruyt et al. (2009)

state that energy security is based on four dimensions, namely accessibility, availability, affordability and acceptability. This characterises energy security as a mix of economic, geological, geopolitical and environmental/social factors. In this context energy security only matters insofar as a lack of it undermines services that are core to the operation of the state and to human existence, such as energy supply to domestic and industrial users that enable their sustainability as economic and social agents (Alhajji, 2007; Bradshaw, 2009). This means that security is not simply about quantity of energy available but also the price of access to energy. This latter indicator is important because the price mechanism does not alter user behaviour and price rises alter the social welfare and economic performance of the state (Barrett et al., 2010). Such narratives upon security find direct resonance within the state's infrastructural mandate whereby energy security directly impacts upon social cohesion, economic integration, state control and development (Kalicki and Goldwyn, 2013). As such, energy security is about the enablement of the state and its needs as a rational actor to assert and maintain its power within a given space through the sustenance of energy flows at stable prices within a territory (LaCasse and Plourde, 1995).

Framed in these terms, direct parallels between security of supply and realism (Dannreuther, 2010) exist based on two themes. The first is that states are motivated by access to and the control of natural resources of which energy is regarded as the most important and critical to state power and interest (Chester, 2010). Second, competition for resources is intense and the state is in competition for these resources – a theme fuelled by theories related to peak oil, resource wars and resource curse. Thus, the intense competition for material resources to fuel growth increases the potential for conflict between states (Klare, 2001). This realism is based on the presumption that security of supply through the GES is second best to indigenous supplies.

The GES is subject to human and natural processes, and events – both isolated and continuous – can undermine the state's infrastructural mandate with the associated political, economic and social risks that emerge from this failure (Bohi and Toman, 1996; Müller-Kraenner, 2008). Expressed in these terms, energy security reflects a desire to reduce state vulnerability by securing low risk supplies and developing secure transmission, distribution, storage and processing infrastructure (Cherp and Jewell, 2011). In the terms adopted by Barrett et al. (2010), based on a framework developed by Stirling (2009), states require a national energy system that is stable, durable, resilient and robust (see also Hughes, 2009). This suggests that energy security (expressed in terms of the territorial state) is a function of the ability to control or influence events that impact upon the performance and efficacy of the national energy system (NES) both internally and externally to the state.

According to Yergin (2005), those states that are in energy deficit need to base their energy security strategy upon diversifying sources of supply to give them enough inbuilt resilience to resist instability. This approach point recognises that states have a vested interest in the creation and preservation of a stable market for energy. According to Yergin (2005), states have come to recognise that security of energy supply is a global public good which needs to operate in the interests of all states and all parts of the global energy system. Yergin (2011) draws this conclusion from analysis of the global oil system (energy security is often seen through the lens of oil due to its tradability and the imbalances between supply and demand) and places an increased prominence on international organisations as a counter-balance towards anarchy in the system (Verrastro and Ladislaw, 2007). The fear is that the state-based self-interest in the acquisition of energy sows the seeds for conflict. However, evidence by Cohen et al. (2011) suggests a mixed picture for the diversification of energy, with gas supplies exhibiting more diversity than oil (Pascual and Elkind, 2010).

***

The key infrastructures within the GES are those where there is the greatest intensity and volume of international flows. Consequently, when examining the forces for integration and fragmentation within the GES, the focus is mainly upon gas and oil infrastructures where the processes of international interaction tend to be strongest and where the greatest impact upon the state's infrastructural mandate is felt.

FORCES FOR INTEGRATION WITHIN THE GES

As with other physical infrastructures such as transport and telecommunications, the main forces for integration within the GES lie within its soft infrastructure component. As argued earlier, the drivers of integration within the GES are ultimately based on the spatial variation between the supply/reserves of fuels and their consumption, especially where the demand for energy outstrips the availability of domestic resources. The list for the forces for integration within the GES outlined next is by no means definitive but it does highlight the main factors securing and preserving flows of energy around the global system.

Hegemonic Power

Within realist literature, there has been considerable debate on the role of the hegemon, notably with regard to its stabilising force within the international system (Gilpin, 1987; Agnew, 2005). Through operating extra-territorially in its own interests, the hegemon can create – via its sustenance of system stability – mutual benefits for all states. This stabilising force is tantamount to an international public good (Kindleberger, 1986; Haggard and Simmons, 1987). A strong hegemonic presence has been almost a permanent feature of the GES throughout its evolution (Yergin, 2005). Throughout the 20th and into the twenty-first century, hegemons (especially the US, but more latterly China) have been central to the creation, sustenance and stabilisation of the international energy system (Stokes and Raphael, 2010). As noted by Yergin (2005), this was initially linked to geopolitics and the geo-economics of western oil company international expansion in the formative years of the GES. Over time, and with the rise of resource nationalism and increased state ownership/control of reserves, this role has been increasingly encompassed, ensuring that the main transit routes between the points of extraction to the point of consumption remain uninterrupted and free from state or non-state intervention. Although hegemon action has often been limited to the global commons or communal transit points, the history of the GES has demonstrated that hegemons are also capable of direct territorial incursions to enable the efficacy of the GES (Yergin, 2005, 2011).

Klare (2008) has noted how this pro-activism in securing energy flows has extended beyond global hegemons to regional powers (such as China and India) on the pretext of accessing the necessary materials to generate welfare gains for their citizens through economic growth and development. This underlines not just the collective interest in sustaining energy flows into and throughout the GES but also that states increasingly use a combination of hard and soft power in the competition for these resources (Nye, 2004; Podobnik, 2006). There have been (and continue to be) numerous examples of powerful states utilising hard power extra-territorially (mainly within global commons but with third party territorial support) to ensure that core international channels remain open to ensure energy flows for their own (but also, by implication, other states') benefit. Until relatively recently, the literature was dominated by discussions on the source for energy as a global zero sum game in which global powers were drawn into increasingly adversarial relationships in their desire to secure the necessary resources. This was fuelled in no small part by the 'peak oil' thesis (Klare, 2001, 2008).

However, the fear created by the peak oil thesis has proved unwarranted through a combination of technological innovation and the rise of unconventional sources of oil and gas. These trends are altering state behaviour with a shift in the pro-activism required by specific states. This has its most evident expression in the case of the US, which is predicted to become a net exporter of energy in the coming decades. This rise in US domestic energy production is coupled with the identification of extensive reserves within contiguous states (such as Canada and Mexico), as well as in relatively benign zones (such as Brazil) of the global economy such that the degree of hard power needed to be exercised by this hegemon will diminish. This applies not just to the US; other powers will also seek to diversify supply to more benign suppliers. For example, China has been establishing more international transmission infrastructure with the states of the FSU and other territorially contiguous states (Leung, 2011). This perhaps suggests that soft power starts to increase in salience as states seek to generate the necessary energy flows.

The logic of the exercise of hegemonic power in the late 20th/early 21st centuries has been shaped by the political instability of those segments of the global economic system (most notably the Middle East and North Africa) which have operated as the world's major suppliers of energy for much of the post-war era. It is a moot point, as noted by Kandiyoti (2012), as to whether these states are unstable due to oil or whether the existence of large hydrocarbon reserves exacerbates existing in-built friction. Whatever the reason, it is evident that the global and regional powers have had to exercise large amounts of hard and soft power to sustain energy flows over the past five decades. In terms of hard power, much of this has been utilised to preserve free flow of oil through the main maritime bottlenecks around the Arabian Peninsula, notably the Strait of Hormuz through which 80 per cent of maritime-based oil flows on its way to Asian and western markets. However, to some degree, shifting dynamics within the GES (notably the rise of China as a major energy consumer) have created new bottlenecks that are more state-specific, such as China's much discussed Malacca dilemma. Thus, despite increased US energy self-sufficiency, the GES (and its sustained integration) is likely to remain a key focal point of action for powerful states. This will not only be through keeping the broad transmission channels of the system open but also through the ability of such states to shape broader issues in the GES, such as the advancement of renewables, climate change strategies and energy security strategies.

International Infrastructure

The capability of international infrastructures to operate as forces for integration is dependent upon the geopolitical/geo-economic context in which they are developed and operated. International pipelines are the most evident exhibit for the process of international energy integration. They reflect the spatial disparities between supply and demand for gas, oil and other fuels. Pipelines are a function of the need for some states to export and for others to import fuels. Transnational pipelines are the most tangible evidence of a transnational system by enabling the transmission and distribution of energy between states. The logic of geo-economics is that states have incentives to engage in the supply of energy through pipelines and also to operate as points of transit within the system. The building of pipeline systems and the supply of energy is a means by which states can exercise power beyond their economic and political weight within the global system. In short, the maintenance of the security of energy flow has become a powerful weapon for states within geo-economics and geopolitics. This is especially true for states that would otherwise be peripheral to the international system. It is the supply of oil from the Middle East that renders this region such a salient concern for the global economy.

The number of pipelines across the GES is increasing because oil and gas have to be transported further distances as demand grows; localised reserves are exhausted; new sources are further away from the location of demand and because some of these new suppliers or suppliers facing new geopolitical considerations, such as the Caspian Region, are landlocked. In short, ever more extensive pipelines systems across and between contiguous and non-contiguous states are an adaptive response to the political economy of oil and gas, as well as to the decreasing proximity between places of consumption and usage. This construction of new pipelines has also been driven by adaption of states to shifting geopolitics; by the vulnerabilities of states to infrastructural bottlenecks within the global system and by the need for the international system to exhibit sufficient capacity to cope with supply disruptions. These pipelines also reflect the energy strategies of consuming states in terms of their energy mix and energy security. This process has been assisted by technological advances that directly facilitate the deployment of pipelines in less hospitable environments, such as in deep-lying maritime locations.

Although pipelines are still being developed in Europe, it is Asia, notably Turkey, China and India, that is the focus of many of the ongoing developments in this area of international infrastructure. In each of these cases, the trend towards more pipelines reflects a shift in energy priorities as domestic energy strategy moves towards reducing urban air pollution – a trend which has resulted in a sustained rise in the demand for gas as states have shifted towards gas-powered power generation and a need for more transnational gas pipelines. China, for example, is seeking to extend and expand the number of pipelines feeding into its territory as a means of security through diversity – on this basis, a pipeline from Siberia is planned to expand supplies into China. In the process, a reorientation of its export supply routes eastwards will give Russia reduced dependency on European markets. Although less proactive than China in the development of international pipeline infrastructure, India is also exploring the possibility of the construction of gas pipelines from Turkmenistan, Iran and Russia. Elsewhere in Asia, Japan is also the focus of new transnational pipeline infrastructure as it seeks to shift its energy strategy away from nuclear power.

International Governance

Although state primacy within the GES, as manifested by the notion of energy security for example, seems to offer little scope or need for strong international governance systems, it cannot detach the needs of national energy systems from the complex forces operating within the GES (Florini and Sovacool, 2009). The notion that the GES is governed by market forces is, to a large extent, illusory – energy is so central to state power and stability that all governments to a greater or lesser degree intervene within the national energy system. These interventions are at all ends of the energy value chain from production and transit through to consumption, and are largely intended to militate against market failures within the energy system. Alongside these state-based actions are a series of inter-governmental international organisations (including international institutions, global summits, public–private partnerships and multilateral development banks) whose functions are to coordinate the actions and strategies of all players within the GES to facilitate system stability (Florini and Sovacool, 2009; Goldthau and Witte, 2009, 2010). The core argument of many of the advocates of a more integrated and coherent international governance system for energy is that this system is a global public good exhibiting a host of public goods problems such as externalities, market failures, coordination problems and competing interests (Karlsson-Vinkhuyzen et al., 2012). As such, local governance is only effective within the context of the global system, especially in relation to issues such as energy supply security, energy poverty and environmental externalities (Van de Graaf, 2013). Moreover, cooperation also arises from the desire to prevent bilateralism emerging as states that are net energy importers create a series of exclusive agreements to secure their own needs at the expense of others (Florini and Sovacool, 2011).

At the forefront of the strategy to stabilise the GES is the IEA – a club of oil consumers, consisting of the leading 29 industrialised states (that is, the members of the OECD). It is widely accepted as the most influential international government organisation in the GES and was formed as a counterbalance to the instability created by the 1973 oil crisis to create stable market conditions and security of demand and supply for its member states, with the explicit aims of securing oil 'on reasonable and equitable terms' and of creating a system to manage oil supply emergencies. The influence of the IEA is based on the absence of a single powerful global energy organisation – without some degree of coordination, the system could descend into chaos. The IEA is the only major international body with the capability to engage and analyse energy policy in its totality, covering diverse issues such as environmental, supply, and security themes. Although it is often portrayed as a consumer-led body, the IEA also includes some oil producers but, unlike OPEC (see later), the IEA is more committed to open energy markets.

The cornerstone of the IEA is the stockpiling system, which obliges members to keep a minimum number of days' consumption of oil and gas in reserve in case of supply disruption. These stocks are drawn on in times of market instability (Van de Graaf, 2012). Through this mechanism, the IEA has helped to coordinate responses amongst consuming nations to a series of shocks and disruptions in global oil markets, including the 1990–91 Gulf War; preparations for the wrongly anticipated Y2K disruptions at the millennium; the aftermath of the 2001 attack on the World Trade Centre in New York and the Iraq War. Throughout the existence of the IEA, the strategic petroleum reserves of its members have helped deter market manipulation, despite the non-compulsory nature of the IEA's recommendations and the fact that four energy exporting members have no restocking obligations. Moreover, only 21 of the IEA's members have gas emergency stockpiles.

The IEA also provides data to states to allow more effective energy planning at the national level. This demonstrates the effectiveness of the mandate of the IEA and that the organisation has moved beyond the issue of energy security to tackle other important issues of interest to the sustenance of the GES, namely environmental protection and economic development (Van de Graaf and Lesage, 2009; Lesage and Van de Graaf, 2016). It also shows that the IEA has been adaptable to shifting contexts, even though there is a strong case that this adaptability is incomplete. The IEA's emergent adaptability has been apparent in its response to the increased multi-polarity of the GES which has seen it has engage more with non-IEA members. However, its ability to manage a stable GES when an increasing share of energy consumption and production is taking place outside its members remains questionable. In these circumstances, it is likely that the IEA will evolve further and place greater emphasis on developing a common soft infrastructure that enables states to gain know-how in areas such as access to clean energy research and technology, especially in areas such as renewable technology, energy efficiency and cleaner fuel technology.

The Energy Charter Treaty (ECT) also seeks to promote stability within the GES by creating harmonious conditions of foreign direct investment (FDI) across the energy sector and for non-discrimination in the trade and transit of energy materials. The Treaty also provides mechanisms for the resolution of inter-state disputes and for the promotion of energy efficiency and seeks to explore methods to lower the harmful effects of energy usage. The development of the ECT was particularly intended to provide continuity of supply and investment against the backdrop of the dissolution of the Soviet Union, which could have introduced new risks and instability into the GES. The focus is mainly on central and Eastern Europe but the principles contained in the Treaty have created interest elsewhere within the GES, notably within the Asia-Pacific region. The ECT is seen as especially valuable in creating the benchmark for transit systems (especially for the states of the FSU), notably in creating – via inter-governmental agreement – security of transit. As such, the ECT recognised that an effective international pipeline system requires the necessary supporting political, technical, financial and legal environment. These rules – which mirror the rules of transit under the United Nations Convention on the Law of the Sea (UNCLOS) – are explicitly covered in Article Seven of the ECT. To support this process, the ECT aims to facilitate investment in national infrastructure to sustain transit systems.

Though the ECT was enabled by the 2008 G8 Energy Ministerial Meeting, Russia was unwilling to allow transit that would effectively allow non-Russian companies to buy gas in Central Asia and ship it to Europe, by-passing the existing arrangements whereby Russia operated as the intermediary. In Russian eyes, this would allow its pipeline system to move beyond its control. Thus, although Russia was perceived by the architects of the ECT as potentially the most important signatory of the ECT, Russia's abstention from ratification of the Treaty has undermined its effectiveness.

The rise of the IEA (as a consumers organisation) was a direct response to the power that OPEC states had over the supply of oil and their ability and desire to use (where necessary) the supply of oil as a geopolitical and geo-economic weapon. However, over time the latter has come to dominate the former as OPEC's power over the supply of oil into the GES has diminished (Lesage and Van de Graaf, 2016). In 1976, OPEC's crude oil share of total world oil production was nearly 60 per cent (BP, 2016a). By 2015, it had fallen to just over 30 per cent as new oil reserves came on-stream. Despite this, OPEC states continued to account for over

80 per cent of global proven crude oil reserves (OPEC, 2015a). OPEC's objective is to stabilise oil markets for the producers of oil and to create market stability. In terms of the infrastructure needs of the GES, this stabilising role is needed to bring forth the high levels of capital expenditure required to establish the necessary export infrastructure. Indeed, one of the major casualties of the sharp fall in oil prices during 2014–16 was capital expenditure by major oil companies (OPEC, 2015a). Although this did not impede system integration, the shortfall will have an impact on system capacity, resilience and redundancy. However, the attempts of leading OPEC members to stabilise conditions within global oil markets have met with limited success.

Liberalisation

The liberalisation of energy markets at regional and state levels is linked to shifting governance requirements and has increased the logic behind integration of the global energy system. Intuitively, the push towards liberalisation encourages access to cheaper fuels than would be available domestically, thereby creating international markets for energy and an associated requirement for enhanced cross-border governance of this trade. Part of the logic of NES liberalisation is that it enhances access to the capabilities of international energy companies in areas such as access to risk capital, technical expertise, diverse asset portfolios and the ability to build relationships with customers worldwide through their refining and marketing activities and strong brands that transcend national boundaries. In short, by allowing greater market access to energy MNCs, energy liberalisation is a powerful force for GES integration. In some senses, the formalisation of liberalisation domestically and the creation of the capability of domestic suppliers to obtain the cheapest energy supplies embeds the longstanding globalisation of energy systems. It also implies that the operation and stability of the market is an effective guarantor of security of supply. This has been persistently called into question.

As the international trade in energy was historically concentrated, cartelised and/or controlled by a few major energy companies, the rules of the global trading systems (first under the General Agreement on Tariffs and Trade (GATT) and more latterly the WTO) did not deal with the specifics of energy as it was felt that the broad rules of state trading, for example, were adequate (Malumfashi et al., 2009). However, as more energy exporting states joined the WTO and as others imported ever larger quantities of energy, so the salience of these rules grew. Given its particular physical characteristics that influence the means of storage, transportation and distribution, energy has many unique features. These are compounded by the resilience of many state monopolies (despite the liberalisation trend) and particular pricing methodologies that lead many to contend the basic rules of the WTO are not really appropriate for energy because the WTO rules are concerned with import barriers. However, there are few import barriers to energy as most states seek to increase imports not exclude them. Indeed, the main trade barriers are derived from the export side where export duties, for example, have been used as revenue increasing devices. However, WTO rules do not address supply monopolies or cartels, or such issues as the pipeline transit rules that have derailed Russia's ratification of the ECT.

In practice, much of the focus on liberalisation is not on primary energy supply but on production further down the industry value chain, such as electricity generation and supply. As such, the impact on primary market integration is less direct and is mainly a product of competition between electricity providers looking to source from low cost foreign suppliers (Pollitt, 2012). The impact on infrastructure is more indirect as operators seek to build up import/export infrastructure as a means of adapting to this process of change. One of the most evident examples is the long-term switch by the UK from domestically produced coal (seen as expensive) towards imported coal. Indeed, between 1953 and 2012 coal imports rose from 3 million to 39 million tonnes, with the largest increase coming during 1983–92 when there was large-scale closure of UK coal mining capability (IEA, 2015a). This a process mirrored across many high cost coal producers such as Spain, Germany and Poland (BP, 2016a). Such strategies only work when there is relatively political and economic stability between trading states (such as within Europe) and across transit states to minimise potential disruption. In short, there has to be confidence that rising imports do not endanger security of supply. This suggests that states might look to diversify as well as liberalise supply.

Security through Diversity

The lasting legacy of the use of energy as a geopolitical weapon by both OPEC and non-OPEC oil suppliers has been two-fold (Lesbirel, 2004). First, there have been sustained attempts to increase the indigenous supply of energy through innovation and efficiency (Bielecki, 2002). Second, there have been efforts to deepen and broaden the GES by encouraging new sources of overseas supply. This is not a novel strategy and has been followed by leading industrialised states since imported oil became a dominant fuel within their respective energy mixes (Yergin, 2005). Such oil diversification strategies are not simply a matter of entering and re-entering the market to obtain energy at reasonable prices with minimal

Table 5.8 Drivers of oil import diversification

Country specific	Systemic
<ul><li>Oil dependence ratio</li><li>Total oil imports</li><li>Changing oil imports</li><li>Middle East oil import ratio</li><li>Non-regional oil import ratio</li><li>Total oil stocks</li><li>Vulnerability perception</li><li>Past experience</li></ul>	<ul><li>Political, economic, social and security instability in exporting regions</li><li>Supply disruptions</li><li>Non-market strategies</li><li>Exporter concentration</li></ul>

Source: Vivoda (2009a)

risk. Other factors clearly come into play related to the quality of the crude offered, freight costs, the infrastructure of the exporting state and its production capacities (Stringer, 2008). These strategies are often also influenced by inter-state political relationships, the quality of transport infrastructure, the existence of and commitment to policy and the availability of military resources to enforce supply agreements if necessary. Clearly, the more proximate the reliable source, the better it is for states such as the US and Canada with their extensive pipeline systems. There are also issues involving local refining capacity and transmission infrastructure which have long development lead times (Vivoda, 2009a, 2009b). Moreover, as much as states try to reduce risk by diversifying supplies, they are unable to isolate themselves fully states from the broader market risks embedded within energy systems such as those create by unstable prices (Neff, 1997). The main criteria affecting oil diversification strategies are highlighted in Table 5.8.

Within the contemporary GES, China has been a notable follower of a security through diversity strategy. It has not only taken a keen strategic interest in obtaining energy (through pipelines) from Central Asia and Russia, it has also sought oil reserves in Africa, making the accompanying investment in infrastructure required to transport the energy resources into the main global transmission routes. However, the focus on obtaining oil from Africa does not – according to Downs et al. (2000) – reduce China's vulnerability because the cost of transporting it to China means that China will tend to sell the material into the open market or exchange it for Arabian or Asian oil, which is easier to transport to the Chinese market (Taylor, 2006). This, in turn, means that China will remain dependent upon hegemonic protection of the main sea lanes, thereby retaining a degree of supply vulnerability (Downs et al., 2000). However, this is a rather pessimistic assessment and does not reflect China's access to unconventional sources internally or that China, via its string of pearls policy, could be increasingly proactive in diversifying its supply (Downs, 2004).

Security through diversity has also been evident in the international transmission of gas. This has been especially evident in the case of the EU where the increased risk of disruption by Russia of its gas supplies has led several states to advance the development of LNG infrastructure to enable them to access supplies from further afield, including Australia and especially Qatar (Ratner et al., 2013). While the EU relies less on imports of gas than of oil, the share of imports in total gas consumption is expected to increase to 80 per cent (up from 60 per cent in 2015) by 2035 (BP, 2016a). In practice, the EU relies on four main suppliers (Norway, Russia, Algeria and Qatar) for its gas but it has been seeking to increase supplies from two, albeit relatively unstable, states – Nigeria and Libya. This diversification strategy has clearly been driven by the erratic nature of Russia and its ability to exploit gas as a geopolitical weapon. It has also resulted in increased pipeline connections with North Africa and consideration of the exploitation of resources in the Eastern Mediterranean (Bilgin, 2011; European Commission, 2013, 2014). However, the ability to tap into these sources depends on market prices, especially in terms of the extent to which they stimulate new field development. There are concerns that Russia has been trying to thwart these diversification plans (via the state-controlled company Gazprom) by developing its own alternative pipelines into the EU and by attempting to co-opt EU companies into this process by offering these concerns a stake in such, and other, related projects. It has also – according to Ratner et al. (2013) – attempted to use its geopolitical influence in FSU states to dissuade them from taking part in attempts by the EU to diversify supply away the Russia. Part of the EU's strategy is to build better intra-EU infrastructure to allow energy (especially electricity) to flow across its borders.

Cohen et al. (2011) suggest that there is, in fact, little evidence of a concerted shift in sourcing of oil in the decade to 2011. There is anecdotal evidence that diversification is increasing. For example, although the US buys oil and oil products from over 40 states, it has switched to sourcing proportionally more of its oil from contiguous territories and away from long distance supplies, but these flows tend to be low in volume and there is a still a residual dependence on conventional sources of oil. According to Cohen et al. (2011), however, diversification of gas supplies has increased markedly. To these authors, the fact that gas is a growing component of TPES for many developed and developing states points to an increase in energy security. The US has successfully managed to diversify its supply away from the Middle East and now just over 10 per cent comes from the

Middle East. The US has been especially active in developing regional systems involving Canada and Mexico to aid its energy security.

Security through diversity also works through supply side channels. As the competition between those states that rely on energy revenues increases and as buyer power consequently increases, there is increased pressure upon states to access new markets to secure new revenue streams. This has been evident as traditional energy importing states attempt to reduce their imports. This has arguably had its most evident expression in the shift in Russian strategy resulting from changing geopolitics and other market pressures, which has led many European states to seek alternatives to reliance on Russian gas. Thus Gazprom, Russia's monopoly exporter, needs new markets. The result is that Gazprom has turned its attention to Asia. This pivot, especially regarding increasing exports to China, requires new cross-border infrastructure (both pipelines and LNG terminals), notwithstanding the fact that China is also subject to pre-existing and emergent competition and is also seeking to diversify its own supply. To this end, Gazprom is planning to build two pipelines into China (the Power of Siberia and the Altai pipelines). However, there have been major concerns regarding the capability of Gazprom to finance these pipelines and the extent to which China will want to rely upon these networks as part of its diversification strategy.

FORCES OF FRAGMENTATION

Given the history of the GES, it can be argued that the forces for fragmentation are as strong, if not stronger, than the forces for integration. For states, external dependence upon energy supplies represents a key vulnerability. The disruptions to flows caused by infrastructural failure represent a key risk within the system. However, such forces for fragmentation can be both positive and negative for the state of the GES, with some measures being openly discriminatory whilst others seek simple import substitution.

National Energy Strategies

The desire to reduce state dependence upon external energy sources of supply is understandable. For consumer states, there is an inbuilt desire to increase self-sufficiency through development of indigenous supplies (Helm, 2002). Indeed, the GES is a relatively new phenomenon created by rising demand and an inability of indigenous resources to meet this additional demand. The trend amongst the leading industrialised states is to develop active energy strategies in two ways: first, by underscoring the centrality of energy infrastructures to state territoriality through their designation as critical infrastructures and, second, by pushing for domestic preference through greater indigenous energy production. Building up supplies from unconventional and renewable resources to replace exports is a long-term strategy. Nonetheless, greater discretion and lower external dependence is a rational strategy for the state, but full energy autarky will remain elusive for all but a few states (Aribogan and Bılgın, 2008).

For many states, the logic of energy security is low external dependence upon primary energy supplies. However, the argument that energy strategies are natural sources of fragmentation within the GES is countered where security is defined on a transnational basis with intensive exchanges based on benign and productive relations between states. In the EU, for example, energy strategy simultaneously seeks to foster domestic supplies whilst increasing imports from benign suppliers. As such, reliance upon external suppliers does not always represent vulnerability. This is reflected in attempts to generate energy security through national energy systems that generate certainty of flows through a mutually supporting inter-state energy system. This integration boosts internal security through the creation of a common energy system but also acts as a collective counterbalance to the power of big regional suppliers. However, these links have been slow to develop in practice, with the central measure of an internal energy market being especially slow to implement.

In terms of primary energy supply, such strategies have brought about a shift towards a more diverse energy mix (notably with increased emphasis upon indigenous renewable resources), together with complementary demand-side initiatives such as the promotion of greater energy efficiency. Through such methods, the state seeks to generate its own flows and to draw on the international system only when unavoidable. This implies that the evolution of the GES will be shaped by domestic preferences regarding issues such as energy mix. These, in turn, will be shaped by the relative salience of industrial policy themes or through the political salience of domestic environmentalism. In many states, rising wealth and the growing strength of non-governmental organisations (NGOs) have exercised a powerful influence over energy mix. In many developed states, the need for public acceptance of the energy mix is a key factor in energy strategy, notably in matters relating to nuclear power and shale gas development, for example. The shift towards low carbon solutions will encourage development of an energy infrastructural system that is highly localised and will replace the current system where supply is based on scale through the integration and interconnection of energy infrastructure.

The great potential conflict – as a cause of instability within the GES – is between the energy security of consuming nations and the logic of resource nationalism. The critical infrastructure for producing states lies in the export system, but for consuming states its essence is in the ability to secure reliable flows throughout their territory. For this reason, some states seek direct ownership and control of these assets. In both producing and consuming states, there has been growing concern over the control of energy infrastructure by non-domestic entities that may use their assets to assert control over states or utilise assets for their own ends. As such, many states, even within polycentric systems, retain the right to control and expropriate assets should the security of the state be under threat. This has had its most high profile expression in the form of resource national-ism which is based on the idea that property rights over valuable national resource located within a state belong to the state and should be used for its benefit.

In practice, the main motivation for resource nationalism is not energy security per se but the use of natural resources for exports to generate rev-enues to promote wider economic development and growth and is directly linked to the state of the commodity cycle (Stevens, 2008; Bremmer and Johnston, 2009). The aspiration for direct ownership/control of these resources has led some states to violate FDI codes by seeking the direct expropriation of domestic energy companies from overseas ownership. Mabro (2007) argues that resource nationalism reflects an energy strategy that mistrusts foreign ownership where the energy commodity in question is the state's main source of export revenue. This is not confined to devel-oping or emerging states because developed states have also imposed extra taxes or costs upon foreign-owned businesses if they feel that these com-panies are harnessing too much rent or if the state feels it is not getting a large enough share. As such, expropriation may be direct through a change of ownership or indirect through changes in taxes or licencing (Vivoda, 2009a; Click and Weiner, 2010). In this way, energy is treated as a strategic good where the state seeks to use the resource to increase its power, both internally and externally. Resource abundance has allowed some resource-rich countries to embrace the 'rentier state' model of governance in which the state is able to avoid taxation by deriving either all, or most, of their revenue through rents achieved from the cultivation of their natural resources (Mahdavy, 1970).

Much of the current debate within the GES stems from the close links between resource nationalism and state capitalism whereby the focus of state ownership of these resources is on improving the quality and stand-ard of living of its citizens (Joffé et al., 2009; Ward, 2009). However, this only works when demand for and revenue obtained from this resource is rising or, at the very least, stable. Moreover, resource nationalism becomes vulnerable when the state relies on markets that can switch to alternative supplies (Adelman, 2004). This has been typified by Russia which has sought new markets in Asia as the EU has sought new supplies to offset Russia's control over gas delivery systems.

In the 2000s, energy nationalism spread throughout much of the global economy (from Russia through to Latin America) driven, first, by rising prices and, second, by the fact that some states felt that they were not getting a large enough share of the rising revenues (Mares, 2010; Porter, 2012). Rising radicalism in states such as Venezuela also played a part. In practice, oil nationalism had mainly lain dormant – it had just needed the right set of conditions to re-emerge (Mabro, 2007). A backlash against no-liberalism in some quarters also underpinned the rise of resource national-ism. However, the fact that resource nationalism proved resilient in the face of falling energy prices through 2014–16 reinforces the conclusion of Ward (2009) that the resource nationalism is also driven by other, non-price inter-related factors such as climate change, resource scarcity, sustainable development and the alleviation of energy poverty.

Energy Poverty

The World Economic Forum (WEF, 2010) defines energy poverty as 'the lack of access to sustainable modern energy services and products'. Much of the literature on energy poverty has a domestic focus based mainly on the absence of or lack of penetration of electricity networks (which is beyond the scope of this chapter). However, the absence of these 'secondary systems' can also represent a failure of some energy-poor states to be connected to the GES (Sagar, 2005). The literature on energy poverty says very little on the role of the GES as a cause of, or even as a solution to, this problem. Instead, it emphasises the absence of indigenous production without addressing the role that integration into the GES could play in the process of reducing energy poverty. Low levels of GDP and of industriali-sation do not attract the investment needed to supply these markets.

The absence of a mature energy system impacts upon the state infra-structural mandate not only through limiting the scope for economic development but also by limiting social and territorial integration and energy security. However, it is prosperity and development that dominate energy policy narratives: the United Nations Development Programme emphasises that none of the Millennium Development Goals can be met without major improvements in the quality and quantity of energy services in developing countries. Sovacool (2012) estimates that around 2 billion people have low levels of energy usage, with many of them relying on localised rudimentary/traditional primary supplies such as wood and biomass with some corresponding negative effects on the environment.

This problem is compounded in developing states by the high cost of other fuels and energy services and by low primary energy supply and/ or the capability to import and distribute energy throughout their territory. Moreover, where there is an indigenous supply, domestic capital and know-how can often be in short supply, thereby limiting the capability to utilise these resources. This reflects not merely the absence of domestic and external facing infrastructure but also of the necessary soft infrastructure.

Paradoxically, energy poverty is also evident in some locations that are net exporters of energy, especially within the Arab world where energy production is geared for export and non-indigenous consumption (El-Katiri and Fattouh, 2011). Low levels of income, particularly away from urban centres, often reinforce a reliance on traditional fuels and lead to underdevelopment of rural regions. Sagar (2005) claims that the focus of developing states in energy policy is on domestic industry and not on rural areas where energy poverty is most severe or even on those urban areas where energy poverty is also apparent. Four out of five people without a regular energy supply live in rural areas of the developing world, mainly in South Asia (Asian Development Bank (ADB), 2013) and sub-Saharan Africa, which together account for more than 95 per cent of the global total (IEA, 2015b). The pattern of electricity deprivation is set to change, however, because 95 per cent of the increase in population in the next three decades will occur in urban areas (IEA, 2015a). In 2013, more than 2.7 billion people – 38 per cent of the world's population – are estimated to have relied on the traditional use of solid biomass for cooking, typically involving inefficient stoves in poorly ventilated spaces (IEA, 2015a). This is an increase of around 40 million since 2012. In Africa, coal is the main fuel in South Africa. Most other African states are heavily dependent upon bio-energy, despite some of them possessing significant coal reserves. Oil and gas remain largely peripheral in the energy mix of sub-Saharan African states (IEA, 2014b).

Energy resources in sub-Saharan Africa as a whole are more than sufficient to meet regional needs, both now and into the foreseeable future. This abundance of resource holds true across the range of energy resources – remaining recoverable resources of oil are sufficient for around 100 years at current levels of production; coal for more than 400 years and gas for more than 600 years (IEA, 2015b). Sub-Saharan Africa holds around 7 per cent of the world's conventional oil resources and 6 per cent of world gas resources. However, three-quarters of these oil reserves are held in two countries (Nigeria and Angola), with the next largest (South Sudan and Uganda) accounting collectively for only 9 per cent of the total. Gas is also concentrated in Nigeria (two-thirds of all resources in sub-Saharan Africa), with most of the rest in South Africa. Moreover 85 per cent of

African gas and oil is exported to western and eastern markets (IEA, 2014b). Thus, although the region is rich in energy resources, it is poor in supply, comprising less than 4 per cent of global energy demand despite having 13 per cent of global population (IEA, 2014a). This reflects the unevenness with which resources are spread throughout the continent and emphasises the need for a regional energy infrastructure that enables intra-African energy trade. The infrastructure inadequacy is not only about pipelines but about inadequate trans-African road, rail and maritime networks, especially within landlocked states. However, the focus of energy providers on western and Asian markets also means little immediate incentive to develop intra-African systems: a fact compounded by low population densities and poor governance of energy systems (notably through illegal extraction and corruption) through much of sub-Saharan Africa. However, the IEA (2015a) estimates that by 2030 the production in several states, including South Sudan, Niger, Ghana, Uganda and Kenya, will start to fall, resulting in a worsening of the energy deficit. This will become especially problematic as trends such as rising economic growth, urbanisation, industrialisation and an emerging middle-class all point to rising demand for energy within sub-Saharan Africa.

Whilst indigenous production is seen as central to alleviating Africa's energy problems, its infrastructural weaknesses are central to achievement of this goal. In addition to problems mentioned earlier, the absence of refining capacity means that African oil often has to be exported to refineries overseas and re-imported, thereby reinforcing import dependence for oil products such as diesel, kerosene and gasoline which is forecast to reach 75 per cent by 2040, even for Africa's major oil producers (IEA, 2015b). Moreover, many of the importing states, as well as the landlocked neighbouring state, often rely upon a single point of entry with limited capacity to offload imported products and suffer from the absence of inland storage capacity and intra-African pipelines. Lack of infrastructure is not the only problem: the dominant position of state utilities in many states often causes a divergence between state and regional priorities – these countries are mandated to drive security of supply based upon indigenous production.

Energy Transmission Choke Points

Choke points are those locations that impede or restrict energy circulation and which cannot be easily bypassed through any reasonable alternative (that is, one that does not add markedly to financial costs and delays). The absence of alternatives is compounded by one or more of the following: limited physical capacity, high intensity of usage and uncertain governance. For energy, the issue of choke points emerges largely from the maritime transmission system because many of these flows (mainly oil) pass through passages, capes and straits which exhibit these characteristics (Komiss and Huntzinger, 2011). These choke points mainly concern oil transportation – those in the gas sector are not yet significant, although they can be expected to increase in line with increasing LNG exports from the Middle East.

Although there are approximately 200 choke points globally, only a handful are of strategic importance (Mitchell, 2010). Their vulnerability arises from their proximity to nations/regions where navigation risks are increased as a result of political instability and the actions of both state and/or non-state actors (Komiss and Huntzinger, 2011). Ultimately, it is a matter of conjecture as to the salience of these choke points to the GES as their efficacy is dependent upon the energy strategies of states and the extent to which oil production remains concentrated in the Middle East where many of these choke points are located (Mitchell, 2010). The main maritime choke points are identified in Table 5.9. Emmerson and Stevens (2012) extend the concept of choke points beyond these simple narrow transmission channels identified to include key production and processing hubs in potentially vulnerable areas such as Saudi refineries in the Persian Gulf.

The Strait of Hormuz can be regarded as a particular vulnerability, with 88 per cent of all oil from the Persian Gulf (or 20 per cent of global oil production) passing through this channel. Attempts to circumvent this

Table 5.9   The main global maritime oil choke points

Choke point	Mb/d (2013)	Nature of limitation	Nature of threat
1) Strait of Hormuz	17	Narrow channels	Iran/terrorism
2) Strait of Malacca	15.2	Size of ship (300,000 dwt)	
3) Cape of Good Hope	4.9	None	Piracy/terrorism
4) Bab El-Mandab	3.8	None	None
5) Suez Canal	3.2	Size of ship (200,000 dwt)/ convoy size	Piracy/terrorism
6) Danish Straits	3.3	Not defined	Piracy/terrorism
7) Bosphorus	2.9	Ship size (200,000 dwt)/ length	None
8) Panama Canal	0.85	Ship size (65,000 dwt)	Flow restrictions None

Source: Business Insider (2015)

potential block through establishment of overland channels across the Saudi Peninsula have been made but these have limited capacity (at best, less than a third of the capacity of the Strait of Hormuz). This vulnerability is reinforced when LNG is added to the equation. However, there is a consensus that this threat is more imagined than real as effective blocking would be strategically (politically and economically) disastrous for Iran, as well as for other states, and is also not feasible militarily (Luft and Korin, 2004; El-Katiri and Fattouh, 2012).

With increased US self-sufficiency and greater European supply diversity, the focus of state vulnerability on these choke points is shifting to Asia, which imports 50 per cent of its oil from the Middle East. These vulnerabilities differ markedly across Asia – states such as South Korea, India and Japan depend for over 70 per cent of their oil on the Middle East (Koyama, 2004). These issues have been especially evident in China's so-called 'Malacca Dilemma' (although particularly associated with China, the Malacca Dilemma is also a concern for Japan, Korea and other northeast Asian states), where over 80 per cent of Chinese oil imports are channelled through the Strait of Malacca, a body of water that is just 1.5 miles wide at its narrowest point (Ogle, 2010). This narrowness is seen as the prime risk as a terrorist attack could easily block the channel (Shaofeng, 2010). To counter this, China, as the regional hegemon, has started to develop alternative supply channels into its territory through new pipelines from the east through Myanmar and Eurasia (Mitchell, 2010). It has also started to extend its influence over the South China Sea to allow it to control and/or readily deploy military power in this area (Rodrigue, 2004). Furthermore, to militate against the Malacca Dilemma, the Chinese government, through the China Overseas Port Holding Company, has taken over operational control of Gwadar port in Pakistan. This is a deep-sea port which provides an extra route to market for oil export from the Caspian Sea and Central Asia and offers an alternative transit route for China should the Strait of Malacca choke point ever become constricted (Luft and Korin, 2004).

Emmerson and Stevens (2012) suggest a number of options to militate against any instability created by these vulnerabilities, including creating or utilising alternative transit routes, increasing regional stockpiles of energy and developing more effective mechanisms for the exercise of hard and soft power (Nye, 2004). To this end, the UN and the EU embarked upon an anti-piracy initiative off the coast of Somalia as part of a commitment to keep international maritime channels open. Evidence from the International Maritime Organization (IMO, 2014) suggests that Somali-based piracy has declined markedly and that most incidences of piracy now originate from Indonesia and Malaysia (IMO, 2014). The Carter

Doctrine (which states that 'any attempt by an outside force to seek the control of the Persian Gulf region will be regarded as an assault on the vital interests of the United States of America' – President Jimmy Carter in his State of the Union Address, 23 January 1980) has been key to the stability of flows through the Persian Gulf, especially in 1990 and 2003 when conflict was sparked in the region. However, the implementation of this doctrine has come at a substantial economic cost (up to US$1 trillion for the 2003 Gulf War). Increasingly, as the risk to Asia from these choke points grows, so its regional powers have also become more proactive in the policing of these vulnerable locations.

Climate Change

The process of climate change can fragment or disrupt the GES. Extreme climate conditions and weather events which, according to the World Energy Council (2015a), have increased by 400 per cent between 1980 and 2014, can have a serious impact upon key infrastructures. These events damage local infrastructure and run the risk of disrupting international flows with a subsequent legacy for price (WEC, 2015b). This was evident in the gas sector, for example, following Hurricane Katrina and its impact on US gas export infrastructure (Skea et al., 2012). Climatic challenges to facilities are also heightened in places where key parts of the global infrastructure system are below sea level. Indeed, many of the world's largest oil and gas facilities (including Ras Tanura in Saudi Arabia and refineries in Rotterdam) are only slightly above sea level, leaving them vulnerable to events and processes that could disrupt supply on a national, regional and global basis.

Aside from these cascade effects, climate change can also impact on system integration through states' adaptive strategies which steer national systems away from large-scale energy systems towards greater localised production. Whilst commitments to renewables will make only a relatively small percentage contribution to total consumption (for example, the EU 'plans' to generate 20 per cent of energy consumption through renewables by 2020), they do place a descaling pressure on the GES. Moreover, states are exhibiting greater sensitivity to those energy infrastructures that have high environmental impact. The IEA (2015a) has identified the inconsistency of national climate change policies and their potential to generate market disruption, price volatility and stranded investments as a serious hazard for oil and gas companies. This is typified by the case of the transnational XL pipeline between the US and Canada. This inter-state pipeline worked (in narrow economic terms) in the interests of the transit state (the US) and the exporting state (Canada) as well as potential importing states.

However, the pipeline was halted on environmental grounds, demonstrating that increases in pipeline capacity to enhance energy security are but one side of the policy debate and highlighting the challenge for oil and gas companies who are increasingly forced to locate in increasingly remote locations as easy to access resources decreases.

Cyclical Factors

Much energy infrastructure is privately owned and investments in system capacity are based on investor expectation as to the price of the commodity transported. Due to its high capital demands and issues of market instability, the supply side of the energy sector is slow to respond to price movements. Energy projects operate with long-lead times with an incentive to keep producing irrespective of price movements. The infrastructural component of the GES is exposed to price volatility, highlighted by the sharp drop in oil prices between 2014 and 2016. The inbuilt strategy of operators in such periods of price instability is to sweat existing operations, cut costs and defer spending on new projects, especially those that are not close to completion.

Cutting back infrastructure spend was a common response to lower oil prices by non-OPEC producers which undertook large cuts in upstream oil and gas capital expenditure. For example, multiple upstream projects were postponed in Canada once oil prices started falling. This took a sustained period of time to feed through into supply due to the long lead times for new investment. This has also applied to LNG projects, many of which were small, speculative and simply uneconomic with falling prices. Australian producers cancelled a number of large projects (for example, Shell and its Arrow LNG project). Moreover, floating LNG facilities were also hit with both Woodside and BHP Billiton cancelling big projects. Cancellations have also occurred to Russian and Canadian LNG projects. In the oil sector, large refinery projects were cancelled in Brazil, the Middle East and Russia. Overcapacity remained an issue in Europe where many refiners reduced their capacity (for example, Total, the French oil major, shut a major refinery in April 2015). In Asia, refining capacity is also either being mothballed or shut (IEA, 2015a).

Geopolitical Issues

The intertwining of energy and geopolitics is a well-established theme in academic and practitioner literature. As mentioned earlier, hegemonic power has been a pivotal factor, both negatively and positively, not merely in preserving flows but also – in a number of instances – in determining the source of flows (Yergin, 2011). A notable example throughout the 1990s was US attempts to change Iran's behaviour by limiting the latter's access to the GES and by applying pressure on importing and transit states to limit transnational flows (Stevens, 1998). This highlights how hegemonic power can be a source of fragmentation as well as of integration within the GES. The most significant geopolitical infrastructure link to the GES has been to the international pipeline system, especially where it crosses multiple territories. For Kandiyoti (2012), this geopolitical risk lies in both the construction and the operation of these systems. Pipelines are only as good as their ability to sustain flows through these systems. However, experience has shown that these systems are prone to interruption as a result of transit disputes or of disputes between buyers and sellers (Stevens, 2000).

The issue of GES fragmentation often arises from transit systems where there is no overarching governance system, thereby enabling a sovereign state to ignore any agreements should it wish. Conflicts emerge as states' interests diverge or if one party feels they are at a disadvantage. This situation has worsened as demand for these transit systems has increased and as the space over which they extend has grown increasingly fragmented, especially in the aftermath of the dissolution of the Soviet Union and, to a lesser extent, following the break-up of Sudan. Transit problems have also arisen where the politics of the transit state have changed and are more hostile to the transit terms or to the logic of the transit route. This has occurred in the Middle East, as demonstrated most markedly by the Iran–Iraq conflict and the interdependence of transit systems between these two states (Barry, 2013). Stevens (2009) suggests that the stability of a transit system depends upon the security of the pipelines; the value of transit fees to states; importance of FDI to transit states; the dependence of the transit state on the 'off take' from the pipelines; the availability of suitable alternative routes and competition between producing and consuming states for markets (Parra, 2004). Transit problems can be magnified by broader ongoing problems between neighbouring states.

Arguably, the greatest geopolitical pipeline challenges and risks have their origin in the fragmentation of the integrated Soviet system resulting from the dissolution of the Soviet Union and the emergence of newly independent states which laid claim to those segments of the old Soviet pipeline system located in their territory. The net effect was to fragment the underlying soft infrastructure of the old Soviet system even though the physical integration of the system remained intact. The claims made by states over their segments of the old Soviet system led to increased disputes over transit fees and fuel prices, increased interference in the transmission of energy and, as Kandiyoiti (2012) claims, even outright political blackmail.

At the core of these disputes have often been attempts by Russia – as the regional hegemon – to reintegrate the old Soviet infrastructure system, thereby making the ex-Soviet republics dependent upon Russia through exploiting their dependence on the Russian transit system and drawing them into its sphere of influence. For Azerbaijan, the main oil/gas producing ex-Soviet republic, this has been a constant problem which it has sought to resolve through the development of alternative pipeline systems (Henderson and Mitrova, 2015).

Russia's geopolitical strategy also has a consumer-facing component as Russia is seeking to lock importing (mainly European) states into the Russian system, thereby limiting the EU strategy of securing security through diversity (see later) (Baran, 2007). However, if this was the strategy, then it has had limited success with the EU pushing harder for diversity and with Russia having to seek new markets (Christie, 2007). For example, a combination of EU insistence that major pipelines transiting its territory should be subject to its rules for open energy markets which, among other things, requires separation of production and sales from transmission networks, and EU sanctions on Russia following its annexation of Crimea resulted in December 2014 in Russia's cancellation of the South Stream gas pipeline project. South Stream had been intended to bypass Ukrainian territory, an advantage in Russia's eyes as flows through this transit state had a history of disruption. Stern et al. (2015) argue that the cancellation of South Stream demonstrates the EU's proactive strategy to achieve security through diversity and to avoid integrating into the Russian system any further.

This systemic geopolitical instability also increased as a direct legacy of the 2011 Arab Spring which, according to BP (2016b), caused oil supply to fluctuate by as much as 3 mb/d. In 2014, it was estimated that such supply disruptions were well above the long-term historical average of around 400,000 b/d. The historical peak of over 4 mb/d in 1991 was a direct result of the instability created by Iraq's invasion of Kuwait, as well as by the collapse of the Soviet Union. Much of the disruption created by the Arab Spring was driven by disruption to Libyan oil production. This experience has highlighted how oil exporting states are vulnerable to localised infrastructure attacks by non-state groups, which destabilise the state where such infrastructures are central to state power and its revenue earning capabilities. Such strategies have been widely deployed by insurgents throughout the Middle East and North Africa (Anderson and Browne, 2011). These events have elicited a response from major importers whereby they seek to use the instability created by the Arab Spring to develop new energy strategies that not only further diversify supply but also spur the development and establishment of new sources of indigenous oil production. Moreover, other suppliers have used this instability as an opportunity to increase routes to major export markets.

Fragmented Governance Structures

Whilst there has been progress in the development of international governance to generate stability in the GES, its capability to do so remains limited by the non-compulsory nature of these measures – a function of the fact that the GES is an amalgam of state-based systems that interact through transnational flows of energy. According to Goldthau and Sovacool (2012), the ability to create an effective international system is hindered not only by the plethora of international and national organisations with a direct interest in the operation of the GES, but also by the lack of cooperation between them (Florini, 2008). To them, the GES needs an overarching agency to oversee the multi-player mandates that form, shape and prevent the effective operation of the GES. For the IEA, stronger international governance is important to shape soft infrastructure in states where such supporting systems are underdeveloped. According to the IEA (2015a), there is a strong link between effective governance and the state of the national energy system. Stable governance is seen as a direct stimulus for inward investment in national energy systems. Indeed, comparison of the share of investment in GDP with a composite indicator for standards of governance in different sub-Saharan countries demonstrates a clear relationship in many countries between low levels of capital formation and weak governance (IEA, 2015b).

However, Dubash and Florini (2011) claim that the IEA, the main international energy focused agency, has simply not adapted to the changing structure and form of the GES. The IEA as the primary energy-centric body does not equate to a WTO-like body and has limited scope in terms of geography and issues. The most evident emerging problem is that the IEA cannot effectively act as a legitimate agent for energy users when it excludes new high energy intensive users such as China and India (Verleger, 1987; Florini and Sovacool, 2009, 2011; Nordhaus, 2009). Debates within the GES have also moved on, with governance needing to reflect the interconnections between energy security, climate change and energy poverty (Cherp and Jewell, 2011). Heubaum and Biermann (2015) claim that the mission of the IEA has been slowly evolving in response to the new pressures within the GES, arguing that this is not a top-down process but has emerged as a result of its pursuing of an energy-centric mandate (Van de Graaf, 2012).

The inclusion of large non-IEA consumers (especially in Asia) is needed not only to offer a holistic stabilising influence over the GES but also to recognise that the IEA's shifting mandate on climate change requires that all large consumers need to be involved in the process of shifting the energy mix to meet the needs of this evolving system (Van de Graaf, 2013). An expansion of membership should increase its effectiveness as a stabilising force within the GES (Baccini et al., 2013). Whilst the IEA is working towards closer cooperation with many of the BRIC (Brazil, Russia, India, China) states, the process remains incomplete, especially as the IEA Treaty formally limits membership to OECD states, and the unanimity to alter this does not exist. Moreover, it is far from certain that many of the large consuming states currently outside of the IEA would actually want to join. Whilst China has been working with the IEA in a number of areas, it does not regard membership of the organisation as either necessary or sufficient to bringing the state into the global energy governance system.

The IEA has also had a rather adversarial relationship with OPEC, although this has improved with dialogue under the International Energy Forum. Nonetheless, there is a profound difference between OPEC and IEA states, with the former committed to production quotas and the latter committed to open energy markets and with an aversion to cartelised systems (both nationally and internationally). However, the long-lasting legacy of the 2014–15 oil falls and the rise of unconventional oil may alter this fragmented relationship as both sides share is a desire to avoid market instability. To this end, these bodies have formed agreements in areas such as investment, transparency, regulation of financial markets, better data (through the Joint Oil Data Initiative), and shared market analysis, technology and energy efficiency.

CONCLUSION

The GES – like transport and telecommunication sectors – is formed from the interaction between separate state-based energy systems (which are at vastly different levels of maturity) to secure adequate supplies of energy to protect a state's infrastructural mandate. As such, at the core of the GES is the desire by states to secure and sustain flows of energy through the inter-action of national energy systems. Dependence upon the GES can create state vulnerability arising from energy insecurity and is something many developed states are seeking to reduce as they seek greater indigenous production. Thus, the GES is a contingent system based on spatial dis-parity of energy demand and supply and is something rational states will seek to rely upon less. Despite these forces for integration within the GES, the forces for fragmentation are also strong. The forces for fragmentation are both consumer and producer led, with the pattern of GES shaped by state desire to increase indigenous production but also by the exclusion of large segments of the global population from this system. These are compounded by the fact that energy remains a hot-bed of geopolitical and geo-economic strategy by producing states – something that may over the longer term undermine the efficacy of the system.

REFERENCES

Adelman, M.A. (2004) 'The real oil problem', *Regulation*, *27*(1), 16–21.
Agnew, J.A. (2005) *Hegemony: the new shape of global power*. Philadelphia, PA: Temple University Press.
Alhajji, A.F. (2007) 'What is energy security? Definitions and concepts', *Middle East Economic Survey*, *50*(45), (5 November).
Anderson, D.M. and Browne, A.J. (2011) 'The politics of oil in eastern Africa', *Journal of Eastern African Studies*, *5*(2), 369–410.
Ariboğan, Ü. and Bılgın, M. (2008) 'New energy order politics neopolitics: from geopolitics to energeopolitics', *Uluslararasi Iliskiler*, *5*(20), 109–32.
Asian Development Bank (ADB) (2013) *Asian Development Outlook*. Manila: Asian Development Bank.
Baccini, L., Lenzi, V. and Thurner, P. (2013) 'Global energy governance: trade, infrastructure, and the diffusion of international organizations', *International Interactions*, *39*(2), 192–216.
Baran, Z. (2007) 'EU energy security: time to end Russian leverage', *Washington Quarterly*, *30*(4), 131–44.
Barrett, M., Bradshaw, M., Froggatt, A., Mitchell, C., Parag, Y., Stirling, A. and Winzer, C. (2010) *Energy Security in a Multi-Polar World*. Energy Security in a Multipolar World, Working Paper, accessed 24 February 2016 at www.ex.ac.uk
Barry, A. (2013) *Material Politics: Disputes along the Pipeline*. Chichester, UK: John Wiley.
Bielecki, J. (2002) 'Energy security: is the wolf at the door?', *The Quarterly Review of Economics and Finance*, *42*(2), 235–50.
Bilgin, M. (2011) 'Scenarios on European energy security: outcomes of natural gas strategy in 2020', *Futures*, *43*, 1082–90.
Bohi, D.R. and Toman, M.A. (1996) *The Economics of Energy Security*. Dordrecht: Kluwer Academic Publishers.
BP (2016a) *Energy Outlook to 2015*, accessed 3 March 2016 at www.bp.com
BP (2016b) *Statistical Review of World Energy*, accessed 5 March 2016 at www. bp.com
Bradshaw, M.J. (2009) 'The geopolitics of global energy security', *Geography Compass*, *3*(5), 1920–37.
Bremmer, I. and Johnston, R. (2009) 'The rise and fall of resource nationalism', *Survival*, *51*(2), 149–58.
Business Insider (2015) *These Eight Narrow Chokepoints Are Critical To the World's Oil Trade*, accessed 6 May 2016 at http://uk.businessinsider.com/worlds-eight-oil-chokepoints-2015-4
Cherp, A. and Jewell, J. (2011) 'The three perspectives on energy security:

intellectual history, disciplinary roots and the potential for integration', *Current Opinion in Environmental Sustainability*, *3*(4), 202–12.

Chester, L. (2010) 'Conceptualising energy security and making explicit its polysemic nature', *Energy Policy*, *38*(2), 887–95.

Christie, E. (2007) *Oil and Gas Dependence of Eu-15 Countries*. wiiw Research Report No. 343, Vienna: Vienna Institute for International Economic Studies.

Click, R.W. and Weiner, R.J. (2010) 'Resource nationalism meets the market: political risk and the value of petroleum reserves', *Journal of International Business Studies*, *41*(5), 783–803.

Cohen, G., Joutz, F. and Loungani, P. (2011) 'Measuring energy security: trends in the diversification of oil and natural gas supplies', *Energy Policy*, *39*(9), 4860–69.

Cornot-Gandolph4, S. (2014) 'China's coal market: can Beijing tame "King Coal"?', OIES Paper CL 1, Oxford: Oxford Institute for Energy Studies.

Dannreuther, R. (2010) 'International relations theories: energy, minerals and conflict', *Polinares*, *8*, 1–24.

Dieckhöner, C., Lochner, S. and Lindenberger, D. (2013) 'European natural gas infrastructure: the impact of market developments on gas flows and physical market integration', *Applied Energy*, *102*, 994–1003.

Downs, E.S. (2004) 'The Chinese energy security debate', *China Quarterly*, *177*, 21–41.

Downs, E.S., Mesic, R., Charles Jr., T., Bowie, C.J., Buchan, G. and Levaux, H.P. (2000) *China's Quest for Energy Security*. Santa Monica, CA: Rand Corporation.

Dubash, N.K. and Florini, A. (2011) 'Mapping global energy governance', *Global Policy*, 2 (Supplement 1), 6–18.

El-Katiri, L. and Fattouh, B. (2011) *Energy Poverty in the Arab World: The Case of Yemen*. Oxford: Oxford Institute for Energy Studies.

El-Katiri, L. and Fattouh, B. (2012) *On Oil Embargos and the Myth of the Iranian Oil Weapon*. Oxford Energy Comment, Oxford: Oxford Institute for Energy Studies.

Emmerson, C. and Stevens, P. (2012) *Maritime Choke Points and the Global Energy System: Charting a Way Forward*. Briefing Paper EERG BP 2012/01, London: Chatham House.

Energy Information Administration (EIA) (2014) *Global Natural Gas Markets Overview: A Report Prepared by Leidos, Inc.*, August 2014, EIA Working Paper Series, accessed 5 April 2016 at www.eia.gov

Energy Information Administration (EIA) (2016) *International Energy Outlook*, May 2016, accessed 26 March 2016 at www.eia.gov

European Commission (2013) *EU Energy, Transport and GHG Emissions Trends to 2050 – Reference Scenario*. Luxembourg: Publications Office of the European Union.

European Commission (2014) *Communication from the Commission to the European Parliament, the Council, the European Economic and Social Committee and the Committee of the Regions. A Policy Framework for Climate and Energy in the Period from 2020 to 2030*, Com(2014) 15 final.

Florini, A. (2008) *Global Governance and Energy*. Working Paper 1. Singapore: Centre on Asia and Globalisation, National University of Singapore.

Florini, A. and Sovacool, B.K. (2009) 'Who governs energy? The challenges facing global energy Governance', *Energy Policy*, *37*(12), 5239–48.

Florini, A. and Sovacool, B.K. (2011) 'Bridging the gaps in global energy governance', *Global Governance: A Review of Multilateralism and International Organizations*, *17*(1), 57–74.

G8 (2014) *Global Energy Security (G8 St Petersburg Summit)*, Official Communique, accessed 25 March 2016 at www.ioc.u-tokyo.ac.jp/~worldjpn/documents/texts/summit/20060716.O1E.html

Gilpin, R. (1987) *The Political Economy of International Relations*. Princeton, NJ: Princeton University Press.

Global Energy Observatory (GEO) (2015a) *Current List of Oil Pipelines*, accessed 22 March 2016 at http://globalenergyobservatory.org/

Global Energy Observatory (GEO) (2015b) *Current List of Gas Pipelines*, accessed 22 March 2016 at http://globalenergyobservatory.org/

Goldthau, A. and Sovacool, B.K. (2012) 'The uniqueness of the energy security, justice, and governance problem', *Energy Policy*, *41*, 232–40.

Goldthau, A. and Witte, J.M. (2009) 'Back to the future or forward to the past? Strengthening markets and rules for effective global energy governance', *International Affairs*, *85*(2), 373–90.

Goldthau, A. and Witte, J.M. (2010) *Global Energy Governance: The New Rules of the Game*. Washington, DC: Brookings Institution Press.

Hafele, W. and Sassin, W. (1977) 'The global energy system', *Annual Review of Energy*, *2*(1), 1–30.

Haggard, S. and Simmons, B.A. (1987) 'Theories of international regimes', *International Organization*, *41*(3), 491–517.

Hall, D.C. (1992) 'Oil and national security', *Energy Policy*, *20*(11), 1089–96.

Helm, D. (2002) 'Energy policy: security of supply, sustainability and competition', *Energy Policy*, *30*(3), 173–84.

Henderson, J. and Mitrova, T. (2015) *The Political and Commercial Dynamics of Russia's Gas Export Strategy*, OIES Paper NG 102. Oxford: Oxford Institute for Energy Studies.

Heubaum, H. and Biermann, F. (2015) 'Integrating global energy and climate governance: the changing role of the International Energy Agency', *Energy Policy*, *87*, 229–39.

Hughes, L. (2009) 'The four R's of energy security', *Energy Policy*, *37*(6), 2459–61.

International Energy Agency (IEA) (2014a) *Africa Energy Outlook: A Focus on Energy Projects in Sub-Saharan Africa*. World Energy Outlook Special Report, Paris: IEA.

International Energy Agency (IEA) (2014b) *World Energy Investment Outlook (Special Report)*. Paris: IEA/OECD.

International Energy Agency (IEA) (2015a) *World Energy Outlook 2015*. Paris: IEA.

International Energy Agency (IEA) (2015b) *Key World Energy Statistics*. Paris: IEA/OECD.

International Energy Agency (IEA) (2016) *World Energy Outlook*, accessed 6 June 2016 at www.oea.org

International Gas Union (IGU) (2015) *LNG Report*, accessed 26 March 2016 at www.igu.org

International Maritime Organization (IMO) (2010) *Annual Piracy Report 2014*, accessed 23 March 2016 at www.imo.org

Joffé, G., Stevens, P., George, T., Lux, J. and Searle, C. (2009) 'Expropriation of oil and gas investments: historical, legal and economic perspectives in a new age of resource nationalism', *Journal of World Energy Law and Business*, *2*(1), 3–23.

Kalicki, J.H. and Goldwyn, D.L. (eds.) (2013) *Energy and Security: Strategies for a World in Transition.* Baltimore, MD: John Hopkins University Press.

Kandiyoti, R. (2012) *Pipelines: Flowing Oil and Crude Politics.* London: IB Tauris.

Karlsson-Vinkhuyzen, S.I., Jollands, N. and Staudt, L. (2012) 'Global governance for sustainable energy: the contribution of a global public goods approach', *Ecological Economics, 83,* 11–18.

Kindleberger, C.P. (1986) 'International public goods without international government', *The American Economic Review, 76*(1), 1–13.

Klare, M. (2001) *Resource Wars: The New Landscape of Global Conflict.* New York, NY: Henry Holt & Co.

Klare, M. (2008) *Rising Powers, Shrinking Planet: The New Geopolitics of Energy.* New York, NY: Metropolitan Books.

Komiss, W. and Huntzinger, L. (2011) *The Economic Implications of Disruptions to maritime Oil Chokepoints.* Arlington, VA: Center for Naval Analysis.

Koyama, K. (2004) 'Energy policies in Asia', in Lynch, M. (ed.), *Risk and Uncertainty in the Changing Global Energy Market: Implications for the Gulf.* Abu Dhabi: Emirates Centre for Strategic Studies and Research, pp. 77–108.

Kruyt, B., van Vuuren, D.P., De Vries, H.J.M. and Groenenberg, H. (2009) 'Indicators for energy security', *Energy Policy, 37*(6), 2166–81.

LaCasse, C. and Plourde, A. (1995) 'On the renewal of concern for the security of oil supply', *The Energy Journal,* 1–23.

Lesage, D. and Van de Graaf, T. (2016) *Global Energy Governance in a Multipolar World.* Abingdon, UK: Routledge.

Lesbirel, S.H. (2004) 'Diversification and energy security risks: the Japanese case', *Japanese Journal of Political Science, 5*(01), 1–22.

Leung, G.C. (2011) 'China's energy security: perception and reality', *Energy Policy, 39*(3), 1330–7.

Luft, G. and Korin, A. (2004) 'Terrorism goes to sea', *Foreign Affairs, 83*(6), 61–71.

Mabro, R. (2007) *Oil Nationalism, the Oil Industry and Energy Security Concerns.* Madrid: Real Instituto Elcano.

Mahdavy, H. (1970) 'The pattern and problems of economic development in rentier states: the case of Iran', in Cook, M.A. (ed.), *Studies in the Economic History of the Middle East,* Oxford: Oxford University Press, pp. 428–67.

Malumfashi, G., Matteotti-Berkutova, S., Nartova, O., De Sepibus, J. and Bigdeli, S.Z. (2009) *Energy in WTO Law and Policy.* Helsinki: National Centre for Competence in Research and World Trade Institute.

Mares, D.R. (2010) *Resource Nationalism and Energy Security in Latin America: Implication for Global Oil Supplies.* Houston, TX: James A. Baker III Institute for Public Policy, Rice University.

Mitchell, J.V. (2010) *More for Asia: Rebalancing World Oil and Gas.* London: Chatham House.

Müller-Kraenner, S. (2008) *Energy Security: Re-Measuring the World.* London: Earthscan.

Neff, T.L. (1997) *Improving Energy Security in Pacific Asia: Diversification and Risk Reduction for Fossil and nuclear Fuels.* Project commissioned by the Pacific Asia Regional Energy Security (PARES) Massachusetts Institute of Technology, Center for International Studies.

Nordhaus, W.D. (2009) 'The economics of an integrated world oil market'. Keynote address, International Energy Workshop, Venice, Italy, 17–19 June.

Nye, J.S. (2004) *Soft Power: The Means to Success in World Politics*. New York, NY: Public Affairs.

Ogle, K. (2010) 'The geopolitics of Chinese energy security', *Journal of Military and Strategic Studies*, *12*(3), 183–213.

Organization of the Petroleum Exporting Countries (OPEC) (2015a) *World Oil Outlook*, accessed 25 March 2016 at www.opec.org

Organization of the Petroleum Exporting Countries (OPEC) (2015b) *World Oil Report*, accessed 25 March 2016 at www.opec.org

Parra, F. (2004) *Oil Politics: A Modern History of Petroleum*. London: IB Taurus.

Pascual, C. and Elkind, J. (eds.) (2010) *Energy Security: Economics, Politics, Strategies, and Implications*. Washington, DC: Brookings Institution Press.

Podobnik, B. (2006) *Global Energy Shifts*. New Delhi: The Energy and Resources Institute (TERI).

Pollitt, M.G. (2012) *The Role of Policy in Energy Transitions: Lessons from the Energy Liberalisation Era*. Cambridge Working Paper in Economics 1216, accessed 5 April 2016 at www.eprg.group.cam.ac.uk/

Porter, G. (2012) *The New Resource Regionalism in North Africa and the Sahara*. Paris: Sciences Po Centre de Recherches Internationales.

Ratner, M., Belkin, P., Nichol, J. and Woehrel, S. (2013) *Europe's Energy Security: Options and Challenges to Natural Gas Supply Diversification*. Congressional Research Services, accessed 15 March 2016 at www.crs.gov

Rodrigue, J.P. (2004) 'Straits, passages and chokepoints: a maritime geostrategy of petroleum distribution', *Cahiers de géographie du Québec*, *48*(135), 357–74.

Sagar, A.D. (2005) 'Alleviating energy poverty for the world's poor', *Energy Policy*, *33*(11), 1367–72.

Schernikau, L. (2010) *Economics of the International Coal Trade: The Renaissance of Steam Coal*. Amsterdam: Springer.

Shaofeng, C. (2010) 'China's self-extrication from the "Malacca Dilemma" and implications', *International Journal of China Studies*, *1*(1), 1–24.

Skea, J., Chaudry, M. and Wang, X. (2012) 'The role of gas infrastructure in promoting UK energy security', *Energy Policy*, *43*, 202–13.

Sovacool, B.K. (2012) 'The political economy of energy poverty: a review of key challenges', *Energy for Sustainable Development*, *16*(3), 272–82.

Stern, J., Pirani, S. and Yafimava, K. (2015) *Does the Cancellation of South Stream Signal a Fundamental Reorientation of Russian Gas Export Policy*, Oxford Energy Comment. Oxford: Oxford Institute for Energy Studies.

Stevens, P. (1998) 'A history of transit pipelines in the Middle East: lessons for the future', in Blake, G.H., Pratt, M.A. and Schofield, C.H. (eds.), *Boundaries and Energy: Problems and Prospects*. Leiden, The Netherlands: Kluwer Law International.

Stevens, P. (2000) 'Pipelines or pipe dreams? Lessons from the history of Arab transit pipelines', *The Middle East Journal*, 224–41.

Stevens, P. (2008) 'National oil companies and international oil companies in the Middle East: under the shadow of government and the resource nationalism cycle', *The Journal of World Energy Law and Business*, *1*(1), 5–30.

Stevens, P. (2009) *Transit Troubles: Pipelines as a Source of Conflict*. London: Chatham House.

Stirling, A. (2009) 'What is security? Some key concepts'. Presentation to Sussex Energy Group seminar on *UK Energy Security: What Do We Know, and What Should Be Done?* London, January 2009.

Stokes, D. and Raphael, S. (2010) *Global Energy Security and American Hegemony.* Baltimore, MD: John Hopkins University Press.

Stringer, K.D. (2008) 'Energy security: applying a portfolio approach', *Baltic Security and Defence Review*, *10*, 121–42.

Taylor, I. (2006) 'China's oil diplomacy in Africa', *International Affairs*, *82*(5), 937–59.

Van de Graaf, T. (2012) 'Obsolete or resurgent? The International Energy Agency in a changing global landscape', *Energy Policy*, *48*, 233–41.

Van de Graaf, T. (2013) *The Politics and Institutions of Global Energy Governance.* Basingstoke, UK: Palgrave Macmillan.

Van de Graaf, T. and Lesage, D. (2009) 'The International Energy Agency after 35 years: reform needs and institutional adaptability', *Review of International Organizations*, *4*(3), 293–317.

Verein der Kohlenimporteure (VBIK) (2015) *Annual Report 2015*, accessed 25 March 2016 at http://english.kohlenimporteure.de/news/annual-report-2015.html

Verleger, P.K. (1987) 'The evolution of oil as a commodity', in Gordon, R.L., Jacoby, H.D. and Zimmerman, M.B. (eds.), *Energy: Markets and Regulation.* Cambridge, MA: MIT Press, pp. 161–86.

Verrastro, F. and Ladislaw, S. (2007) 'Providing energy security in an interdependent world', *Washington Quarterly, 30*(4), 95–104.

Vivoda, V. (2009a) 'Diversification of oil import sources and energy security: a key strategy or an elusive objective?', *Energy Policy*, *37*(11), 4615–23.

Vivoda, V. (2009b) 'Resource nationalism, bargaining and international oil companies: challenges and change in the new millennium', *New Political Economy*, *14*(4), 517–34.

Ward, H. (2009) 'Resource nationalism and sustainable development: a primer and key issues', Working Paper 2, International Institute for Environmental Development.

Winzer, C. (2012) 'Conceptualizing energy security', *Energy Policy*, *46*, 36–48.

World Economic Forum (WEF) (2010) *Energy Poverty Action*, accessed 3 April 2016 at www.wef.org

World Energy Council (WEC) (2015a) *World Energy Issues Monitor.* London: World Energy Council.

World Energy Council (WEC) (2015b) *The Road to Resilience − Managing and Financing Extreme Weather Risks.* London: World Energy Council.

World Trade Organization (WTO) (2015) *International Statistical Review 2015*, accessed 4 March 2016 at www.wto.org

World Trade Organization (WTO) (2016) *World Trade Statistical Review 2016*, accessed 4 March 2016 at www.wto.org

Yergin, D. (2005) 'Energy security and markets', in Goldwyn, D. and Kalicki, J. (eds.), *Energy and Security: Toward a New Foreign Policy Strategy.* Baltimore, MD: John Hopkins University Press, pp. 51–64.

Yergin, D. (2011) *The Quest: Energy, Security, and the Remaking of the Modern World.* London: Penguin.

6. Reflections on the Global Infrastructure System

The embeddedness of infrastructures deep within socio-economic systems can undermine fuller analysis within the framework of international political economy (IPE). Moreover, debates on globalisation tend to focus on international flows and their impact upon the sovereignty of the state and its ability to express territoriality within its demarcated space (see, for example, Held et al., 1999). This volume attempts to add to this literature by assessing the dependence of these global flows (and the power structures embedded within such cross-border movements) upon spatially fixed assets, namely what is termed here the 'national infrastructure system' (NIS). Such a conceptual treatment is justified by the growing focus within practitioner and academic communities that infrastructures are subject to functionally and spatially complex processes, such that not only do single pieces of infrastructure have other infrastructure embedded within them, but that this infrastructure is frequently physically dislocated to the extent that it can be located in another state's territory or within the global commons (for example, Rinaldi et al., 2001). This concluding chapter brings together the themes addressed within this volume to facilitate a more holistic understanding of the processes shaping the global infrastructure system (GIS).

THE NATURE OF THE INFRASTRUCTURE SYSTEM

At its core, infrastructure is central to the operational dimension of the territorial state. Perhaps because there is a large degree of consensus about this amongst academics and practitioners, infrastructure (as an enabler of territoriality) has not attracted significant interest within the IPE community. This relative paucity of research may also reflect two other factors: first, the deep embeddedness of infrastructures within territorial systems means they are only noticed when they fail; and, second, infrastructure itself has become increasingly amorphous (Star and Bowker, 2006; Neumann, 2006). This latter point has been evidenced by the recognition that a state's infrastructure can be considered and treated as a complex system. Such complexity recognises that no single piece of infrastructure stands apart from others to the extent that the ability of a piece of infrastructure to act as infrastructure depends upon the infrastructure embedded within it (Howe et al., 2016). This complexity manifests itself in many ways (for example, Rinaldi et al., 2001). However, this volume addresses the spatial complexity of infrastructure systems under the pressure of the adaptive tensions created by the rising intensity of global flows.

Expressed within the terms of state territoriality and its place within the international system, the notion of infrastructure changes again where the idea of territorial infrastructuring is considered a strategic act by the territorial power (Mann, 1984; Taylor, 1996). In short, infrastructuring is the strategic act of turning a bordered space into territory over which the state can assert sovereignty via the creation of a NIS, which comprises the totality of interconnected networked infrastructure within the demarcated borders of the state but which is embedded within and interacts with other NIS (Brenner, 1999). This has led to a burgeoning literature on critical infrastructure (especially within the context of increasingly polycentric NIS) where criticality (that is, the centrality of specific infrastructures to state territoriality) legitimises and rationalises state infrastructuring (that is, the state's direct investment and involvement in the NIS). The logic of market failure, which is still embedded within much of the literature, suggests that without this infrastructuring function the NIS would be underdeveloped and challenge the welfare gains expected (Edwards et al., 2009).

In a global system of states, state infrastructuring is central to territoriality. It is through this process that the major functions and objectives of the state are achieved, notably in regard to its ability to legitimise itself, not only by improving the welfare of its citizens but also by exercising its neo-Weberian roles through establishing and embedding its territorial strategies. This volume refers to this as the 'state's infrastructural mandate' and argues that the state has to infrastructure to fulfil its core functions, namely territorial control, integration, security and growth. Whilst each dimension of the infrastructural mandate can be subdivided into several supporting themes, this volume argues that they are ever-present themes within the state-based global system as the state seeks to preserve and enhance its position within a set territory. In so doing, state infrastructuring is subject to a number of tensions (both inter- and intra-territorial), to which the NIS has to adapt to preserve its territoriality.

A major source of tension originates from the redefinition of territoriality (and consequently the infrastructural mandate) by the forces of globality. This tension supports Brenner's (1999) argument that territorialisation is historically specific and, as a result, infrastructures – as territorial configurations – are subject to a constant process of change and are updated and reconfigured in line with the changing demands upon them (Harvey, 1999). In a global system of flows, many have argued that using the state as the sole unit of analysis in IPE is dated (see, for example, the debate raised by Agnew, 1994). Arguably, the most salient expression of this is within debates surrounding the 'territorial trap'. Briefly, this entails the argument that – in terms of NIS – infrastructural relations are not confined solely by flows within the borders of the state and that externally sourced or destined flows can have an impact upon or beyond the territory. This is reflective of the network society of Castells (2009) and also of the re-scaling of activity within the national systems, both upwards to the global level and down to the subnational level. There is much debate on the space of flows (that is, how technology reshapes spatial arrangements) however this often happens without a focus on the supporting structure of space. The structuring of space is key to enabling the space of flows. The structuring of space is enabled by the infrastructural systems that underpin the flows that shape the globalising system (Held et al., 1999).

Although infrastructures are polycentric, multi-scalar systems, the spatial fixity of such assets (despite the emergence of global flows) and the high risk, multi-dimensional nature of infrastructure has led to the view expressed in this volume that infrastructuring remains a core function of the state (see the debates raised by Samli, 2010). Whilst many developed states have sought to devolve infrastructuring to local bodies to develop subnational infrastructures (at regional, urban or community levels), the position adopted in this volume is that these levels are integral to the NIS and its territorial functions. Moreover, the shift towards polycentrism (where the NIS evolves through the interactions of the state and non-state actors) are also core to the NIS. For example, neither the development of private systems within the NIS (which ultimately needs to interconnect to the public system to achieve end-to-end connectivity) nor the regulated provision of infrastructure run contrary to the state's infrastructural mandate. The state retains the power to influence the form and nature of infrastructuring by non-state bodies operating within its territory. As a consequence, the polycentric NIS has multiple sources of development, but the state, either through its own investment or its sanctioning of mandate compliant structures, remains the primary driver.

Although not the sole source of adaptive tension within the NIS, globality is nonetheless a potent force for change (Organisation for Economic Co-operation and Development (OECD), 2015). Infrastructures may be territorially fixed but the flows that move over and between them are not solely for the benefit of or sourced from within the system over which they are moving. Some argue that this reinforces the argument that – in a global system of flows – the territoriality of the state cannot be neatly confined to the borders of the state (Keating, 2013), given that infrastructure lies at the heart of the contradictions between fixity and motion in the circulation of capital (Harvey, 1985). As such, this argument stresses that capital is inherently globalising, overcoming all geographical barriers and creating the 'annihilation of space through time'. This reflects the Marxist notion of the inherent and inevitable spatial expansion of capital. The desire of states to benefit from this expansion incentivises them to produce an NIS that enables this space–time/cost compression. In Harvey's words, 'spatial organisation is necessary to overcome space' (1985, p. 145). However, in creating such time-space compression assets, the state renders itself vulnerable to the very forces it is seeking to capture.

This volume takes a neo-realist perspective and does not suggest that states simply open up NIS in the face of the overwhelming force of global flows (Dunne and Schmidt, 2005). It remains the case that 80 per cent of the flows over the NIS are solely for national needs – an example of what Ghemawat (2003) has termed 'semi-globalisation' and which is also reflected in themes addressed by Hirst and Thompson (2002). The issue is one of adaptability, not subservience to globality, as states seek to shape these flows to preserve and fulfil their infrastructural mandate. States compete with each other to attract those flows that enhance their position. In this sense, state infrastructuring has direct parallels to the capital stock of a firm, notwithstanding that the state has broader geostrategic/geopolitical aims and motives. However, extra-territorial infrastructuring remains the exception rather than the rule and international infrastructure cooperation is based on interconnection and interoperability that create pan-regional infrastructures.

THE STATE-BASED GLOBAL INFRASTRUCTURE SYSTEM

Globalism implies that NIS are increasingly porous systems subject to cross-border flows that have the potential to alter the core components of the infrastructural mandate. The globality of infrastructure systems can represent both a threat and – less often noted – an opportunity for infrastructure systems and the attainment of the infrastructure mandate. In understanding emergent geostrategies, it is necessary to explore the shifting context across the identified processes. The global stretching of relations suggested by the maturity of modernity has made users less place-bound as they build new relations and rely less on heritage (Giddens, 1985; Beck et al., 2005). The conventional legacy of these shifts is spatially complex infrastructure systems where (as noted earlier) the power relations engendered within them can no longer solely be confined by borders. The state becomes a 'leaking container' subject to both internal and external flows of power which are shaped by the infrastructure that connects a given territory to flows from other systems to which it is connected (Taylor, 1995; Castells, 2009). The extent to which this shift in relations represents a shift in civic society with globality becoming the norm within intra-territorial relations is a moot point (Brenner, 1999; Held et al., 1999). As a matter of practical territorial interaction (unless a state adheres to autarky or isolationism), infrastructures are global in the sense that any location is ultimately accessible from any other.

The logic of the welfare state suggests that states have a direct incentive to moderate flows across borders, especially where the de- or re-territorialisation of flows can be expected to have a detrimental impact upon civil society (Majone, 1996). As such, states would conventionally infrastructure to enhance or preserve the welfare of its citizens through the filtering, monitoring and moderating of movements across borders. This strategy seeks to keep NIS as islands within a global system and to sustain fragmentation of the global system in the name of welfarism. However, the emergence of the competition state as a legacy of the move towards neo-liberalism has led to a shift in narratives on the development of the NIS towards supporting the competitive positioning of the state and of the enterprises located within it (Fougner, 2006; Cerny, 2010). This implies a lowering of the protective 'walls' around territories and the freer flow of tangible and tangibles into the state and a consequent diminishing of gateway infrastructure as an instrument of state power.

The interdependent nature (both spatially and functionally) of infrastructure as complex economic, political and social systems means that any single piece of infrastructure can fail in a multitude of ways, with the ultimate cause of failure lying deep within the system (Rinaldi et al., 2001). System dependencies vary over space, with key hubs and links proving especially salient for the maintenance of global movements. The complexity of infrastructure systems is created not only by physical structures and the physical dependencies between different infrastructures at any single point in space and time, but also because relationships formed across systems are not tied to any single system. In short, global usage creates systemic interdependencies as users exploit freedom of movement. As national systems, NIS are formed to support national needs (that is, all those users located within a territory), but using the demarcated territory as the sole unit of assessment for the impact of infrastructure understates its interactions with the global system. Within a state-based GIS, states are seen as embedded within but not subservient to global forces (Guzzini, 1998). Thus, states retain a high degree of control over NIS as a means of influencing outcomes within their own territory. Within this process, there exists the capability of the state to fragment the system, either through benign neglect or through domestic infrastructuring strategies which exert more control over cross-border flows.

The NIS is a complex system comprising a set of infrastructures that rely or interoperate with external infrastructure systems as a means of enabling territoriality (Hall et al., 2012; Hall et al., 2016). The logic of globality is that at least part of this process is externally determined by the ability of the NIS to engage with and capture those international flows necessary to support economic activity, development and/or growth. For highly infrastructured developed states (that is, those with universal – or very close to – access to core economic infrastructures), the state faces either a choice to allow full movement of flows that allow them to penetrate deep into the territory or (as often happens) the state seeks to moderate those flows. For these reasons, states maintain gateways to control access to the NIS (especially evident within communication components of the NIS, such as transport and information). The balance of these issues is reflected by the relationship between the forces for integration and fragmentation within the GIS, many of which are overwhelming shaped by state-based processes.

FORCES FOR INTEGRATION

When the NIS is conceived as a state-based system that interacts with other state-based systems across both territorial and non-territorial zones, this state primacy confirms that the adaptation to global pressures reflects, at least partially, a discretionary process by states to seek closer links with non-domestic systems. Viewed through the lens of neo-realism, the integration process is driven by the state's perception that proactive engagement with global forces can enhance, or at the very least not run contrary to, attainment of the infrastructural mandate (Buzan, 1996). As such, the logic of NIS integration is driven by the benefits that states can gain from closer integration with the global system and reflects, to a greater or lesser degree, the dependency of the fulfilment of the infrastructural mandate upon external flows. The pro-active engagement with global flows through closer cooperation in soft infrastructure or through the seamless interoperability of physical system underpins the competition state and the state's use of such strategies as a means of positioning within the global economy (Fougner, 2006).

An indirect contributor to the pattern of integration within the GIS has been technological advances, both in terms of the capabilities of specific infrastructures and of access technologies. In the case of the former, convergence between the main infrastructure sectors has occurred. In practice, this functional convergence has always been present but never fully explicit and had its most evident expression in the mutual dependence between energy and transport systems. However, this process has been rendered considerably more explicit by the increased alignment of information infrastructure with energy and transportation infrastructures, which has allowed greater efficiencies across these infrastructures and greater flows without a corresponding increase in high capital, sunk cost investment. This has also had the impact of enhancing time-space convergence across the GIS (Harvey, 1999). In terms of access technologies, there has been an evident rush to scale and a push for greater volumes over existing infrastructure with minimal adjustments. For example, there has been a push to consolidate flows through high volume mega-ships.

When looking across the main infrastructure sectors, there are a number of common themes within the GIS that are shaping the form and pace of NIS integration. The first of these is cooperation. Cooperation is often treated as a feature of a neo-liberal perspective on the global system. However, Jervis (1999) argues that neo-realism allows for cooperation where it works to the mutual advantage of all states. As such, cooperation is not driven simply by efficiency factors, as suggested by authors such as Keohane and Nye (2001), but also by the needs of the state to preserve its legitimacy. The most obvious rationale for the latter type of cooperation is the collaboration by states to generate system stability. This stability has three elements: ensuring the certainty of flows and, therefore, the avoidance of disruption; fostering of the security of flows; and ensuring that flows that are being de- or re-territorialised offer no challenge to the infrastructural mandate. Across the three infrastructure sectors examined within this volume, there are evident differences between states and sectors. The forces for collaboration appear strongest within transport, especially in relation to containerisation and combined with the need to facilitate flows (OECD, 2015). In energy, cooperation is between consumers and, to a lesser extent, between producers and consumers. The role of collaboration in this sector is to work in the interest of states to ensure that each can continue to access sufficient energy supplies as energy supply chains grows ever more stretched and to secure markets for producers. In the case of the internet, cooperation is at a formative stage: many states continue to prefer unilateral action due to the unpredictability of flows and the sources of disruption within.

The uncertainty over flows and the possibility of disruption to flows, especially within the non-territorial component of the global system, shows that cooperation can be a reactive strategy by states. It can be argued that the move toward unilateral state actions in internet filtering, for example, reflects a core uncertainty regarding the impact of flows and how security is created. It is also evident that not all vulnerabilities are evident at the point of infrastructuring. Cooperation in extra-territorial areas is therefore a rational strategy where there are sources of uncertainty within the system or ambiguities over the source and nature of the risk. Cooperation can be seen as a logical strategy where there is a desire/need to preserve system openness in a global system characterised by ambiguities over the form, nature and type of risk.

Although there is some evidence of cooperation at the regional level, international governance as a force shaping the form and nature of state infrastructuring is of limited salience. Agreements across the sectors examined in previous chapters are inter-governmental, with states being allowed considerable discretion in terms of the conventions embedded within such agreements. Moreover, it is evident that across many of the agreements specified, there are major omissions that directly impact on the efficacy of the system to exhibit true globality. For example, the US has opted out of the UNCLOS, and China and Brazil are just two countries who have opted out of international air transit agreements. Moreover, at the time of writing, there is little evidence of states wanting to establish an international governance system for the GII. Indeed, there is a growing body of evidence that states are beginning to assert power more effectively over flows into national information infrastructures, as highlighted by the popular narrative on the 'splinternet'.

Structuralists within IPE (notably, Strange, 1998) highlight that the forces for integration are sourced from a wider range of sources than state strategy alone: multinational companies (MNC) also operate as sources within the process. The shift towards polycentrism within and across NIS does offers plenty of evidence for private and other non-state activity in the development of NIS. The last decade (especially given that infrastructuring has come to be seen as a possible partial solution to the stagnation of western economies) has seen a plethora of policy pronouncements that seek to diversify the financing, operation and other aspects of infrastructuring beyond the state (Hall et al., 2016). The existence of integrated capital markets and dedicated infrastructure funds have highlighted how this capability has become – to some degree – decoupled from the state (Clark et al., 2013). However, the impact of these forces does not necessarily lead to a push for full integration of NIS. These pressures depend upon the nature of the MNC business model and how connectivity supports this and are also a function of the extent to which system fragmentation can either hinder or support the nature of the model. This fragmentation of GIS is not always a hindrance to multinational operations where such separation allows for higher rents (OECD, 2008). Furthermore, such organisations remain subject to state infrastructuring strategy and the need to fulfil the infrastructural mandate. This creates a paradox whereby a global system does not always need a fully globally integrated industry value chain. This leads to the conclusion that MNCs can be a force for integration within the GIS, but they are not a deciding force given that there are many other factors that shape the nature of both firm and state strategy. Whilst network effects appear powerful drivers for such strategies, they are not a definitive *raison d'être* for multinational infrastructure companies who can operate within the constraints of and even benefit from systemic fragmentation.

This is not to deny that extra-territoriality has been a powerful force upon state infrastructuring and in enabling the infrastructural mandate. This has become more evident as value chains become increasingly dispersed and diversified. Indeed, a common feature is the involvement of hegemonic powers in facilitating the sustenance of flows (Taylor, 1996). The substance of the global trading system depends upon a consensus of the needs for flows and of the right of transit between points of embarkation and destination. As such – and the US has been a powerful force sustaining this (more recently this has also applied to others such as China and the EU) – rights of access through the commons as well as key territorial transit points are vital for energy and logistics systems. By securing passages and access to these parts of the globe, hegemonic power has proved to be a powerful force for integration of NIS through its role in facilitating flows. Such security is an international public good as many of the benefits to states from hegemonic actions are an unintended consequence of the hegemon securing its own interests.

FORCES FOR FRAGMENTATION

Forces leading to the full globality or integration of infrastructure systems have not rendered the state subservient to global flows. Nonetheless, there is plenty of evidence that states, to varying degrees, are dependent upon external flows and develop infrastructure accordingly. This has its most evident expression in the energy sector where energy security for many states is tied closely into the sustenance of transnational energy flows (Emmerson and Stevens, 2012). Such dependence reflects the multi-faceted sources of fragmentation or potential for disruption within the global system which can arise from individual NIS, transit states and/or the global commons. Thus, as much as a true global system (as defined in Chapter 2) might be elusive, there is still a dependence upon international flows to which NIS have to adapt.

One of the main issues at the level of the state and inter-state flows inhibiting the development of a truly global infrastructure system is the unevenness of development and levels of maturity of the NIS globally (see OECD, 2006a, 2006b; World Bank, 2015). It is evident across all three main infrastructure sectors that there are wide variations in the quality of and access to infrastructure across the GIS. In some places, such as land-locked states or small island developing states, this is due to a combination of low levels of development and remoteness from the main global chan-nels for flows. This can be compounded by low levels of internal infrastruc-ture which limit the ability of global flows to penetrate deep into a state. This is also true of gateway infrastructure where, notably in transport and energy, the absence of key gateways has proved to be an inhibitor of the integration process.

This problem is compounded by rogue states that intentionally frag-ment the system. The literature on rogue or failed states (for example, Bilgin and Morton, 2004) frames the debate in terms of security. In this context, rogue states are defined as those whose intent is to opt out of the norms and conventions of the international politico-economic system to the extent that they create disruption within it. In terms of the GIS, rogue states tend to follow a proactive policy of discrimination and bias towards 'illegitimate' agents to the extent that they limit the globality, plurality and modularity of the infrastructure system under their jurisdiction. These states will have a soft infrastructure system whose function is to generate a governance system with strong centralised control over infrastructure and which works to control and/or impede the free flow of traffic across borders. For example, some such states have used their key position in energy transit networks to restrict energy supply and to use this position as a political weapon.

The nature of the failed state stands in contrast to the rogue state. In the latter, there is a deliberate strategy of creating discontinuity through the soft infrastructure/hard infrastructure interface. In the case of the former, there is an absence of an institutional system to control and protect traffic flows within the jurisdiction of the state, which impedes the development and operation of infrastructure within this domain. For example, the absence of a government in Somalia allowed piracy to flourish, which in turn generated impediments to the free flow of traffic in key logistics networks. This highlights a blatant risk associated with the creation of the GIS where interdependence between national systems is open to subver-sion or outright attack for political, strategic or opportunistic reasons. Rogue and failed states stand in juxtaposition to each other: one exercises total control, whereas there is a complete absence of control in the other (Bilgin et al., 2007).

Whilst the notion of the rogue state suggests a proactive stance towards generating bias in the GIS, the issue of divergence in the approaches to the integration of NIS is more constrained. Such divergences often belie a commitment to the GIS but can reflect both the uneven implementation and a lack of consensus on the core principles underpinning the system. Discrepancies can result from reactive forces or a sclerotic system that is resisting the forces of integration that drive the GIS. Such divergences, whilst not contrary to the operation of the GIS, limit its ability to operate as a truly open system with distributed governance. These divergences can manifest themselves through a number of channels, such as divergence over ownership preferences and control patterns on infrastructure or the desire of the state to use infrastructure as a tool of industrial policy (Orr and Kennedy, 2008). The consequence of such divergences is that global infrastructure networks (GIN) will be malformed in some places and immature in others, depending on how policy actions impair the structure of the pluralist–modular system and how it impacts on traffic flows.

Divergences have had a notable impact within telecommunications where constraints upon the flow of traffic across the global information infrastructure have been imposed by states seeking to control the type of content that can be accessed by the local population but are sourced internationally (Malcomson, 2015). Across the globe, a number of states have imposed 'firewalls' (Goldsmith and Wu, 2006). These are virtual controls on the form and type of content accessible within a given territory where access to this content contravenes accepted social and political norms and is perceived as a threat to the social and political fabric of the state. Although restrictions are placed on the flow of traffic, they tend to be applied consistently and in a non-discriminatory manner and, as such, may not undermine fully the territorial integrity of the GIS (Drake et al., 2016). Similar barriers also exist with energy and transport where states have aligned their strategic interests to strong national control of key infrastructure sectors.

There is an abundance of both anecdotal and research-based evidence to highlight the link between divergences in soft infrastructure and the existence of legacy and incumbent interests within a given territory (for example, OECD, 2015). The issue is one of sclerosis in the adaptability of soft infrastructure created by the political influence of legacy interests and their desire to preserve the power. These interests depend on system fragmentation, the retention of existing market structures and on a tightly regulated system of interconnection, interoperability and access (OECD, 2006a, 2006b). In such a context, legitimisation of the GIS becomes extremely difficult: modular providers are unable to connect and traffic flows are strictly controlled. Inevitably, this involves political interaction manifesting itself in an embedded soft infrastructure that limits plurality. This does not necessarily preclude modularity, but it does occur via arrangements between the state and the incumbent that seeks to control the spread and usage of any given module that links to its core architecture.

This legacy system is based on a desire for strong centralised control of the national infrastructure system in which governance patterns enable the state to retain control of a core strategic asset. This can occur for reasons of security, because the incumbent is a branch of government and/or because the need or desire for private finance is limited. Incumbent interests are especially pertinent given that infrastructures are frequently characterised by a history of strong state control in which incumbents either remain state-owned to some degree or retain a degree of influence over network development. Whilst such power has diminished in many larger states, many smaller states retain strong legacy interests.

As mentioned earlier, the open nature of the GIS can leave the system vulnerable to disruption through attacks, either on infrastructure itself or through the use of these channels to attack other targets. This raises the prospect of states seeking to protect their territorial security by ensuring that critical infrastructures are sufficiently controlled to limit such threats. In practice, this means that states in fear of such disruptions can attempt to control key hubs; limit the form and type of cross-border flows; restrict pluralist governance systems and practice discriminatory legitimisation processes on issues of asset ownership and control (OECD, 2008). Inevitably, such practices hinder the efficacy of the GIS. There is ample anecdotal evidence across all infrastructure sectors of states citing security to justify their exertion of influence over the structure and globality of its critical infrastructure. For example, in creation of the global information infrastructure, widespread restrictions have been placed on technology so that states can monitor external and internal threats (see opennet.net for a review of ongoing restrictions). In the aftermath of 9/11, the US sought to tighten security at major infrastructure entry points, especially regarding the perceived weaknesses of container ports. With this in mind, the US resisted the acquisition by Dubai World of key US container ports following its acquisition of P&O (Graham and Marchick, 2006).

The use of disconnection for reasons of security, however, poses a number of problems. The most immediate is the extent to which the security is legitimate rather than merely disguised protectionism, which, in turn, can give rise to retaliatory actions. Furthermore, within the GIS there has to be recognition that a state's critical infrastructure does not exist in isolation from other infrastructure. In practice, this means that the integrity and security of any state's infrastructure is determined, at least in part, by actions taken elsewhere within the system. This suggests the desirability of states addressing common security concerns through common fora such as, for example, the UN's actions on cyber-security. This pressure has intensified as states have realised how convergence has increased the vulnerability of critical infrastructure from globally sourced cyber threats (Rinaldi et al., 2001).

Underscoring the salience of the state-based system is the importance of geopolitics as a force shaping the global flows into and out of NIS as well as across the global commons. The role of hegemons as a force in building infrastructure to enable and sustain flows and their role in preserving flows through the commons have already been mentioned elsewhere (Taylor, 1996). However, it is evident in other sectors that geopolitics has long operated as a powerful restraint upon the effective operation of the GIS. In energy, some states have restricted transit of energy across their territories as a means of seeking to place pressure upon either the source or the destination of the flows (Klare, 2009). Other cases, namely some states which are the source of flows, have sought to restrict flows to other states as a means of exerting power over the destination state or the transit state who may rely upon transit fees. Whilst these examples do not offer a definitive list of the means through which states can seek to utilise NIS to disrupt flows, they do serve to underline the dependence upon external NIS as a means of enabling and facilitating the ability of the state to attain its infrastructural mandate.

CONCLUSION

Infrastructure is central to an international system characterised by globalising flows. It is through the existence of and access to these physical structures that the impact of the global flows is felt through their capability to penetrate deep into the state-based system. For a true global system to exist, this volume argues that global flows need to flow unimpeded between and within states – a situation which remains elusive. Although global flows are a salient force within the international system, the unevenness with which infrastructure is developed and accessed, both within and between states, represents a significant hurdle to development of a genuine GIS. In some cases, this fragmentation is generated by issues related to the unevenness of economic development and its legacy for the national infrastructure system; in other cases it is an intentional state strategy to monitor, filter or even restrict flows as states seek to preserve their territoriality within a globalising system.

REFERENCES

Agnew, J. (1994) 'The territorial trap: the geographical assumptions of international relations theory', *Review of International Political Economy*, *1*(1), 53–80.

Beck, U. (2005) *Power in the Global Age: A New Global Political Economy*. London:
Polity Press.

Bilgin, P. and Morton, A.D. (2004) 'From "rogue" to "failed" states? The fallacy of
short-termism', *Politics*, *24*(3), 169–80.

Bilgin, P. and Morton, A.D. (2007) 'Rethinking state failure: the political economy
of security', in Lambach, D. and Debiel, T. (eds.), *State Failure Revisited I:
Globalization of Security and Neighborhood Effects*. Institut für Entwicklung und
Frieden, INEF Report, p. 87.

Brenner, N. (1999) 'Beyond state-centrism? Space, territoriality, and geographical
scale in globalization studies', *Theory and Society*, *28*(1), 39–78.

Buzan, B. (1996) 'The timeless wisdom of realism?', in Smith, S., Booth, K. and
Zalewski, M. (eds.), *International Theory: Positivism and Beyond*. Cambridge:
Cambridge University Press, pp. 47–65.

Castells, M. (2009) *The Rise of the Network Society. The Information Age: Economy,
Society, and Culture*, Vol. 1, 2nd edn. Chichester, UK: Wiley Blackwell.

Cerny, P.G. (2010) 'The competition state today: from raison d'état to raison du
monde', *Policy Studies*, *31*(1), 5–21.

Clark, G.L., Dixon, A.D. and Monk, A.H. (2013) *Sovereign Wealth Funds:
Legitimacy, Governance, and Global Power*. Princeton, NJ: Princeton University
Press.

Drake, W.J, Cerf, V. and Kleinwachter, W. (2016) *Internet Fragmentation: An
Overview*. World Economic Forum, Future of the Internet White Paper, accessed
5 September 2016 at www.wef.org

Dunne, T. and Schmidt, B.C. (2005) 'Realism', in Baylis, J. and Smith, S. (eds.),
The Globalization of World Politics, 3rd edn. New York, NY: Oxford University
Press, pp. 162–83.

Edwards, P.N., Bowker, G.C., Jackson, S.J. and Williams, R. (2009) 'Introduction:
an agenda for infrastructure studies', *Journal of the Association for Information
Systems*, *10*(5), 6.

Emmerson, C. and Stevens, P. (2012) *Maritime Choke Points and the Global Energy
System: Charting a Way Forward*. London: Chatham House.

Fougner, T. (2006) 'The state, international competitiveness and neoliberal
globalisation: is there a future beyond 'the competition state?', *Review of
International Studies*, *32*(1), 165–85.

Ghemawat, P. (2003) 'Semiglobalization and international business strategy',
Journal of International Business Studies, *34*(2), 138–52.

Giddens, A. (1985) *The Nation-State and Violence*, Vol. 2. Berkeley, CA: University
of California Press.

Goldsmith, J. and Wu, T. (2006) *Who Controls the Internet? Illusions of a Borderless
World*. Oxford: Oxford University Press.

Graham, E.M. and Marchick, D. (2006) *US National Security and Foreign Direct
Investment*. Washington, DC: Peterson Institute Press.

Guzzini, S. (1998) *Realism in International Relations and International Political
Economy: The Continuing Story of a Death Foretold*. London: Routledge.

Hall, J.W., Henriques, J., Hickford, A. and Nicholls, R. (2012) *A Fast Track*

Analysis of Strategies for infrastructure Provision in Great Britain: Technical Report. Environmental Change Institute, University of Oxford, UK.

Hall, J.W., Tran, M., Hickford, A.J. and Nicholls, R.J. (eds.) (2016) *The Future of national Infrastructure: A System-Of-Systems Approach*. Cambridge: Cambridge University Press.

Harvey, D. (1985) *The Urbanization of Capital*. Oxford: Blackwell.

Harvey, D. (1999) 'Time-space compression and the postmodern condition', *Modernity: Critical Concepts*, *4*, 98–118.

Held, D., McGrew, A., Goldblatt, D. and Perraton, J. (1999) *Global Transformations: Politics, Economics and Culture*. Cambridge: Polity Press.

Hirst, P. and Thompson, G. (2002) 'The future of globalization', *Cooperation and Conflict*, *37*(3), 247–65.

Howe, C., Lockrem, J., Appel, H., Hackett, E., Boyer, D., Hall, R., Schneider–Mayersom, M., Pope, A., Gupta, A., Rodwell, E., Ballestero, A., Durbin, T., el-Dahdah, F., Long, E. and Mody, C. (2016) 'Paradoxical infrastructures: ruins, retrofit and risk', *Science, Technology and Human Values*, *41*(3), 547–65.

Jervis, R. (1999) 'Realism, neoliberalism, and cooperation: understanding the debate', *International Security*, *24*(1), 42–63.

Keating, M. (2013) *Rescaling the European State: The Making of Territory and the Rise of the Meso*. Oxford: Oxford University Press.

Keohane, R.O. and Nye, J.S. (2001) *Power and Interdependence*. London: Longman.

Klare, M. (2009) *Rising powers, Shrinking Planet: The New Geopolitics of Energy*. Basingstoke, UK: Palgrave Macmillan.

Majone, G. (1996) *Regulating Europe*. London: Routledge.

Malcomson, S. (2015) *Splinternet: How Geopolitics and Commerce Are Fragmenting the World Wide Web*. New York, NY: OR Books.

Mann, M. (1984) 'The autonomous power of the state: its origins, mechanisms and results', *European Journal of Sociology*, *25*(2), 185–213.

Neumann, M. (2006) 'Infiltrating infrastructures: on the nature of networked infrastructure', *Journal of Urban Technology*, *13*(1), 3–31.

Organisation for Economic Co-operation and Development (OECD) (2006a) *Infrastructure to 2030: Telecom, Land Transport, Water and Electricity*, accessed 4 May 2015 at www.oecd.org

Organisation for Economic Co-operation and Development (OECD) (2006b) *Infrastructure to 2030 (Volume 2): Mapping Policy for Electricity, Water and Transport*, accessed 4 May 2015 at www.oecd.org

Organisation for Economic Co-operation and Development (OECD) (2008) *Protection of Critical Infrastructure and the Role of Investment Policies Relating to National Security*, May 2008, accessed 5 February 2016 at www.OECD.org

Organisation for Economic Co-operation and Development (OECD) (2015) *Fostering Investment in Infrastructure*, accessed 5 May 2016 at www.oecd.org

Orr, R.J. and Kennedy, J.R. (2008) 'Highlights of recent trends in global infrastructure: new players and revised game rules', *Transnational Corporations*, *17*(1), 99–133.

Rinaldi, S.M., Peerenboom, J.P. and Kelly, T.K. (2001) 'Identifying, understanding, and analyzing critical infrastructure interdependencies', *IEEE Control Systems*, *21*(6), 11–25.

Samli, A.C. (2010) *Infrastructuring: The Key to Achieving Economic Growth, Productivity, and Quality of Life*. Dordrecht, NL: Springer.

Star, S.L. and Bowker, G.C. (2006) 'How to infrastructure', in Lievrouw, L. and

Livingstone, S. (eds.), *Handbook of new Media: Social Shaping and social Consequences of ICTs*. London: Sage, pp. 230–45.

Strange, S. (1988) *States and Markets*. London: Pinter Publishers.

Taylor, P.J. (1995) 'Beyond containers: internationality, interstateness, interterritoriality', *Progress in Human Geography*, *19*(1), 1–15.

Taylor, P.J. (1996) *The Way the modern World Works: World Hegemony to World Impasse*. Chichester, UK: Wiley.

World Bank (2015) *Development Indicators 2015*, accessed 3 April 2016 at www.worldbank.org

Index